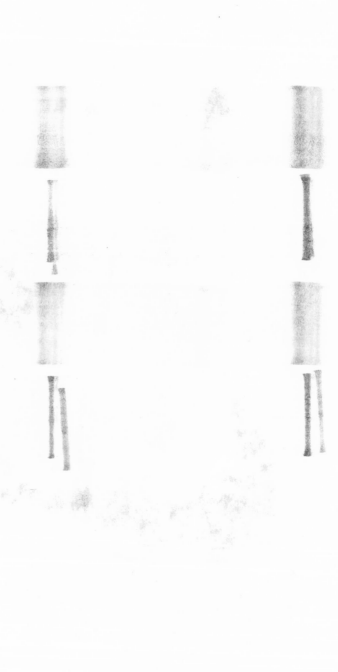

Strategies of Reticence

Silence and Meaning
in the Works of
Jane Austen,
Willa Cather,
Katherine Anne Porter,
and Joan Didion

Strategies of Reticence :

Silence and Meaning
in the Works of
Jane Austen,
Willa Cather,
Katherine Anne Porter,
and Joan Didion

JANIS P. STOUT

91568

University Press of Virginia

Charlottesville and London

Printed in the United States of America

Library of Congress Cataloging-in-Publication Data
Stout, Janis P.
    Strategies of reticence : silence and meaning in the works of Jane
  Austen, Willa Cather, Katherine Anne Porter, and Joan Didion / Janis
  P. Stout.
      p.   cm.
    Includes bibliographical references.
    ISBN 0-8139-1262-8
    1. American fiction—Women authors—History and criticism.
2. Silence in literature.   3. Austen, Jane, 1775–1817—Criticism and
interpretation.   4. Cather, Willa, 1873–1947—Criticism and
interpretation.   5. Porter, Katherine Anne, 1890–1980—Criticism and
interpretation.   6. Didion, Joan—Criticism and interpretation.
7. American fiction—20th century—History and criticism.
8. Feminism and literature.   9. Women and literature.   I. Title.
PS376.S54S76 1990
813.009'9287—dc20   89-29777
                                                              CIP

Contents

Preface

And so by degrees the silence is broken.

——— VIRGINIA WOOLF ———
"DOROTHY OSBORNE'S LETTERS"

Traditional beliefs about the nature and role of women have included a notion that silence is an appropriate condition for women, an aspect of their rightful submissiveness, or even a natural state, a manifestation of women's innate passiveness. Studies of women's silences by writers who dispute such beliefs have generally emphasized repression. Carol Christ, for example, begins *Diving Deep and Surfacing* with the statement, "Women's stories have not been told." She continues, in a litany of negation, "Without stories a woman is lost. . . . She is closed in silence."[1] Adrienne Rich speaks of "anger uttered in silence" and of "a lot of poems" she "couldn't write" because of needing to act out the accepted role of woman.[2] Her gender stifled her freedom to speak, as a poet and as a revolutionary.

There can be no doubt that silence, as a form of imposed repression, has been a major part of women's experience historically. Even when the stifling of women's free speech has not been deliberate, it has been effectual. The privileging of male roles in patriarchal societies means that women are conditioned, if not directly enjoined, to limit their speech. To be sure, such conditioning may not be overt. Factors such as undervaluing women's voices in decision-making situations, praising soft-spokenness, and casting women as "ladylike" figures, lacking authority or rationality, produce (en-gender) self-limitation almost as efficiently as rules ("women should be silent in church") and denial of the vote impose it from outside. Stylistic qualities of reticence or withholding in writings by women must necessarily be viewed as having some relation, however unclear, to the general societal squelching of women.

My emphasis here, however, will not be on silences and reticence as effects so much as on silences and reticence as consciously or unconsciously chosen strategies for effect. I will be concerned primarily with the "speaking silences" of four women writers: Jane Austen, Willa Cather, Katherine Anne Porter, and Joan Didion—a group that spans a considerable time period as well as the distinction between American and British literatures. Austen, the exemplar of the reticent style as rhetorical strategy, worked around 1800. The other three are clustered in the twentieth century, when women have taken an unprecedented role in the production of both popular and literary fiction, as well as poetry. Even so, in a time when the situation of women and of women writers is (in some ways, at least) changing very rapidly, they are of different moments. Cather's work is chiefly of the earlier twentieth century, the second and third decades, while Porter's partly overlaps but mostly succeeds hers, and Didion's continues to the present. In addressing the work of each of the four, I will be discussing attributes of style and fictive vision that have been recognized before but have not, I believe, been sufficiently explored.

My selection of these four is based in part on my own response as a reader. They are writers I find interesting, aesthetically pleasing, richly rewarding. But beyond personal preference the reasons for my selection of these particular writers derive from the distinctive yet comparable ways in which their work manifests qualities of silence, withholding, or reticence. These qualities are not, of course, peculiar to the four I have chosen. They are qualities of style or of vision that have been recognized as being genuinely important in women's literature generally. Austen, Cather, Porter, and Didion are not *the* four, in the sense of the obvious and only four, women writers who might be studied in this way; other women writers also make distinctive use of the reticent style. But these four are writers whose work variously devolves upon these qualities, and realizes and uses them in a central and determining way.

The inclusion of Jane Austen in a book given preponderantly to the study of American writers calls for special explanation. Let me first say what I am *not* doing: I am not undertaking an "influence study" in the sense that used to be so familiar. As a matter of fact, I do believe that Austen has been crucially influential upon these and upon all women writers of our time whose voices are those of reserve or indirection, as Austen's was a voice of reserve and indirection. But my belief is largely intuitive, based on perceived similarities and on the monumental presence of Austen in the literary heritage of women who are, as these three have been, well-informed readers. More specifically, the high regard in which Cather held Austen is well established, in her brief and often-quoted comment that Austen "certainly had more common sense than any of them"—that is, the women writers she was discussing—"and was in some respects the greatest of them all."[3] In any event, I have not pursued statements of this kind because it has not been my purpose to demonstrate influence, but similarity—or, more precisely, these writers' varied sharing in a larger pattern in women's literature.

Austen is here because she is the fountainhead of the strategically reticent style in the novel as we know it. It was Austen who managed to transform the discreet feminine silence prescribed by a system of social decorum into not only a thing of art but also a persuasive rhetoric. Whether or not the other writers considered here directly learned from Austen (and I would argue that Cather plainly did and Porter and Didion almost certainly did), we as readers need to learn what Austen does with the reticent style so that we can better understand what Cather and Porter and Didion, who are more obviously engaged in using that style for feminist ends, are doing. The fact that Austen, too, was engaged in the examination of gender roles in her own society, and that her reticent style is employed persuasively in questioning those gender roles, is all the more reason to see her as a precursor of these, and other, women writers who employ strategies of reticence. But primarily she is here because of her importance in perfecting the technique and because of our need to understand that technique as thoroughly as possible as we examine others' use of the same and similar techniques. The difference of time and of national literature is, I believe, only a superficial problem. The sharing of gender and the sharing of rhetorical method are far more important than disjunctions of time and place, especially when dealing with a writer who has been so well known as Austen has.

In short, we see by careful study of Austen how a reticent style can become a rhetorical strategy. We then examine the ways in which that rhetorical strategy is employed by three modern and postmodern writers who have employed a rhetoric of silence and withholding in more aggressively feminist ways than Austen did—and indeed, as we move from Cather to Porter to Didion, in increasingly aggressive ways.

Some explanation of my use of the word *reticence* is needed as well. The word is commonly used to connote restraint in confronting unpleasant or uncomfortable subjects, particularly a shyness or reserve about discussing sexual matters. In this sense, of course, reticence has traditionally been a quality more of women's experience, and of women's speech, than of men's. And until quite recent years women's writings were more often reticent with regard to sexual or scatological matters than men's. Therefore, this traditional meaning of the word is operative here. Because it is a word that may imply a link with women writers of an earlier time and with the constraints on women exerted by ideas of propriety, I have found it a convenient word for my title. But I use it only as a figurative indication of a much larger complex of silences and curtailments in women's fiction. Joan Didion cannot be called reticent in the more traditional sense. In that, she is sharply distinguished from Austen or from Porter or Cather. But she participates, nevertheless, in the larger stylistic and rhetorical strategy being considered here.

My method in this undertaking is conspicuously open to the charge of what Mary Jacobus calls the American "flight toward empiricism."[4] Since I regard myself as being avowedly and cheerfully empiricist in my intellectual affinities, I can hardly resent such an imputation. I would, however, modify somewhat Jacobus's account of the results of the "flight" she speaks of. Rather than leading to an "insistence on 'women's experience' as the ground of difference in writing," I believe that a grounding in empiricism should, and I hope that in my own case it does, lead to an *emphasis* on women's experience as *a* ground for difference in writing. That distinction, I believe, is important and manifests, not an absence of theory, but a different theory.

I am deeply (but happily) indebted to friends and colleagues who have given me both encouragement and the benefit of their wide reading and insight. Beth Rigel Daugherty was a source of enlightenment and of lively give-and-take on the question of the "woman's voice" long before I began actually writing this book. She generously shared with me her thoughts on the introductory chapter as it evolved toward the form in which it appears here. Robert W. Burch also gave me reassurance and astute suggestions as I worked on the introduction. In my thinking on Austen I especially benefitted from talking with Robert L. Patten, William Bowman Piper, and Susan K. Gillman. Sylvia A. Grider shared her thorough familiarity with Cather and helped me to clarify many things. Ann Fisher-Wirth both challenged and cheered me toward clarification of what I meant as well as how I said it. I especially thank her for the phrases "mode of decorum" and "mode of anguish," which I have seized upon and incorporated. Cynthia H. Foote at the University Press of Virginia has afforded me the benefit of her keen perception and good judgment, for which I am grateful.

Most of all, my colleague in the academy and my husband, Loren Daniel Lutes, has consistently, by example and in discussion, challenged me to think more clearly and buoyed me up when I have felt discouraged.

Portions of chapter two have appeared in different form in *Studies in the Novel* 14 (1982): 316–26. Portions of chapter four have appeared in *Essays in Literature* 12 (1985): 285–94 and in *Philological Quarterly* 66 (1987): 259–78. I thank the editors of these journals for permission to reprint.

Strategies of Reticence
Silence and Meaning
in the Works of
Jane Austen,
Willa Cather,
Katherine Anne Porter,
and Joan Didion

CHAPTER ONE

Introduction:
Silence, the Critic, and
the Good Little Girl

*Now the Sirens have a still more fatal weapon than
their song, namely their silence.*

——————————— FRANZ KAFKA, *Parables* ———————————

Lying is done with words, and also with silence.

——————————— ADRIENNE RICH ———————————
"WOMEN AND HONOR: SOME NOTES ON LYING"

Novels, like people, have personalities of their own. Some are
more outgoing, more assertive, than others. Some play by the
rules, while others quietly subvert the rules, and some proclaim
their freedom from all rules. Some speak politely; some yell and
swear. Some are deeper than they seem. As we talk with various
people, we weigh their words differently, we listen with different
levels of attention. With some people, we take into account the
conditions—recent griefs, old grudges, significant hearers standing nearby—that may be restricting what they say. With some,
more than others, we note the raised eyebrow, the shrug, the little

smile that betrays an unspoken meaning. The weight of the tacit is equally present as we read. We hold a bundle of paper, we look at words printed on the page, but our reading, if it is skillful, also takes into account the pressures that may have restricted or shaped what was written down. It takes into account as well the spaces around and between the actual words of the text: the silences.

Books are not people. However pleasing the analogy, we cannot carry our knowledge or our expectations of the one directly and entirely over to the other. The conditions that impinge on the one are not entirely the same as those that impinge on the other. Even the conditions affecting one specific person do not necessarily and in the same way affect that person's books. If they did, and if we really could treat books and persons as if they were the same, or even if we knew with any confidence the extent of their commonality, the familiar critical debates over biographical method, historicity, and intentionality would have ended long ago. They have not. We continue to be interested in authors, as well as their books, though the coextensiveness of the two interests remains in dispute. To be more specific, and to approach more nearly the interests of the present study, we continue to believe that it makes a difference whether the writer of a given book is male or female. But the nature of the difference that it makes is one of the most pressing uncertainties in literary scholarship today.

The extent to which we read a book as we "read" a person, noticing the pauses and the gestures and the failures to mention certain topics or experiences, and the degree of our own docility or scepticism as we do so, is another of those issues. The "reading" of textual silences, of what is not actually there but might have been there or is evoked by what is there, especially when writers call attention to the fact of such omissions, limitations, or outward pointings, is among the liveliest and most provocative developments in criticism in the past twenty years—and not in deconstructive criticism alone. Wayne Booth called attention, almost thirty years ago, to the function of authorial silences in the "art of communicating with readers" in fiction.[1] When the "reading" of silences is superimposed upon the equally debated issue of the difference it makes that a writer is a woman, we have a yet more challenging question and one that is just beginning to be asked.

Criticism has traditionally concerned itself with texts, with sets of words, objects made of words. The poem was a well-wrought urn, a solid thing; the novel, a well-made novel. We looked at their components, the pieces out of which they were assembled or the stuff—clay, color, glaze—that went into the urn, and we looked at the way that stuff, that solid material, was shaped. But with structuralist and poststructuralist critical innovations, texts have been reconceived as permeable, open, no longer things so much as processes, occasions. It is that reconception that has brought with it a concern not only with the matter and the shapes of texts but with their spaces, their openness.

Silence is an aspect of that openness. It is one of those elements in the novel that "move against obvious statement, against presences, against things, against the assertions of positivism."[2] Silence or withholding is an aspect of, or at times a metaphor for, those "fractured surfaces" which, in Frank Kermode's words, mark a break with fictions that "make false sense by means of a false realism" and which therefore constitute a "perpetual invitation" to interpretation. For Kermode and for other critics as well, that invitation, that openness, constitutes the life of a living literature.[3]

Traditional textual scholars, particularly those whose interests are directed toward the earlier periods, the Renaissance and pre-Renaissance, have long contended (the word is not accidental: they have struggled) with lacunae in texts. But that is a different matter. In that case, the assumption is that something used to be there, and the effort is to find or convincingly recreate what is missing. The standard remains one of completeness or fullness. The lacunae or emptinesses of damaged or maltransmitted texts are unintended silences. They exist because some outer force—time or fire or offended righteousness—did violence to the author's intention, which was an intention of fullness.

The lacunae with which critical scholars now often concern themselves, and with which I am concerned here, are viewed not

3

as accidental gaps, but as intended or at least significant and signifying spaces, spaces which are fully integral to the text as read.
Such silences may be deliberately placed for effect, and thus may
represent very conscious manipulation of the expressive medium;
or they may, though fully significant in the reader's experience of
the text, arise from authorial intentions not fully conscious. Silences may be imposed by social constraints of various sorts, such
as prevailing assumptions about morality or propriety, what
should and should not be said and by whom. In any event, they
are part of the text and are quite legitimately interesting to the
critic in their own right.

Such an interest has established itself, however, with growing
frequency and elaboration, only in the past twenty years or so. It
was stimulated in the 1950s and 1960s by a handful of essays and
suggestive studies by such artists and scholars as John Cage, Max
Picard, Susan Sontag, Erich Heller.[4] These critics found in the
turn to silence or vacancy a powerful defining attribute of modern
and postmodern art—indeed, of the modern and postmodern
sensibilities. Silence meant, to Cage and to Sontag, a clearing
within which the perceiver might achieve a new realization of
quiet processes going on all the time but unnoticed, drowned out
in the twentieth-century general noise. They found in silence, as
well, a new means of expressing the artist's integrity, as refusal to
speak began to mean not only the turning away from modern life
and modern trash in revulsion, but a refusal to sully art with
trivial expression.

At about the same time, Booth's *Rhetoric of Fiction* greatly advanced the critical understanding of, and interest in, the modes
of persuasive communication between writer and reader and the
ways in which a reader's creative interactions may be evoked. In
examining the "disguised rhetoric of modern fiction," Booth not
only lucidly considered the various communicative functions of
limited narrative point of view but, much to our purposes here,
also explored narrative strategies in which the author and the
reader share a "secret communion" carried on "behind the narrator's back." At such times, in Booth's words, the resourceful
author "may wink and nudge" but "may not speak." Much of the

current critical engagement with authorial silences is directed toward understanding that winking and nudging. Booth is particularly helpful, for my purposes, in his elucidation of ways in which narrative strategies enlist the reader's sympathies in the establishment of a specific point of view represented by a narrative center and of ways in which the reader is led to take delight in arriving at a collaborative tacit understanding. "Whenever an author conveys to his reader an unspoken point," he astutely observes, the author thereby "creates a sense of collusion against all those, whether in the story or out of it, who do not get that point."[5]

The work of these critics at mid-century has more recently issued in a spate of books and articles exploring the silences of particular writers or silence itself as a concept or as a metaphor or sign. Some of these critical works concern themselves directly with the ways in which authorial silences invite the participation of the interactive reader or performer in the creation of meaning.[6] And it is not only in relation to literature that the interest in silence has developed. Following Cage, the concept of silence or openness of meaning-structures has also loomed large in the study of avant-garde music (in particular, indeterminate music) and certain of the visual arts, such as minimalist painting, in which blank spaces have assumed great importance.[7] A number of other critics have taken up the study of silence as metaphor or sign and the affective or conceptual values it summons in contemporary literature.

A philosophical or meditative interest in the concept of silence, literal silence—that which preexists the all-creating Word and presumably waits, deathlike, when our noisemaking ceases—is not new. Silence has long been the subject of serious, even religious or quasi-religious, meditation and of elevated or at times rhapsodic praise. Silence is golden, we have been told. It is restorative. Wordsworth expected us to recover our souls in the silence of lone communion with nature. Newspapers have published celebratory stories of slot machines which, for a quarter, will provide three minutes of silence—not literal silence, of course, but what passes for silence, a relief from the added noise the jukebox produces the rest of the time. Thomas Carlyle, in one of his more frequently quoted aphorisms, told us that "Speech is of Time, Silence is of Eternity." The image is of a kind of sublime absoluteness, what Picard calls a "pure existence ... like uncreated, everlasting Being."[8] It is that quality of sublimity which George Steiner, following in the tradition, celebrates in his 1966 essay "Silence and the Poet": "It is just because we can go no further, because speech so marvelously fails us, that we experience the certitude of a divine meaning surpassing and enfolding ours. What lies beyond man's word is eloquent of God."[9]

We must admit, though, that Steiner's pronouncement, however it may move us to assent, has about it a ring of pious mustiness, the ring of a voice out of the past. And the reason for that is not trivial. It has to do, in part, with the shift from belief to disbelief that there is anywhere there beyond the point of our own furthest speech. Though it is indisputable that silence continues to carry connotations of serenity, stillness, and a perspective beyond the everyday (thus its appropriateness for comment on empty chatter), it is more likely, in twentieth-century literature, to evoke a set of connotations having to do with death, emptiness, alienation, and perhaps unutterable revulsion, unspeakableness. As Steiner himself indicates in *Language and Silence*, a sense of silence as the appropriate response to prevailing "linguistic devaluation and dehumanization" is more indicative of contemporary feeling than is a sense of silence as evoking awe. The recourse to silence becomes a means of pronouncing absolute judgement on the debasing horrors of modern history (particularly, as Steiner argues, on the horrors of the Holocaust), by excluding them from the realm of discourse.[10]

Steiner's argument raises the issue which is at the heart of my own present study, that is, the issue of silence as rhetorical strategy. But I want to reserve that issue for the moment in order to explore more fully the critical thinking of the past decade relative to the affective and conceptual qualities of silence as it appears in contemporary literature. I hope to show not only how my concern with the strategies of reticence employed by certain women writers grows out of a well-established body of criticism but how, in turning to feminist concerns, we add a new dimension to the preceding critical interest in textual silences.

Traditional celebrations of silence, like Carlyle's or Steiner's, were directed toward the experience or the idea of a literal silence, an absence of (obtrusive) sound. Recent critical interest in silence has been directed more toward figurative silences, such as moments in texts when the expected or potential words do not actually appear on the page. More generally, it has been concerned with absences of all sorts—with silence, as Ihab Hassan says (in what is probably the most sustained excursus on the place of silence in the broad sweep of twentieth-century literature), not as concept, but as metaphor. Postmodern literature, Hassan declares, "moves ... toward the vanishing point." In the work of certain avant-garde writers (he cites Genet and Beckett), words appear ... on the page only to declare themselves invalid. The postmodern writer or reader turns toward silence, not for edification, but as the expression of an obsessionally nullifying sensibility. The import of the metaphor of silence, as Hassan reads it, is utterly negative, partaking of nothingness and of nihilism. Silence provides, not an intuition of God, but "an intuition of the great emptiness behind the meticulous shape of things." As metaphor, it summons meaning, but the meaning it summons is nonmeaning. It is the chosen vehicle of a vision of invalidation. Arraying modern against postmodern in parallel lists of defining qualities, Hassan opposes to the modern closedness, solidity, and "totalization" a postmodern cluster of value traits including "Decreation/Deconstruction," "Absence," "Indeterminacy," and "Exhaustion/Silence."[11]

That this would be so is scarcely surprising; Hassan's list is perspicacious, but not revelatory. What is striking, here and elsewhere in Hassan's work, is the bleakly negative quality of much of his descriptive language with regard to the postmodern and the avant-garde, as well as the metaphor of silence. Postmodernism, in this vision, carries little of that sense of ludic sportiveness that we often associate with the postmodern in literature as well as, of course, the poststructuralist in criticism.

Hassan indeed avows his perception that the "boundary state" we call silence is shaped by "the negative" and that his book is in fact devoted to "negative silence," silence as negation. Enumerating (in yet another list) the attributes of silence in the postmodern context, he takes the reader through a litany of bleakness: "abrogation of any communal existence," "disrupt[ion of] human systems," "separation from nature," "misogyny to necrophilia," "self-repudiation of art," "de-realiz[ation of] the world," "solipsis[m]," "complete devaluation," "total accusation of life." In the end he does allow for the possibility that silence may, as it were, overstep its bounds and cause "the affluence of being" to "flood the abyss." But his emphasis is overwhelmingly on what Hassan himself terms an "outline of negativity."[12]

In a social era tormented by clutter—visual, aural, temporal—silence may, however, both rest and restore us to ourselves. The very absence that in one context speaks to us of the meaninglessness of life may, in another, remind us that mundane distractions have not yet blotted out all openness of potentiality. The vacant sky of an Ansel Adams photograph carries a very different emotional freight from that of the vacant streets and surfaces of an Edward Hopper cityscape. Hassan's are one set of "meanings" of silence, but they are not the only set.

Indeed, though I find Hassan's work very helpful—it is both extremely suggestive in itself and illustrative of the interpretive leaps made by theorists of the past decade or two—I would want to make a sharp distinction between that work and my own, which is considerably different in its intentions and its methods. Hassan is interested in the avant-garde and the surrealistic; I am interested, to a much greater degree, in the realistic. Hassan is interested in symbolism; I am interested in rhetoric—that is, in the function and the meaning-effects of silence in relation to the communicative and persuasive aspects of texts. Even the "negative" values Hassan enumerates may, in fact, be used rhetorically in what we might call a positive, or at least an illuminating, way. To be sure, he allows for such a use himself when he mentions the possibilities of discovering "cunning equivocations" and of "purifying the language," or "accus[ing] common speech." The phrases describe precisely the kind of rhetorical use that women writers often make of silence.

A more moderate and moderating value framework of the sort that Hassan allows for but does not present is explored by J. A. Ward in his book *American Silences*. Ward's interpretation of both verbal silence and its visual analogues encompasses not only the emptiness of the ontological void and the loneliness of the silent vision, but the awesomeness of space (reminiscent of Carlyle's pronouncement in *Sartor Resartus*) and the bare hope of open possibility. In his introductory comments, Ward observes that Ernest Hemingway "encumbers his protagonists with a surrounding chorus of banal voices."[13] The hero's silence on matters of importance shows up, by contrast, the vocal trash of those who speak at length on trivia. A silence of this kind may (does) convey disaffection and radical disillusion, but it performs the presumably corrective function of providing the ground against which more comfortable but more radically debased values can be displayed and exposed.[14] Silence becomes the voice of integrity.

Neither Ward nor Hassan considers the silences of women artists. Hassan, indeed, is emphatically masculinist. Not only does he concern himself almost exclusively with male writers within a critical realm of discourse unimpacted by feminist scholarship, but the language in which he writes of these concerns is staggeringly masculinist, with its references to what "men of letters know" and how "men" (apparently in the traditional inclusive-exclusive sense) "manage reality."[15] What Hassan does not consider in his discussion of the trope of silence as negation is the intensification of that trope when it is applied to women. In being defined, as Simone de Beauvoir has shown, as Other, woman becomes object to man's subject and is thereby silenced. She is the emptiness that awaits the creating Word. She is made the ally, in her silent objecthood, with "unconsciousness and, finally, death."[16] Carrying so great a weight of attribution, woman speaks of and through silence out of a tradition of being silenced.

The silences of women writers, then, do not simply provide yet another example of what may be considered a characteristic at-

tribute of their literary period. They constitute instead an intensified, doubly weighted version of it. Indeed, if we approach the
silence and withholding of a woman writer's work only through
the analytic terms set up by a critic such Ihab Hassan, we are
likely to disregard a great deal of the social, linguistic, and literary
pressure arising from what Sandra Gilbert and Susan Gubar re-
fer to as "the reality of gendered human experience."[17] That reality has both tended to enforce silence and compounded the
significance of that silence.

The twentieth-century women writers I take up here speak as
members of the modernist and postmodern literary periods,
which have been peculiarly characterized by silence. (Sontag's
characterization is apt: they have been a time "noisy with appeals
for silence."[18]) But they speak also as members of a class on whom
silence has been imposed. In addition, they speak as interpreters
of that silence and as rhetorical strategists who turn silence back
on their repressors as a weapon. My concern here is not only with
the silences of women writers, then, and the uses they have made
of their silences, but with the profound difference in our understanding of the meaning and significance of their silence that
arises from opening the discussion to the issues of feminist study.

It has been said, brutally, that the only good Indian is a dead
Indian. Not so pointedly verbalized, but much more widely believed, it would seem, is the axiom that the only good woman is
a quiet woman.[19] Cordelia's voice was soft and low, Lear tells us,
"an excellent thing in woman." In some places in Europe in the
Middle Ages a voice loud enough to be heard next door was
sufficient cause for a man to divorce his wife. Victorian women
were expected, so the folklore has it, to "suffer and be still." Certainly Victorian notions of proper social behavior worked toward
the repression, that is, the silencing, of women.[20] Mary Poovey, in
a study of early Victorian ideas of female propriety (based in part
on an impressive survey of instructional handbooks for women),
finds that behavioral patterns of docility, evasion, and accommodation—patterns we might take as behavioral equivalents of silence—were indeed "women's learned or internalized responses"
to the actual "social situation" of women.[21] Even today—though,

one hopes, decreasingly so—women are conditioned toward quiet and passivity.[22] It is commonly assumed that male children will be rough and noisy (assertive, self-expressive) while female children are expected to be quieter, easier to manage (unassertive, self-denying). Such expectations have far-reaching effects. Sociolinguists tell us that, in actual empirical study, women speak fewer words than men do in virtually any public situation and are interrupted by male listeners far more often than they interrupt men: the woman is no more expected to "lead" in conversation than she is in ballroom dancing.[23] The proper woman—in the past and still, or at least until very recently—is the quiet one. The properest, it would seem, is the quietest.

The late nineteenth century saw, in Gilbert and Gubar's words, "the rise of feminism and the fall of Victorian concepts of 'femininity.'"[24] Women began to "speak" publicly in a great variety of arenas, as they had already begun to speak, in overwhelming numbers, in the arena of fiction. Yet old ways die hard, and assumptions of innate female submissiveness or of the way things ought to be, innate or no, still survive. In the mid-1950s (I say from certain knowledge) teenage girls were being told they should not call teenage boys on the telephone, but wait (and hope, for otherwise how could they know they were of any value?) to be called. It was not right for girls to take the initiative—to speak up. Besides, no boy would stay interested for long in a girl who let it be seen that she felt a reciprocal interest. Young men, the doctrine went, were by force of nature sexually ravening, but girls did not have that urge and a nice girl would resist—until the right time, when she would respond. That she might have ravening urges herself, that she might appropriately initiate as well as resist and passively respond, was not acknowledged. By 1966 when a man told his wife (in Larry McMurtry's novel *The Last Picture Show*) to hold still during sex because nice women didn't move, the reader knew his statement showed not only his insensitivity but his being terribly out-of-date. But it was still plausible that such a man might say such a thing.

McMurtry's benighted football coach with his wife who dared to move beneath him reflected the well-established "male notion" that women should be desired but should not desire[25]—a differ-ent way of saying that they should be spoken (to) but not speak. Female jouissance is a speaking, a direct and open expression, of the desiring self. Silencing denies autonomy and denies, as well, desire.

Silence is the verbal equivalent of that submissiveness or pas-sivity that is generally recognized as the essential defining attrib-ute of the (traditionally) feminine.[26] Submission to what Mary Daly calls the "false naming" of things and of experience by the male[27] has the direct result of not naming, not asserting a coun-tervoice. Indirectly, it means developing a "vague sense of anxi-ety" or a more profound self-doubt which then leads to the same thing, silence.[28] Like some character in a Henry James novel, women have had to "speak haltingly, in response to a loss of faith in language"—men's language. Their haltingness is the restraint of the weaker in the face of the stronger: women have historically had to watch what they say, with the result that, even under the guise of chatter, they may be actually silent, in the sense of prac-ticing the Jamesian "holding back of words."[29]

Such a holding back means, in Sandra Gilbert and Susan Gu-bar's interpretation of nineteenth-century literature, the buildup of pressure that results in the madwoman's outbursts. Less dra-matically, it means an insidious tendency to say only what is ac-ceptable to men, to let anything else go unsaid, to retreat into conventionalism and rigid forms. In "When We Dead Awaken: Writing as Re-Vision," Adrienne Rich tells of her discovery, when she was beginning to write, that the woman poet most approved by the male critical establishment was the reserved and discreet Marianne Moore, a poet whose resistance is not asserted, but is masked by indirection. Moore was, in Alicia Suskin Ostriker's words, a poet of "necessary timidities and disguises," and Eliza-beth Bishop, Moore's "successor as the eminently acceptable woman poet," has been, like Moore, "esteemed for reticence."[30] But reticence was not to be Rich's way. She traces her own ma-turation as a poet to her arrival at a willingness to break out of what she regarded as stultifying forms and speak openly, aggres-sively.[31]

Silence or effective silence, not being heard or not being free to speak authentically, is a mark of women's repression in a masculinist culture. It is, indeed, a mark of victimization. The myth of Philomela, the raped girl whose tongue was cut out so that she could not speak to accuse her attackers, has been, for all its grotesqueness, a pattern of the actual experience of women in the real world: it is the victim, not the perpetrator, who must keep quiet. In Jane Marcus's words, men have "cut out the tongues of the speaking woman and cut off the hands of the writing woman for fear of what she will say about them and about the world."[32] Speaking submissively and self-doubtingly, keeping to the personal and emotional discourse expected of feminine speakers, has been, in Paula Treicher's words, "acceptable language in the ancestral halls." But "impertinent" speech that challenges the authority of the male's "sentence" of perpetual self-denial and subservience had better be squelched unless one is prepared to pay a very high price indeed.[33] Even in the 1970s and 1980s, Mary Jacobus argues, and even in the French theoretical writing about women and literature that has been taken by many as the authoritative voice of feminist theory, a female language is effectively silenced. The feminine "becomes the repressed term by which discourse is made possible"; it "takes its place with the absence, silence, or incoherence that discourse represses."[34]

For women writers, the situation has been doubly repressive. As *women* they are silenced by virtue of being members of a victimized class—"victimization incurs voicelessness."[35] And as women *writers* specifically, being positioned as the Other to men's subjectivity means being made outsiders to a masculine literary hegemony. It means being caught in a hard bind: as Ostriker puts it, "*true writer* signifies assertion while *true woman* signifies submission."[36] (The ways in which this positioning produces a silencing of women writers are expounded by Joanna Russ in *How to Suppress Women's Writing*, a book which male students generally disbelieve because they have not seen the world as being so prejudicial.[37] "Can't write! Can't paint!" echoes through more pages than Virginia Woolf's. Though Sigmund Freud "equated" dumbness, repressed speech, with "feminine concealment and duplicity"—supposedly innate traits of women—it is equally plausible, Mary Jacobus suggests, that women's reticences and silences are actually the mark inflicted by male intellectual aggression. Men have long betrayed a penchant for theoretical pronouncements about women. But the traits they have been glad to see as the defining attributes of authentic femininity—passivity, absence of logic, centering on domestic emotions—may well be a sign of women's internalization of Freudian/masculine sentence to literary death, that is, the male insistence on women's "incapacity" for producing literature.[38]

Male intellectuals have used theoretical pronouncements on the nature of women as a rationale for silencing them. In the past, the terms in which that theory-based silencing was argued were heavily moralistic. It was not proper, not morally acceptable, for a woman to speak about certain things or, in the view of the more conservative, to speak publicly at all.[39] The proper sphere of women was the home, where they were to serve as a refuge of purity, a haven, for men and to safeguard an ideal of innocence and self-giving which men, exposed to the rougher outside world, could not be expected to maintain. Publication of their writing—or their music or their art—was of dubious suitability at best for a proper, home-centered woman.[40]

In our own century the theoretical rationale has shifted its terms to a less moralistic argument. Psychologizing male intellectuals have used the tortuous and highly conjectural terms of Freudian theory to argue, not that woman *should* be retiring, but that she is inherently so. Juliet Mitchell, wishing to defend Freud and psychoanalysis proper from the ire of feminists, insists that such theories are often not so much Freud's own as those of over-zealous or misunderstanding disciples and interpreters. The Freud "inherited" by feminists, she explains, is "often a long way off-centre," and much of the feminist "outrage" against Freudian theories is a "more-than-justified denunciation of their application."[41] Recent years have seen a "growing tolerance" for psychoanalysis as a method "potentially rich for feminist theory."[42] Even so, whether by Freud directly or by his followers in the Anglo-American clinical and theoretical establishment, the frustrations of women unable to fulfill their urge to creative or intellectual achievement have been attributed to denial of their inherent sexual identity, that is, to penis envy. As one of its central tenets, however, feminist thought insists that such pronouncements are scarcely to be considered disinterested—indeed, that speech is always interested. A different perspective, a different interest, illuminates the bias of such pseudoscientific essentialism. Its interpretive terms are built on the desire to maintain dominance; Freudian psychology has striven to define the female, but the act of definition, from a privileged and interested position—let alone the terms in which that definition has been couched—has been grossly repressive. Responding to Shoshana Felman's question, in "Rereading Femininity," "What does the question—'what is femininity—*for men*' mean for women?" Mary Jacobus answers, accurately enough, "the silencing or elimination of woman."[43]

In the twentieth century, despite waves of feminist challenge (or perhaps because of it), linguistic and literary theorists too have continued to fasten exclusionary labels—though perhaps more subtle ones—upon women. Indeed, according to the view of literary and sexual history presented and richly documented by Gilber and Gubar in *The War of the Words*, male theorists and writers have expressed their misogyny more aggressively and vehemently since women *have* been speaking, despite the ongoing conditioning that tends to squelch them, than in previous centuries, when effective silence could be assumed. So frequently cited a theorist as Jacques Lacan said, in "God and the *Jouissance* of the Woman," that women are "excluded" (from everything? or only from discourse?) "by the nature of things which is the nature of words." Language itself, he is asserting (wishfully?), by its very participation in the natural order, silences women. Robert Graves, in *The White Goddess*, urges that the woman poet should instead be "a silent Muse."[44] The past dies hard.

The result of masculine theorizing about femininity has been that women's stories, as Carol Christ observes, "rarely have been told from their own perspectives."[45] That is, women's interpretations of their own natures, experiences, and concerns have often been devalued in favor of interpretations from a masculine perspective. Women's writings have overwhelmingly been viewed as trivial, formless, or otherwise unworthy. As every reader of anthology tables of contents knows, until recent efforts to re-form the canon, women writers were virtually unrepresented, unrecognized. Even their existence was scarcely known—the work of feminism in literature was first (and is still) a recovery of lost texts, silenced voices. The power structure itself, the control of the literary enterprise by men, who defined what was important and worth publishing by what reflected masculine experience, worked to silence women writers or to define the terms of literary value in such a way that women's texts for the most part dropped from memory.

Another effect of male control of the literary establishment has been to pressure women into adopting evasive and masked presences and the stylistic traits defined as being appropriately feminine. Tillie Olsen, whose now classic book *Silences* is probably the most eloquent sustained lament for the thwarting of creative endeavor, summarizes the stylistic result of the subversion of women's art: "Being charming, entertaining, 'small,' *feminine*, when full development of material would require a serious or larger tone and treatment. Pulling away from depths and complexity. Irony, wit, the arch, instead of directness; diffuse emotion or detachment instead of tragedy. Avoiding seriousness altogether. Concealing intellect, analytical ability, objectivity; or refusing to credit that one is capable of them. Abdicating 'male' realms: 'the large,' the social, the political." Women writers have not only adopted pseudonyms but pseudolanguages as well. What Patrick Moore observes of poet Louise Bogan, "since she wanted to be published, to be heard, she had to restrain her voice," has been true of countless others as well. Alicia Ostriker quotes an array of (male) critics of the 1960's and 70's who use "modesty" as a test of a woman poet's achievement.[46]

The silencing of women by masculine theory and masculine power has, of course, been erected on a very practical foundation of social constraints and demands. Practical means of silencing have included denial of education and social autonomy and time and access to readership. As numerous feminist literary historians have demonstrated in recent years, and indeed at least so long ago as Virginia Woolf's *A Room of One's Own*, women writers have simply had to struggle against more constant and more wearing obstacles than men. Writing—if they were allowed to learn to write—in the scant interstices of time between other, more pressing chores or in the weary late hours after children were put to bed, or, like Jane Austen, slipping their work under the "cover" of letter paper when visitors came into the parlor, they had to be astonishingly perseverent if they were to continue at all. Though gynocritics have discovered far more women writers than the silencing of misogynist canon-formation once led us to believe, it is nevertheless clearly evident that until the nineteenth century, at any rate, women writers were far fewer than men. The wonder is that there were as many as there were.

But beyond the more obvious facts of the male control (until very recently) of the means of publication, language itself has been possessed, owned, by the male. From its pronouns to the arcana of its traditional masculine preserves, such as scholarly Latin, patriarchy "inscribes" the "marginality" of women. Yet it is in the very language of patriarchy that women must speak if they are to speak at all. The problem of the woman writer, at a more fundamental level than that of access to the machinery of publication, is how to "challenge" the "terms" of patriarchy while "necessarily working within them."[47] "Necessarily," because the dream of a woman's language, a language that would "write" the (female) body, remains just that: a dream (and a dream, moreover, that insidiously reintroduces a form of biological essentialism). To be published, to be read, to be accepted even marginally among the critical and academic arbiters of value, the woman must use a language (and a language of forms) that is, if not the property of masculinity, at least so controlled by masculinity as to be, in large measure, a hostile medium. She must manage to inscribe the feminine within forms of discourse established by patriarchy and tainted with misogyny.

Small wonder that so many women writers have used pseudonyms. The temptation to deny one's handicapping identity so as to enhance one's acceptability and chance for esteem must have been enormous. And literary history is rife with examples of female writers who have enjoyed warm receptions so long as reviewers thought they were men. But denial of personal identity is a form of silencing, too, just as thwarting of authorship, denial of a "hearing," and restriction of matter and style and pressure to use evasive language are a silencing.

The woman writer may find another answer, however, to the multifarious problem of silencing by the male hegemony. That answer is to use silence, the very silence that has been imposed, as a tool to undermine the ascendancy that silenced her. Janet Perez notes that in modern Spanish literature, operating within a situation both socially and politically repressive, silence has often been used as part of a "rhetoric of opposition," along with false or devious language such as "circumlocution" and "oblique or elliptical presentation," as a means of resisting censorship.[48] Women writers, facing the "censorship" of masculine prescription, masculine control of the means of publication and the terms of cultural validation, often masculine control of the means to a daily livelihood, have employed a similar means of opposition.

The employment of such a strategy is indeed nothing new, nor is it confined to writers. Silence has been used as a weapon by immemorial generations of women—especially of wives.[49] Silence and various behavioral tropes of silence—mocking submissiveness, unresponsiveness, exaggerated passivity, particularly exaggerated unresponsiveness and passivity in bed: these have been the most effective (often the only) weapons in the arsenal. They are techniques of withdrawal, of refusal to participate, or what is called passive aggression. They are also techniques which involve a miming of the conditions of inequality and denial of personhood in which women have routinely lived. "Very well," such silences say. "If you are the master, if you are the one who has the say in things, go ahead, be master, assert yourself. You see what that does to me—it makes me a dead thing, a mannequin, the corpse of a woman. That's what you seem to want. Now how do you like it?" And so women have been (one would guess) in virtually all cultures, at virtually all known times, great satirists—

through their silences. And by using the force of their silent satire they have often, in small ways, got what they wanted.

Of the four writers considered here—Jane Austen, Willa Cather, Katherine Anne Porter, and Joan Didion—three are, in varying degrees, great satirists (Cather being the exception). Porter is perhaps the least so, Austen probably the most. But all, on occasion, employ techniques of miming of the male power-holders to show up the falseness, the overinflation, of their pretensions. All four of these writers—three of them American, one British; three of them representing the twentieth century, though their productive periods scarcely overlap; one still living and productive—manifest at times the effects of the silencing or repressing of women by a patriarchal social structure. That is, either they themselves as narrative voices or specific characters in their fictions are seen to be at moments unable to speak fully or openly because of the pressure of expectations regarding the proper (subordinate) role of women. Their own writing or the speech of their created characters accommodates itself at times to "the feminine."[50] All of them reveal, however, dissatisfaction with that state of affairs and find ways of evading and undermining it, if not of directly challenging and altering it.

The strategy of resistance most consistently employed by these four writers, who are in many ways so dissimilar, is a sometimes evasive, sometimes aggressive silence. All of them variously use silence rhetorically as an invitation to the reader to perceive more than is said or to perceive the fact of the imposition of silence. More radically, Didion and to some degree Porter turn toward silence as toward vacancy or the void, the invalidation of that which is. That is to say, they participate in the modern and postmodern elevation of silence or emptiness that we have seen discussed in the work of such critics as Hassan, Ward, and Kermode. But that role of silence in their work, that participation in a characteristic trope of their time, is by all odds the least interesting and the least significant aspect of their work. Of more importance than the troping of silence which they have in common with other (male) modern and postmodern artists is the use of a rhetoric of silence which they share with Jane Austen. In their various ways they employ silence or omission—that enforced mark of the feminine—as a rhetorical strategy of subversion, specifically subversion of masculine power.

It is important to point out that the four writers discussed here are not alone in manifesting traits of reticence, either in their own voices or in their created voices, or in using a rhetoric of reticence or silence. Just as reticence is a behavioral pattern shared by many women, so verbal reticence is a stylistic trait of many women writers.[51] This is not to say that devious or accommodative speech is inherently feminine. Very little, indeed, in the behaviors or attributes of the sexes can confidently be said to be inherent. Gender is socially constructed. That being true, however, the commonality of the varying degrees of social constraint within which women have had to work has produced observable commonalities of verbal expression—among them, accommodative, reticent, and (we now know) duplicitous language. These four—Austen, Cather, Porter, and Didion—are by no means the only writers who have employed suppressions and withholdings as an aggressive rhetorical strategy. One thinks of Emily Dickinson or of Edith Wharton or of Anne Tyler. Similarly, in the work of Ann Beattie, according to a recent critic, we must "listen to the tale not being told in order to understand" the "narrative acts" of the stories.[52] No principle of necessity, then, dictates the choice of these four writers for the present study. They are, however, the writers who, in my own reading, have seemed to employ a rhetorical strategy of reticence in the most pervasive and most creatively effective ways, as a principle of fictional energy.

The four writers studied here do not employ strategies of reticence or silence at all uniformly. Sharing as they do a quality of controlled pointedness, they are still in many ways dissimilar. Indeed, that dissimilarity is as important to the understanding of the (female) rhetoric of silence and suppression as is the fact that they not only share the employment of such a rhetorical strategy but employ it for similar ends.

The imposition of reticence or silence for reasons of propriety is seen most clearly, of course, in Jane Austen, who took as her challenge the discovery of a way to speak beyond the limitations she had, of necessity, to observe. At the surface of her fiction she indeed seems to observe the expected behavior patterns; her novels do not raise their voices; but at the same time, she shows us, helps us to see, the straitness of her female characters' bounds and the foolishness of imposing such bounds. That duality, that saying beyond words, lies at the heart of what is perceived as Austen's irony. In Mary Poovey's words, Jane Austen achieved an ironic stance that gave her the "freedom necessary not only to identify" the "ideology" of the proper lady but "always tactfully and with ladylike restraint" to "criticize the way it shaped and deformed women's desires."[53] Austen uses omissions, understatements, and silences mainly for analysis, to isolate and clarify meanings without spreading them boldly before the reader in so many words. She also uses such devices as means of engaging the responsive reader, that is, of stimulating an interactive reading. But in addition, she uses strategies of reticence for revealing and undercutting the relative positions of the sexes. Austen's silences become windows through which the clear-eyed reader sees the falsity and the unfairness of a system of misconceived and misapplied conventions regarding gender.

Willa Cather, writing somewhat more than a century later than Austen, faced far fewer constraints from social forces of propriety. Nevertheless, her fiction is equally marked by the duality of saying beyond words, by "strains, chords, counterparts."[54] She felt acutely the restraint of small-town conventionalisms and responded, first by speaking out in her blunt drama reviews while in college, then by leaving. But even in Pittsburgh and then in New York she felt the strain of being counter to the majority, female in a male world of art, lesbian in a heterosexual society, midwestern in an East Coast literary and artistic establishment. Her novels bear the mark of her reticence, not only about her own life but about all things sexual. Moreover, Cather was, if anything, an even more self-conscious artist than Austen, well and deliberately informed by that remarkably self-conscious theorist Henry James, as well as by the work of others who had directed the novel increasingly into paths of self-scrutiny. Her ideas of art involved a strong commitment to restraint, selectivity, and precise focus. This commitment, combined with her own need for reticence and disguise, produced a fiction not only of spareness and omission but of duplicitousness. Nevertheless, Cather's work also has a rhetorical thrust. Largely by means of the contrast between what is said and what is not said, it illuminates and displays harsh truths about women's lives.

Katherine Anne Porter, born some twenty years later than Cather and establishing herself in literature about the time Cather was flagging as an artist, is much like Austen in the dryness and economy of her tightly reined prose. Like Austen's, hers is a style of clarification. She shows us what we can see if we are willing to pay very close attention. What that is may be an ambiguity, an unresolvable dilemma, but we see its terms more clearly because of her precise delineation. Like Austen, too, Porter expects us to fill in her spare outlines with our own realizations. She shows us things, and if we are perspicacious we will find them uncomfortable; but she does not *make* us uncomfortable.[55] Separated by more than a hundred years, Austen and Porter are more alike than any other pairing of the four. Porter's reticence is generally like Austen's, a mode of decorum. But at times, in both "Old Mortality" and "Pale Horse, Pale Rider," it is also, like Joan Didion's, a mode of anguish.

Didion is a writer very different from the other three in the consistent aggressiveness of her silences. Reticence will seem, perhaps, an odd term to apply to Didion. Certainly she has no maidenly modesty. She is free to address any subject. But she, like the others, refrains from spreading out her fictive world in all its abundance. She gives us its outlines, a sharp detail here or there, a broken-off phrase from a conversation, no more. The rest we must fill in for ourselves—as we do when we read Austen, Cather, or Porter with active engagement. Like Austen and Porter, she is a writer of few books; and like Porter and Cather, her books are typically compact, lean, short. Unlike the pointedness of the others, however, Didion's terseness is aggressive. She assaults the reader, in effect, with four-letter words yelling out of blankness. Her prose is bluntly, tersely angry, and the great spaces of blank paper surrounding it do nothing to soften that anger. Didion hurls silence back into the face of patriarchy.

In the works of all four of these writers, the characteristic style is one of understatement more than inflation, of tautness more than abundance. (This is true for Austen despite undergraduates' complaints about all those words and so little happening.) All four characteristically bring the reader up to the point, then stop, letting that point be made silently, in the space that echoes after the cutting off. By doing so, all four writers characteristically unsettle the reader. And the discomfort created by that unsettling is related, among other things, to the reader's being made aware of the injustice and unreasonableness of the world's patterns of relationships between men and women. None of the four is what we might call an orating feminist. They do not get on soap boxes or stumps; they do not expound and explain feminist arguments. But all four are, nonetheless, subversive feminists, and I believe intentionally subversive feminists, working to overturn the encrusted structures of gender by the mockery or the assault of what they don't say.

CHAPTER TWO

What They Don't Say:
Conversational and Narrative
Withholdings in Austen's Novels

If I loved you less, I might be able
to talk about it more.

———— JANE AUSTEN, *Emma* ————

When Mrs. Bennet goes to visit the ailing Jane, temporarily
housed at Netherfield, in the ninth chapter of *Pride and Prejudice,*
she chatters away as usual while Elizabeth tries vainly to stem the
flood of her mother's foolishness. One exchange in particular is
as remarkable for what it tells us about Austen's narrative technique as it is typical of Elizabeth Bennet's efforts to cope with her
mother.[1]

> Nothing but concern for Elizabeth could enable
> Bingley to keep his countenance. His sister was less
> delicate, and directed her eye towards Mr. Darcy
> with a very expressive smile. Elizabeth, for the sake
> of saying something that might turn her mother's
> thoughts, now asked her if Charlotte Lucas had
> been at Longbourn since *her* coming away.
> "Yes, she called yesterday with her father. What
> an agreeable man Sir William is, Mr. Bingley—is
> not he? so much the man of fashion! so genteel and
> so easy!—He has always something to say to every

body.—*That* is my idea of good breeding; and those persons who fancy themselves very important and never open their mouths, quite mistake the matter."

"Did Charlotte dine with you?"   (2:43–44)

What is interesting here is not so much what either of them says as what Elizabeth does not say. Indeed, she does not directly respond at all to her mother's reproachful discursus on gentlemanly agreeableness—reproachful, because Mrs. Bennet intends it to point up Mr. Darcy's lack of such agreeableness. We can imagine Elizabeth's saying, in ordinary conversation, how fully she agrees or how she in some way or in every way disagrees. We can imagine a less dutiful daughter protesting that Mrs. Bennet talks too much or too unthinkingly or that Sir William Lucas is not everybody's idea of a polished gentleman. Elizabeth says nothing, or nothing, at any rate, in the way of a direct follow-up. She merely changes the subject. After what we imagine as a slight delay, a moment of silence, she asks her brief question about Charlotte.

That moment of silence before she puts her question, that absence of what she might have said but didn't, tells us more clearly than any words could have done how Elizabeth feels about her mother's social gaffes and how she attempts to deal with them. She knows well that Mrs. Bennet's remarks are terribly, rudely pointed; that they lack even the least subtlety; that they are not only an affront to Darcy, their putative target, but a fresh revelation of Mrs. Bennet's own stupidity, not only because she offers the obtuse and self-important Sir William as her standard of excellence but because she imagines that in talking about him in order to get at Darcy she *is* being subtle and clever. Elizabeth knows, too, that to protest now would be not only graceless, since it would further call attention to the effrontery of her mother's outburst, but useless, since there is no hope she could ever make her mother understand what is wrong. Realizing all this, yet maintaining her self-possession (the text indicates no stammerings of dismay, no breezy verbal bustlings), Elizabeth puts the tersely worded question by which she hopes to deflect Mrs. Bennet onto another track.

My point is that if we read the conversation between Elizabeth and Mrs. Bennet, we consider not only what they say and how they say it, but also what they might reasonably have been expected to say and what was not said at all. We read the gaps, the silences, as well as the words. Doing so, we become cocreators in the dynamic of the text, the potential or submerged text as well as the text as printed. That "interaction between text and reader" that has been so great a topic of critical interest in recent years is both stimulated and accommodated by the text's indeterminacy—what is not said.[2] In manipulating dialogue, as well as in other ways, Austen invites the reader's involvement. We find ourselves always evaluating her characters' discourse, always *sounding* it (that is, both hearing it and plumbing its depths), always sifting out the precise meanings from the apparent ones, the false from the true. And then, besides, "hearing" and pondering what they don't say. True reading of significant texts is, perhaps, always an interactive endeavor, but it is particularly so in the case of these texts. And interactive reading is particularly close to Austen's aesthetic intent and the meaning of her work. She did not write for "dull elves" who have to have everything spelled out (spelled, written out) for them.[3] As interactive readers, we enact the effort that her novels emphasize. Tony Tanner points out in his admirably thoughtful study that for Austen the "imperatives of verbal repression were as important as the obligation of communication."[4] For the Austen reader, no endeavor is more important than the painstaking reading of dialogue, and the imperative of reading the lacunae is as pressing as the obligation of reading the printed words.

Examples of elusive or incomplete conversational interchanges, inviting the reader's imaginative involvement, are abundant in Austen's novels. There would be no virtue in any effort at cataloging them. We might mention, however, just one more, the famous scene of indirect communication between Anne Elliot and Captain Wentworth in *Persuasion*. We will have occasion to come back to this complex scene later, but here it would be well to note how much gets said tacitly, in the empty spaces. All readers of *Persuasion* will remember the scene in which Anne and Wentworth, both of them desperate to convey their emotions to the other and to learn whether there is any chance of reciprocation after their long estrangement, manage to communicate indirectly, Anne by means of speech ostensibly directed to another, Wentworth by means of a letter hidden beneath another letter he is writing. Both oral communication (Anne's) and written communication (Wentworth's) have to be doubled and duplicitous in order to achieve their purpose.

To be sure, during the early part of Anne's conversation with Captain Harville, she believes Wentworth is beyond earshot. The remarks to Harville that carry hidden reference to her own situation—remarks chiefly about the constancy of women's feelings—are not intended as covert communications to Wentworth. But after Wentworth drops his pen, she does suspect he is overhearing, and she then goes on to tell Harville, in phrases only ostensibly impersonal, that some reasons for a belief in the capacities of one's own sex "cannot be brought forward without betraying a confidence, or in some respect saying what should not be said" (15:234). By this she means Wentworth to understand that her reasons for insisting on the constancy of women are more personal than she has stated. Arguing that men feel deep emotions, Harville mentions the sadness of going to sea and leaving a beloved wife on shore. In response, Anne concedes men's strength of feeling but claims for women the distinction of "loving longest, when existence or when hope is gone" (5:235)—meaning to convey to Wentworth an inkling of her own continuance in love after his suit was broken off. Meanwhile, Wentworth writes his secret note to Anne while seeming to write a business note. They manage to reach an understanding despite the restraints of company and decorum.

The worthy people of Austen's world, the Annes and Wentworths of her fiction, always manage to communicate much in little. Indeed, their patterns of economical speech and careful silences become a criterion by which the worthy are measured and identified, in contrast to those who say little in much.

In Austen's world, the big talker is almost always either a fool or a villain, or both.[5] Fools may, of course, be redeemed to inclusion in the comic community by virtue of their goodness—the most obvious example being Miss Bates of *Emma*. In Austen's hierarchy of personal merit, the topmost position is occupied by those who possess both goodness and intelligence. But of those who have only one or the other, it is those with goodness, but not intelligence, who take the second position and those with intelligence, but not goodness, who are lower down, ahead of only the Mr. Eltons and the Mr. Collinses who are both foolish and, in varying degrees, vicious. Miss Bates is accorded the novel's tolerance, or more than tolerance—affectionate tolerance. Though less obviously foolish than she, Mr. Weston, a person of only the kindest intentions, also tends to rattle on and to violate with endearing abandon his own resolutions to keep secrets. Mr. Knightley is, of course, *Emma*'s great hero, a man who unites astuteness with warm feelings and moral insight. He is also a man of few words.

Austen applies a standard or garrulous or incisive, glib or weighty speech as a yardstick of merit. Her standard of positive value is a judicious reserve. It is the glib, the fulsome, the verbose who are found wanting, and those of few words who are affirmed. To be sure, she values clear expression and appropriate openness; intelligent, honorable discourse is seen as the hope of society. But discourse is often abused or debased. Austen distinguishes, and expects her reader to distinguish, between qualities of discourse, to distinguish valuable converse from verbal trash.

In *Emma*, in particular, dialogue is the medium of ethical discrimination. By their talk, we know that the Eltons, both Mr. and Mrs., are vulgar, morally insensitive people; that Frank Churchill is deficient in conscience and control; that Emma herself is undisciplined. The positive values associated with reticence and restraint are less easily discerned, since they are conveyed by absence more than by presence; but they are no less real. We are able to value Jane Fairfax, Robert Martin, and above all Mr. Knightley by their restraint, their seemliness, and their understatement.

Moral evaluation by what one doesn't say, rather than does say, is a point in Austen's work that requires particularly alert readers who are able to let the tenor of the whole guide their local readings. One needs to be constantly referring the specific to the general and the general to the specific. In *Emma,* for example (vol. 1, chap. 6), Mr. Elton's wordy ecstasies over Emma's influence on Harriet Smith and especially her attempts at a portrait of Harriet (4:43) are allowed to stand on their own, with no comment by the narrator and only a brief (and, as a matter of fact, mistaken) one by Emma. The unwary might suppose the guiding consciousness of the novel finds nothing amiss here, that is, might take Elton's effusions at face value. Yet our acquaintance with Austen's work as a whole, if not our careful note of what the text is doing just here, enables us to realize that the narrator is tacitly condemning flattery and fulsomeness, not only in Elton, but in Emma herself, who lets her eagerness to promote a match for Harriet with Mr. Elton lead her into ramblings of overstated enthusiasm. Or again, in chapter 9, Emma makes a long speech to Harriet beginning "'When Miss Smiths and Mr. Eltons get acquainted—they do indeed'" (4:74) and going on to indicate her belief that the two are "'by situation called together'" and that a marriage is both desirable and likely. But Emma's superabundant comments are both hasty and incautious. Her speech is another instance of Austen's letting her characters show themselves up by saying too much, while the narrator says nothing. In fact, it is Emma herself with whom Mr. Elton has been wanting to "get acquainted" and with whom, in his eyes at any rate, marriage is the goal.

Verbal restraint is a lesson Emma sorely needs to learn. Throughout the book, her lapses in judgment and in what can only be called goodness are associated with saying too much. Like Frank Churchill, she shows that "readiness to talk" (4:190) which often marks the unworthy in Austen's world. It is an unfortunate flaw, which comes very near linking Emma, to her discredit, with the wrong group—the inane but dear Miss Bates and, even worse, the shallow Elton and the stupid, intrusive Mrs. Elton, as well as glib, deceptive Frank Churchill. The risk that Emma will be incorrectly "placed" on the basis of her unconsidered speech is an aspect of those "difficulties of a high order" that Wayne Booth, in *The Rhetoric of Fiction,* says Austen posed herself. Emma goes on at length—wrongly—about Harriet's supposed social origins and Robert Martin's "entire want of gentility" (4:32), and does incalculable harm in frustrating his affection and confusing Harriet's understanding of her own emotions, status, and expectations. Having no knowledge of the facts and no valid reason to meddle in other people's affections, she should have held her tongue. Her promotion of Mr. Elton's supposed suit is much the same kind of lapse. Subsequently, when the news comes of Elton's engagement to another, Emma's speculations about the character of his intended bride are as unrestrained and as baseless as her manipulative talks with Harriet had been. About Jane Fairfax, too, she gossips entirely too much, and very irresponsibly. Later, after her moral awakening has begun, she can only think of her behavior in that respect with a "blush" (4:399) of shame.

Emma's greatest transgression, her rudeness to Miss Bates at Box Hill, is, of course, a clear instance of saying too much. After the buildup of a great deal of vain chatter with Frank Churchill (vain both in the sense of being empty and in the sense of being puffed with vanity), bringing Miss Bates to her utterly candid admission that she is likely to say "'dull things'" as soon as she opens her mouth, Emma cannot "resist" an urge to show her wit at Miss Bates's expense. Yielding to impulse, she makes her notorious remark about the difficulty of limiting Miss Bates to only three dull comments. Restraint would have been much preferable to so pointed a display of her own readiness of amusing speech. The remark evokes a succession of labored efforts at amusement, thinly veiled sneers, and general discord, largely furthered by a combination of Frank Churchill's double-talk aimed at Jane Fairfax and Emma's own undisciplined vanity. Lacking good will, lacking restraint, but loaded with underlying tensions, the flow of Frank Churchill's comic ebullience reaches "a pitch almost unpleasant" (4:374) which at length wears thin even to Emma. He carries to an extreme the forced wit and lack of judiciousness that have led Emma to violate the most basic principles of kindness. When Mr. Knightley reprimands her as the party is breaking up, she can see not only how unkind but how mindlessly unsubstantial her conversation has been.

In contrast to the Elton-Churchill group of vicious/foolish speakers and the Bates-Weston group of virtuous/foolish speakers, each of which is temporarily joined by Emma at some point, the people of the novel who meet Austen's highest standards of decorum, good sense, and moral discernment are both reserved and reticent. Jane Fairfax is offered as the paragon of the virtues Emma needs to develop—though not, of course, as the highest example of charm, wit, and lovableness: she is not the heroine. And Jane Fairfax is reserved almost to a fault. Indeed, she herself would prefer to have spoken more freely and grieves that she has been blameworthy in that her restraint at times borders on deception, just as Frank Churchill, whose fault she has "caught" by association, deceives by what he omits to say as well as by what he says. But we must not confuse Jane Fairfax's reticence with the effects of the false position in which she finds herself as a result of her secret engagement. Austen is able to distinguish quite precisely between restraint and lack of candor, and to value effective communication quite as highly as she values reserve. It is clear that Jane Fairfax would in any event, quite apart from her enforced caution, be a person who speaks less than she thinks. She is a model of decorum. Even Emma, at her worst, recognizes this, as clearly as she recognizes the good will and tact underlying her friends' expressions of praise when she plays the piano and their comparative silence as to Jane's playing: "'my playing is just good enough to be praised, but Jane Fairfax's is much beyond it'" (4:232).

Indeed, Jane's reserve makes Emma uneasy. She goes on at excessive length in mentally condemning Jane for being "wrapt up in a cloak of politeness, . . . determined to hazard nothing . . . disgustingly, . . . suspiciously reserved" (4:169). But we are not to take Emma's thoughts here as the valuation of the novel. At the time she is reacting in this way to Jane, Emma is still unenlightened, unperfected. Reserve, it seems, is a means of preserving one's social safety, and Emma, who is forever hazarding hers, wants Jane to be more vulnerable than herself, not less so. Whereas Emma's verbal indiscretions threaten to undermine her standing both in the world of the novel and in the estimation of the reader, Jane's reserve establishes her dignity and elicits the explicit endorsement of Mr. Knightley, who pronounces what appears to be the narrator's own judgment that a "'diffidence'" which "'arises from discretion'" is to be "'honoured'" (4:171).

Knightley is, of course, as his name indicates, the novel's standard of perfect conduct, and he is a man of few and inevitably judicious words. Direct to the point of bluntness, he is never unkind or curt. Like Jane, he both thinks and feels more than he says, replying to nonsense monosyllabically. More than once we see him responding to Miss Bates's verbal outpourings with his usual sensible brevity. But he replies tolerantly, without any of that unkindness to which Emma gives way at Box Hill. It is unfortunately true, as readers have often complained, that Mr. Knightley appears somewhat stodgy or stuffy. He has none of that sense of fun, of free play, which makes Frank Churchill so appealing (speciously appealing) and which we know, from the evidence of most of her fiction, especially *Pride and Prejudice,* Austen herself enjoyed. As Tanner points out, Knightley is "as little likely to 'play' with language as he is inclined to dance."[6] But the novel shows us that, given the choice between a specious (even deceptive) witty chatter and a kindly and judicious shortness, we can only prefer the latter.

It is important to acknowledge that Austen never applies reticence as an obvious or unilateral standard, but as one to be governed by circumstances and occasions. An inappropriate reserve such as Sir Thomas's, in *Mansfield Park,* which keeps him at a chilly distance from his own children and lets him forego any effort to learn why his household has fallen into disarray in his absence, is not a mark of decorum but of inadequacy. A withholding based on the desire to mislead people or to create a false impression, such as Frank Churchill's, is simply a form of dishonesty. Reticence about expressing one's own feelings to one's own family, such as Elinor's in *Sense and Sensibility* or Fanny's in *Mansfield Park,* may lead to harmful repressions; or at any rate, from our post-Freudian vantage we judge that it may, though such an idea may have been less clear to Jane Austen. It is not, then, as though Austen has taken a bipolar view of social intercourse. She values open communication. But she values, even more, judicious communication, and this means at times judicious silence. Knightley not only displays but embodies such judiciousness.

In volume 3, when Mr. Knightley represses the social gesture of kissing Emma's hand, we know that it is because he cares too much for her to be able to perform as a mere gesture what would mean a great deal to him. The incident is a pointed indication of the meaning of his similar verbal restraint. Understanding this, we are expected to see that the one occasion in the novel when Knightley lapses into verbal inconsequence is a very significant departure from his characteristic behavior, indicating his emotional turmoil. Emma asks whether his intention to visit his brother in London is not "'a sudden scheme'" (4:385), and he replies, in a thorough muddle of self-contradiction, "Yes—rather—I have been thinking of it some little time.'" This is scarcely the deliberate Mr. Knightley we have come to know and respect! But we are able to assess his emotional disorder here by comparison with the emotional order and verbal restraint he more characteristically displays. It is these qualities which Austen establishes as the yardstick by which to measure foolishness, conveyed in babble, and the yet more culpable failings of irresponsibility, duplicity, or viciousness. The Frank Churchills of Austen's world—a character type including Crawford of *Mansfield Park*, Wickham of *Pride and Prejudice*, and Willoughby of *Sense and Sensibility*—may be glib, but her Mr. Knightleys and her Darcys, however they may lack the readier social graces, are people of sense, forthrightness, and few words. We are never allowed to doubt which Austen prefers.

The development of conversational judiciousness or reserve as a touchstone of positive valuation, which we have examined primarily with reference to *Emma*, is evident in all the other novels as well, though with varying emphasis. In *Persuasion*, which we will consider at greater length below, we see a striking turn toward values of openness and demonstrativeness, even spontaneity, in all sorts of social interaction. Even so, the two characters who are the hallmark of both merit and emotional honesty in a world of dissolving values speak, as they act, with a considerable, and a considered, reserve. In *Sense and Sensibility,* despite recent modulations of what was once the critical consensus that it projected a simplified bipolar vision, we see very clearly that Elinor's reserve is preferable to Marianne's "honesty and spontaneity," which, as David Monagham points out, end, not in better communication, but in injury to those Marianne is concerned to comfort. Therefore, the novel argues, in Monagham's words, that "discretion" is advised.[7] In *Pride and Prejudice,* the passages of bright and sparkling repartee, chiefly between Elizabeth and Darcy, no doubt give the reader a sense that conversation is relatively free flowing. Yet the criteria of reserve and economy, of speaking with care and knowing when to keep silence, are confidently invoked in the moral hierarchy that puts Elizabeth and Darcy at the top, closely followed by Jane and the Gardiners, and perhaps Bingley, with the three foolish Bennet sisters, Mrs. Bennet, and Wickham at the bottom.

Indeed, it is Wickham who, by virtue of his unrestrained speech, is perhaps the most wicked of any of Austen's characters (unless that distinction goes to Aunt Norris, of *Mansfield Park,* whose speech is not only unrestrained but cruel). Wickham is both imprudent, or improper, and deliberately untruthful in what he says. Upon first meeting Elizabeth, he vilifies Darcy (falsely) at length while insisting that of course he would never publicly expose the Darcy family. Elizabeth, who should know better, is taken in; as usual, a glib tongue combined with a handsome appearance is a potent charm for even Austen's superior young women. Elizabeth, too, under the charm of Wickham's attention, falls into excessive talk, as she elsewhere falls into wittiness for its own sake. Like Emma, she must learn restraint.

Perhaps the readiest, and the most obvious, example of the contrast between excessive and reserved speech in all of Austen's work comes in *Pride and Prejudice* in the contrasting marriage proposals—Mr. Collins's proposal first to Elizabeth, then (reported indirectly) to Charlotte, and Darcy's first proposal, against which his second is poised. Mr. Collins's proposal to Elizabeth is one of the great bits of satiric comedy in all of literature. He convicts himself out of his own mouth of being a great fool. Most obviously, his proposal speech is very long, some three pages (2:105–7) as compared to the brief two paragraphs of narration given to Darcy's second proposal and Elizabeth's acceptance. Beyond his mere verbosity, however, Collins's speech is repulsive and ridiculous for its smug self-assurance, indeed its utter self-preoccupation, its inflated formality ("you can hardly doubt the purport of my discourse"), its false claims to emotion ("before I am run away with by my feelings on this subject," he says, while Elizabeth stifles a laugh at the improbability of Collins's ever being run away with by his feelings), and its tactlessness ("your wit and vivacity, I think, must be acceptable to her, especially when tempered with ... silence and respect"). Collins, in short, is not honest; one guesses that he does not know how to be. So it is certainly not surprising that he complacently assumes Elizabeth is not honest either when she rejects him. His insincerity is demonstrated, of course, when he applies to Charlotte Lucas only two days later, again in "long speeches" that only delay the answer Charlotte, in the "pure and disinterested desire of an establishment" (2:122) has already determined to give him.

In the case of Collins's proposals, Austen has no need to maintain decorum. No strong emotion is present which might violate it, and she has no wish to spare Collins but, on the contrary, a wish to hold him up to laughter. Her brevity in the matter of Collins's proposal to Charlotte derives simply from her wish not to repeat what he had already said so ludicrously to Elizabeth. His prolixity, of course, indicates only Collins's lack of emotional substance. He likes the sound of his own voice more than he wants to gain Elizabeth.

The matter of Darcy's first proposal is very similar in that he, too, conveys primarily his own egotism. His opening statement may at first seem like a direct outburst of strong emotion: "'In vain have I struggled. It will not do. My feelings will not be repressed. You must allow me to tell you how ardently I admire and love you'" (2:189). With a little care, however, we can see in it an egotism only a little less extreme than Collins's, though not so ridiculous. His emphasis is not only on himself but on his wish that he did not care for her. And he is scarcely less assured than

Collins: "'You must allow me to tell you. . . .'" Darcy goes on, as tactlessly as Collins, though with more reason, to dwell on "his sense of her inferiority—of its being a degradation—of the family obstacles" (2:189). His lengthy letter of explanation does not have to bear the same censures of pretense or insincerity that Austen attaches to long speeches because, first, it is a convincing explanation (particularly of his dealings with Wickham) and, second, when writing a letter one is relieved of the emotional pressure of a personal presence, and therefore free to be fully detailed, rational without heartlessness, and frank without breach of decorum. The letter begins to change Elizabeth's mind. A long speech, which could be heard only once and would surely have aroused her spirited rejoinder, could not have done that.

In *Mansfield Park*, the contrast of volubility and reserve remains an important moral index, but with the difference that its import is more often made explicit here than in the other novels. Austen actively directs our realization that, for instance, Mary Crawford should not speak so freely about her uncle's lapses as she does (3:57). Mr. Yates's "easy indifference and volubility in the course of the first five minutes" of their acquaintance are taken by Sir Thomas, in explicit indirect discourse, as confirmation of the young man's suspected shallowness (3:183). As so often before, we see that excessive talkativeness marks a character as one of the unacceptable, but here we do not have to judge that for ourselves; we are told.

Fanny, the insistently affirmed heroine and moral center, is reticent to a fault. Literally so: we may well wonder—though the narrator does not—whether her reticence on at least one occasion, that of Sir Thomas's request for an explanation of her refusal to marry Henry Crawford, might not be actually blameworthy. If she had managed to overcome her awe of Sir Thomas so far as to tell him that she had good reason to doubt Crawford's moral character, a great deal of misunderstanding and unhappiness might have been averted. But Austen (and in *Mansfield Park* the narrator virtually *is* Austen; distance between author and narrator almost disappears) does not seem to make that observation or to question, to any degree, Fanny's correctness in withholding that explanation of her actions.

The fact that Austen does so fully affirm Fanny that she cannot entertain any question of her right judgment in such an instance—we might say, so fully that she does not ever present Fanny ironically—is an indication of the larger problem readers have experienced in reading and responding to this text. In Austen's fiction generally the reader engages in an interpretive endeavor guided by the voice of a narrator whose knowledge and understanding, even whose wisdom, surpasses the reader's own, but whose stance vis-à-vis her characters allows fluctuation, exploration, discovery—whose view, in short, is congruent with the reader's own imperfect understanding even while superior to it.[8] But in *Mansfield Park* the narrator is not only assured in her view, but flatly certain of it; she regards Fanny as an absolute, an evaluation no more subject to enlightenment or to the halftones of real human understanding than Fanny herself is subject to moral suasion. The narrator's view of Fanny is a closed book, and the reader's experience is, accordingly, foreclosed. Howard S. Babb, commenting on the narrative point of view in *Mansfield Park*, notes that Austen here presides "all in all . . . more solemnly, I think more openly, than in her other novels."[9]

It is precisely this, the manner in which our comprehension of the author's ethical valuations is established and developed, that accounts for that differentness from the other work that many readers have sensed in *Mansfield Park*. The novel differs from every other work in the Austen canon in the extent to which the reader is told. It is not that the book's values are belabored or made obvious—the ongoing critical discussion of what evaluative standards are being invoked by the theatrical episode or the contrast between Mansfield Park and Portsmouth is evidence that they are not. Probably there is more direct statement in this novel than in the others, and even more moralistic statement. But the narrator's comments are not always direct or obvious. Often they are broadly or obliquely ironic, so that the reader is kept in an ongoing process of deciding what the true intentions are. We read that Mr. Grant "looked" the gentleman, but judge that he only looked it; we read that Mrs. Grant "foresaw" elegance and accomplishments in Mary, but we observe that such elegance and accomplishments are not enough (3:42). The difference is that whether direct or ironic, the narrator's comments are more fully verbalized than in the other novels. They are rarely tacit. Dialogue, too, is more fully elaborated. The reader engages in interpretation, but not in the filling in of strategic lacunae.

Reticence, then, becomes, not a stance of tentativeness, of openness to revelation and of invitation to the participating reader, but a stand against sharing, an absolute standard of behavior. And in *Mansfield Park* the character who best epitomizes reticence does not speak out of the strength of self-control and intellectual curiosity, but out of the weakness of timidity and an urge to self-preservation. To a degree, reticence was always a strategy of weakness. It was, in Austen's time but not uniquely then, a standard of proper female behavior and bearing. The ideal woman was expected to maintain a deferential quiet, leaving it to the lords of the earth to assert their views and their selves.[10] Or to put it another way, reticence was a key aspect of a code of womanly decorum based on a conviction of woman's weakness and need to rely on the protective leadership of her man. Characteristically, Austen turns weakness into strength as she imagines a more just, that is, a feminized, social order. But in *Mansfield Park*, despite her directly expressed wistful hope for "a juster appointment hereafter" (3:468), she merely clothes weakness in the defensive strategies of evasion and repression. Fanny's silences are rarely significant of anything except her timid self-effacement.

I have urged that to read Austen's conversational discourse rightly we must read its silences as well as its spokenness, and that to do so requires the closest attentiveness.[11] In addition, we must read the narrator's silences as well.

In the interchange between Elizabeth Bennet and her mother with which I began, in which Elizabeth changes the subject without any spoken response to what her mother has been saying, the narrative voice, too, maintains silence. The narrator passes over what would seem to be a perfect opportunity for either pronouncements on Mrs. Bennet's foolishness or ironic summations, preferring to let her ill-advised words speak for themselves (as Babb puts it, Mrs. Bennet "stands condemned every time she opens her mouth"[12]) and to let the reader arrive independently at an understanding of Elizabeth's tactics. Indeed, this is Austen's usual method when dealing with the foolishness of a Mrs. Bennet or a Mr. Collins or, in *Emma,* a Mr. Elton. All of these big talkers are allowed to convict themselves out of their own mouths while the narrator stands by, enjoying the spectacle with us.

At times, Austen's technique of narrative silence can be seen as simply an accomplished version of the comic drop, a device for punctuating the text so as to achieve effects of surprise, display, and emphasis. We see that device, for instance, when, after paragraphs of foolishness between Mrs. Bennet and Mr. Collins and after Mr. Bennet's portentous summons of Elizabeth to his study, we come to Mr. Bennet's terse summary of the case: "'Your mother will never see you again if you do *not* marry Mr. Collins, and I will never see you again if you *do*'" (2:112). The change in cadence—to crisply balanced monosyllabic neatness after sprawling phrases in which are cushioned, like fruit in flavored gelatin, various ludicrous bits of inanity—reinforces the satisfying surprise of the turn of events. We could find a great many more instances of this technique in Austen's work, especially in *Pride and Prejudice;* she is very good at it, and it is an important aspect of her characteristic effect of comic undercutting. But my interest here is not so much in the drop from plenitude to terseness as in the drop from plenitude to nothing. Silence. Again and again she follows comic excess with comic absence, a withholding of comment. The device becomes a kind of speechless gesture of display, like pointing a finger, which lets foolish wordiness show up its own foolishness.

Often the underscoring by silence comes at the end of a chapter, where the blank space and the reader's pause can, so to speak, deliver it. Mrs. Bennet's inanity, reported both in direct and in indirect discourse, provides six occasions for such chapter-end cutoffs, and Mr. Collins four. We will look at only two examples: In volume 2, Mrs. Bennet rails bitterly at Mr. Collins and Char-

lotte for their supposed anticipation of the inheritance of Long-
bourn, ending, "'Well, if they can be easy with an estate that is
not lawfully their own, so much the better. *I* should be ashamed
of having one that was only entailed on me'" (2:228). Stop; break.
Enough said, the narrator's silence implies; no more need be
added. And the second example, from the ever-effusive Mr. Collins:

> "You will not, I hope, consider me as shewing
> any disrespect to your family, my dear Madam, by
> thus withdrawing my pretensions to your daugh-
> ter's favour, without having paid yourself and Mr.
> Bennet the compliment of requesting you to inter-
> pose your authority in my behalf. My conduct may
> I fear be objectionable in having accepted my dis-
> mission from your daughter's lips instead of your
> own. But we are all liable to error. I have certainly
> meant well through the whole affair. My object has
> been to secure an amiable companion for myself,
> with due consideration for the advantage of all your
> family, and if my *manner* has been at all reprehen-
> sible, I here beg leave to apologise."   (2:114)

And the chapter ends. It is as if the narrator, too, were reduced
to speechlessness by Collins's outrageous blend of feigned humility and pompous, intolerant self-assurance.

In *Emma,* where the issue of reticence versus fulsomeness is
developed more somberly than in the high-spirited *Pride and Prejudice,* we find fewer instances of this particular device, the end-
of-chapter drop to silence for comic purposes. The comic effects
in *Emma,* when they do occur, are less crisp, more muted. But
the good Miss Bates provides many opportunities for gentle fun,
where Austen is able to draw on the drop from much to little.
During one of Emma's many visits, for instance, Miss Bates goes
on in her usual fashion about Col. Campbell's generosity and Mr.
Knightley's thoughtfulness and what a delightful party last night,
etc. She has just started to repeat every word of a wordy chat
with Mr. Knightley that everyone else has overheard anyway, and
Jane has pointed out that they heard it all—a very obvious ex-

change. "'Oh! yes, my dear, I dare say you might, because you know the door was open, and the window was open, and Mr. Knightley spoke loud. You must have heard everything to be sure. "Can I do any thing for you at Kingston?" said he; so I just mentioned.... Oh! Miss Woodhouse, must you be going?—You seem but just come—so very obliging of you'" (4:245). The drop is not to absolute silence, in this instance, as a comment on all Miss Bates's conversational clatter, but to silence as regarding the main point. Before the chapter break, we drop from billowing verbiage to terse narrative summary that, with its brief understatement, achieves virtually the same effect as the drop to silence. "Emma found it really time to be at home; the visit had already lasted long" (4:246). Coming straight on the heels of Miss Bates's verbal overabundance, this leaves tacit the narrator's acknowledgment of what both Emma and the reader are feeling, that tolerance has reached its absolute limit. Some things, like the excellence of Jane Fairfax's piano playing, go without saying, they don't need shoring up with words, and indeed, out of courtesy, should not be mentioned.

Clearly, Austen uses the drop to silence, or to understatement or evasion, as a mode of tacit commentary on whatever has preceded it. Foolishness and verbosity are not only displayed against silence or compression but are implicitly measured by it, or by the standard of control that compression implies, and are judged inferior. Lack of control, expressed as volubility, becomes associated, as we have seen, with foolishness and often—though not always; witness Miss Bates—with moral deficiency as well. Absence becomes a more positive force than presence. It also becomes, of course, a means of eliciting the reader's active participation. Again and again, the narrator withholds comment on motivation or significance, displaying her character's words and mannerisms but leaving the reader "space" in which to arrive at an understanding of the self-deceptions and repressions that they reveal. Thus, in volume 3 of *Emma,* she shows us Frank Churchill's restlessness and his eagerness to go to the door, masked as concern that somebody may need an umbrella, and leaves it to us to realize that he is impatient to see Jane (4:321). In the same sequence she gives us Emma's thoughts about the ideal man, a man of "general benevolence, but not general friendship" being a man she "could fancy" (4:320), but leaves it to us to realize that this description fits Mr. Knightley very well. Her narrative silence or reticence, then, becomes an emptiness the reader is invited to fill, and, to readers willing to engage in the imaginative effort of filling that emptiness, a source of interest. As Frank Kermode writes, a "text with minimum indeterminacy is a boring text."[13] Austen's texts provide ample, but not always conspicuous, indeterminacy. They are rarely, if ever, boring.

A particularly telling instance of the judgmental withholding of comment occurs in *Pride and Prejudice* when Mr. Collins writes to convey his "condolences" for Lydia's disgrace. The letter is, of course, an exercise in viciousness. Typically longwinded, it closes: "this false step in one daughter, will be injurious to the fortunes of all the others, for who, as lady Catherine herself condescendingly says, will connect themselves with such a family. And this consideration leads me moreover to reflect with augmented satisfaction on a certain event of last November, for had it been otherwise, I must have been involved in all your sorrow and disgrace. Let me advise you then, my dear Sir, to console yourself as much as possible, to throw off your unworthy child from your affection for ever, and leave her to reap the fruits of her own heinous offence" (2:297). After the formal closing (itself inflated with compliments indicated by two "etc."s; John Gardiner's letter, a few pages later, has one) the narrative simply proceeds, without comment, to what happens next. We are given no indignant protestings by Elizabeth or Jane, reading the letter. We have no pronouncements by the narrator on either the pompousness of the style or the crude self-regard of the sentiments. Nor does the narrator remind us how far short of Christian charity the implacable vengeance recommended by Collins falls, or how far he is from fulfilling any rational standard of a true churchman. None of this needs to be said, because it is too obvious to need saying. In effect, the controlling sensibility of the novel—we could call it "Jane Austen"—leaves Collins beneath notice.

We have considered the quality of reticence in Austen's narrative and in her use of direct discourse as a stylistic maneuver for reader involvement and, in general, for subtlety and as an index to ethical valuation. A somewhat different but certainly related matter is the withholding, or even evasiveness, in the expression of emotions that characterizes Austen's people, especially her women. That evasiveness is particularly marked in the expression of romantic and sexual emotions. The reason for this marked constraint on affective expression is scarcely surprising: reticence in communicating emotion is an aspect of the prevailing social decorum of Austen's world. More particularly, it is an aspect of the nature of societal constraints on women. The matter is considerably more subtle than that bare statement would indicate, however, and is bound up with Austen's evident sense of the limitations and shiftingness of language itself.

As many critics have pointed out, the constraint placed on expressions of feeling in Austen's novels is most clearly manifest in her proposal scenes. In these, both dramatized action, or dialogue, and narrative summary and comment are particularly curtailed and problematic. Happily, few critics would now revive the once common view that Austen's restraint at such moments indicates an emotional poverty or coldness on her own part, a supposed limitation that has at times been equated with other kinds of limitation, notably her happy imperviousness to political and social problems. A host of depressingly *ad feminam* readings have implied that, being a spinster, she was unacquainted with how people behaved or spoke on emotionally charged occasions (it doesn't follow) and therefore could not write of them (that doesn't either). Somewhat closer to the mark are those critics who have implied, from time to time, that Austen chose to build her fictions on prudential principles, sticking with what she knew she could do and avoiding the risk of handling material outside her direct ken. Though the overtones of the hedging of one's bets in such an argument are unattractive at best, it does at any rate recognize the role of choice, that is, conscious control rather than helpless deprivation, in the shaping of the fictive structure.

To us it may seem self-evident that Austen knew what she was doing (at least as well as anyone ever does) and that her mind was by no means helplessly formed by societal conditions but was continually questioning, mocking, resisting. Simply to read her letters is to wonder how she could ever have been viewed as a creature enslaved by conventional assumptions or impoverished by a narrow range of experiences. Among recent challenges to that view that stress the aspect of conscious selectivity in Austen's art, Susan Morgan has argued that Austen's suppression of romantic (i.e., sexual) events was a chosen demurral from conventions that defined a heroine's role and significance primarily in terms of her sexual relation to a man. To be sure, the action of the novel still revolves around the heroine's search for and choice of a husband. But the emphasis is shifted. By thwarting reader expectations of a culminating love scene, Morgan argues, Austen asserted the "simple and endlessly influential point" that "women can grow, can be educated, can mature, without the catalyst of a penis"—that is, without sexual experience. The "absence of sex" in Austen's work, by which one includes the absence of passionate expressiveness, far from being the weakness it has at times been considered, is actually a "literary innovation" that freed the novel to treat women characters seriously as developing, fully self-validating agents.[14]

Clearly, Austen's suppressions were, very often at least, chosen strategies, primarily for reader involvement and for conveying a theory of language. That they were at the same time manifestations of culturally imposed notions of appropriateness, or tact, particularly on the part of women, and reactions to those notions, is also clear. To acknowledge that a writer lives in her own time and that, say, battlefield experience at Waterloo might have colored Austen's work differently than a lifetime of, say, tying up dahlias, by providing her a different set of impressions, remembered emotions, and images, is not necessarily to fall into the trap of a naive life/work equivalence. It is reasonable to suppose that life gets carried into work somehow or other. But the extent and quality of the carryover are by no means simple or obvious, and a theory of creativity that bases itself on biographical equivalence ignores the quality of mind and specifically the strategic choices that continually transmute, transform, even recreate the simple passed-through stuff of experience. We can say, then, that bio-graphical and societal factors are important, even that they may appear in unconscious ways or limit the text in unconscious ways, without taking those factors to be determinant. What matters is what Austen did with her experience and the assumptions about propriety that pressed upon her. And what she did—as Porter, Cather, and Didion have also done—was to find her own way of maneuvering within constraints and at times actually to turn the negative weight of conditioning into positive strength.

Austen's heroines—and Austen herself—must create their own expressive space and define their selves within a double set of constraints. They are confined not only by the prevailing ex-pectations governing polite social behavior but also by those more stringent ones governing the proper behavior of women. Both sets of expectations are enormously complex and deeply involved in every aspect of the self and of the literary text. The constraints on a woman's behavior, in particular, pertain most obviously to her sexual conduct and the manner in which she may and may not indicate her interest in a man, or even her willingness to admit his interest in her, but they extend even to the terms and the topics of her ordinary conversation. The pressure of these dual constraints leads to the development of complex "strategies of indirection."[15] We can see these strategies in operation on the level of verbal style in the wittiness and irony of Jane Austen's narrative discourse, which treats indirectly issues that readers often claim are completely excised from her immaculate fictive world. We can see them in operation as well in the larger shapes of her work, the behavior patterns of her women characters and the blocks of material that she chooses to include or exclude, or more charac-teristically, to curtail.

Examples of constrained expressive action are everywhere—in the impossibility of Jane's taking any initiative with Bingley by giving him a direct indication of her feelings, and the resultant misunderstanding of her too-restrained indirect indications; in Elizabeth's inability simply to write to Darcy and tell him she knows she was wrong (a woman can't write a note to a man unless they are engaged); in the enforced passivity in which both of the Bennet sisters, and indeed all of Austen's enamored young women, must sit at home and hope that their young men come to address their suit. Even Emma, who has known Mr. Knightley all her life, cannot say to him that she wishes he would say what is on his mind, but can only suggest that they walk a little further. Jane Fairfax is, of course, as helplessly caught in the toils of propriety as in those of economic necessity, so that she cannot either explain her situation to others or demand that Frank Churchill make good his engagement to her and relieve her of the necessity of accepting a position as governess. All of these characters maneuver within narrow limits to control their own lives.[16]

The effects of such socially imposed reticence are particularly interesting in *Sense and Sensibility* and in *Persuasion*.

Long considered the weakest of Austen's novels, *Sense and Sensibility* shows thoroughgoing evidence of the strain not only of restraint but of actual repression. The delineation of a pair of sisters, strikingly unlike each other temperamentally but engaged in closely parallel actions, strongly suggests that we think of the novel in terms of classic doubling and, further, that the sisters may serve as projections of conflicting aspects of Austen herself. To be sure, the contrast of the two personality types is not so clearcut and simplified as commentators have sometimes implied. If Austen does finally chasten Marianne for her exaggerated sensibility and her disregard of decorum and vindicate Elinor's good sense, she does not do so in such an extreme way as to scapegoat Marianne or deny her attractiveness. Further, far from being devoid of sensibility as a representation of sense alone, Elinor too demonstrates warmth of feeling. The contrast, then, is not unreasonably exaggerated. Yet it does show signs of anxiety over the need to choose one mode above the other and real fear that the sensibility of a Marianne, if given free rein, might prove personally and socially disruptive.[17]

The parallel of the two love plots is striking. In both cases, we have young men who give strong evidence of emotional attachment, then mysteriously withdraw from the scene, and, after a period of bewilderment on the part of the woman, are found to be engaged to another. The attitudinal aspects of the parties are quite dissimilar: Marianne falls into distraction while Elinor represses her emotion; Willoughby proves to have been toying with Marianne while Edward has curtailed his attentions out of a sense of honor. But the shape of the two romantic actions is much alike. In each case, the woman is or should be prevented by decorum from making any effort to resolve her dilemma. When Marianne in typically heedless fashion disregards propriety and writes to Willoughby to invite his renewal of attention, she makes her situation worse by evoking increased societal attention and intrusion. Surprisingly, she seems to encounter little overt disapproval, but, what is worse in her mind, she receives great excesses of pity. It is assumed that she must be severely distracted indeed to behave so unbecomingly. Because of her own forwardness, she is left with no place to hide in the privacy of her (indubitably overindulged) emotions. At the end, when Marianne realizes her mistake, she goes so far as to blame herself for Willoughby's guilt—even though it is clearly demonstrated that he is a practiced villain. In what we might recognize as a typical form of womanly behavior, she feels guilty for having attracted his dishonorable intentions. A heroine, it seems, should not be outgoing and emotionally expressive, but should only wait in passive self-preservation for her male-centered fate to catch her up.[18]

In contrast to Marianne, Elinor not only observes female decorum (which in the novel is identified with good sense) in her own behavior, but has to be always restraining and correcting her impulsive sister. Obliged to disguise, if possible, and atone for Marianne's disregard of social niceties, she must undergo those ordeals of minor falsifying which are essential to the ordinary operation of society. In the complicated course of her love for Edward, leading to their eventual marriage, she is forced to wait passively for the resolution of his mysterious changes in attitude, unable to determine for herself how things stand between them, since the initiative must be entirely his. When Edward comes to visit and behaves coldly, she is "mortified" but, as politeness would dictate, resolves to avoid "every appearance of resentment or displeasure" (1:89). Put in a false position by her knowledge that Edward is engaged to another even while the gossips among whom she lives believe he is engaged to her, Elinor must endure the torments of their incessant teasing without making the least response, because to address the question in any way would be improper. She is caught in a smothering stasis, a kind of social paralysis, as she is screwed down more and more tightly to the conventions decreeing male freedom and female propriety— meaning, passivity.

Austen shows us all this and invites our realization that such a system is unreasonable, then seemingly vindicates Elinor's acceptance of such constraints while punishing Marianne's free spirit. Indeed, as Stuart Tave points out, after she comes to appreciate the example of Elinor's "composure of mind," Marianne excoriates herself for her former behavior—in characteristically "extravagant language."[19] Yet the novel is not without its own questioning of that distribution of reward and punishment. Elinor's reticence is so extreme that she feels herself unable to ask her own sister a question about so delicate a matter as her romantic feelings. "'I long to inquire; but how will *my* interference be borne!'" (1:165). We are inclined to agree when Marianne accuses her of "reserve," though Elinor resents the imputation. Even more unsettling is the parallel between Marianne's and Elinor's reliance on their young men's appearance of affection. Elinor has argued that Willoughby's appearance of devotion to Marianne should not be trusted in the absence of an actual proposal, and her judgment on the point has been vindicated by the discovery that Willoughby is indeed a cad and has been toying with Marianne all along. Even after that vindication of her insight into her sister's peril, however, Elinor uses precisely the same argument from appearances to fly in the face of clear evidence and reassure herself that Edward really cares for her. To be sure, her confidence proves to have been well founded; her love story ends happily. But the parallel hints that it need not have been so. Luck was with her in this instance, but the position of a young woman having only a man's behavior toward her to rely on is, it seems, uncertain indeed.

By combining the story of Elinor's prolonged frustration in romance with a secondary plot involving an even more spectacular romantic victimization (a victimization in which Marianne, of course, conspires by virtue of her intense and heedless sensibility) and two merely glimpsed subplots of victimized females (the two Elizas and Mrs. Palmer), Austen develops in *Sense and Sensibility* a powerful, understated indictment of the social constraints on women's freedom to manage their own lives. The essence of those constraints is the enforced reticence that prevents women from confronting issues directly and resolving their own problems. In the mirroring plots and glimpsed motifs of the novel we see clear demonstration of Mary Poovey's view that Austen's ironic stance gave her a position of freedom from which she could both eluci-date the "ideology" of the proper lady and "criticize the way it shaped and deformed women's desires"—all without violating the decorum of her own "ladylike restraint."[20]

The glimpsed stories of the Elizas and of Mrs. Palmer are ex-amples of the very significant shadow elements in Austen's work, that is, the novelistic omissions and withholdings which illustrate the operation of enforced reticence in her own dealings with heavily emotional material and material related to the plight of women. Such material is typically conveyed indirectly in her nov-els or effectively masked, suppressed, or alluded to without full development. The entire Jane Fairfax subplot is such a shadow in *Emma*. We are told just as much about Jane Fairfax as will serve the theme of ready speech versus reserve and the growth of Em-ma's education. The hardships of a governess's life are raised spec-trally; enough is said that, if we stop to think, we can infer something of the pressure of this form of constraint on women, just as we can infer something of the economic straits of Miss Bates. Of Jane Fairfax's motivation or the basis of her love for Frank Churchill we know virtually nothing. The plight of the exceptionally intelligent woman of limited means and few op-tions who allows herself to enter into a romantic relationship with a shallow young man remains a shadow.[21]

One could say simply that the writer makes choices; she cannot choose to write every story that comes her way. But this is not a matter simply of how many children Lady Macbeth had. Jane Fairfax is present in *Emma* in a way very different from the way

Harriet Smith is present. Austen creates our interest in her, poises her as a foil to Emma, a comment on her, and then refuses to illuminate her for us. The Jane Fairfax story lures us off from the Emma story, but as it does it raises uncomfortable questions. Austen will not go that way; she chooses to write comedy. But neither will she ignore the grim truth. The result is the shadow.

In the troubled romantic comedy of *Sense and Sensibility*, Mrs. Palmer is such a shadow. Particularly in combination with the melodrama of the two Elizas, both ruined by charming men who seduce and abandon them, and in combination with the victimization evident in Marianne's story, the presence of Mrs. Palmer invokes a shadow motif of the plight of the woman as a victim of man, even within the marriage relationship that is the goal of the primary plot, the supposed happy ending. The young and lively Mrs. Palmer is a Mrs. Bennet not so much seen from the inside as seen with sympathy. The wife of a man who finds her barely tolerable because of her inferior mentality (and, without truly heroic endeavor, how could that have been improved in her society?), Mrs. Palmer resorts to a mode of self-deception that effectively represses her awareness of her own misery. "'He is so droll!'" she exclaims of her rude and insulting husband. "'He never tells me anything!'" (1:110). Indeed he does not. He treats her like a stupid child. Or again, "'Mr. Palmer is so droll! ... He is always out of humour'" (1:112). Much as we dislike seeing a person so thoroughly evade the truth, which is that her husband is simply a rude beast and his behavior is not droll at all, we cannot imagine any more effective way for a Mrs. Palmer to deal with her situation. A conspicuously talkative, superficially communicative person, she suppresses authentic communication of her feelings so fully that she can state, without the least evident irony, "'Mr. Palmer is just the kind of man I like'" (1:117). She says so because she had better say so and think so; she has no other option. Again Austen refuses to follow out the theme she has raised multidimensionally, but evokes its presence as a shadow text we "read" only by filling in its emptiness.

In *Persuasion* we see an exposure of the constraints on women similar to that in *Sense and Sensibility* but artistically more fully achieved.[22] Anne Elliot, caught in the prolonged aftermath of her refusal of Wentworth's proposal on the advice of her elders, suffers the stasis of a social inability to act on her own behalf. Not only is she disregarded by her family (she is "a heroine who has great difficulties in making herself heard"[23]) and deprived of any volition as to her own residence or activities, there is literally no one to whom she can express her feelings. When Wentworth returns, the pressure of conventional behavior prevents her, even if her fear of rejection does not, from giving any indication of her continuing love for him or making any effort to ascertain his feelings for her. She must helplessly suffer the romantic overtures of a man she does not with to attract, seeing all the while that his addresses force Wentworth further away, because social expectations give her no means to relieve herself of the unwelcome approach, to clear her own personal space for more authentic behaviors.

It is because the accumulating pressure of such constraint is so well realized as a weight under which Anne is borne down in stasis that we respond so intensely to the minor incident in which Wentworth physically lifts a weight off her. Kneeling down to remonstrate with her "remarkable stout, forward" nephew, she is pinned down to the floor by the child and cannot "shake him off." Then suddenly she feels herself "being released"; she cannot see who, but "some one was taking him from her, though he had bent her head down so much" that she could not move (5:79–80). The action is emblematic of the entire liberating action of the book. Though the reader would, perhaps, like even more to see Anne find a means of taking that action for herself, rather than have the man take it for her, the more important point seems to be that her renewed love affair is a liberating force for her. We see in the general movement of *Persuasion* a heroine who, like Elinor in *Sense and Sensibility,* is convinced that self-effacing service to others is right and that propriety must be respected, but who learns, as Elinor does not fully learn, to "make social conventions accommodate and communicate her feelings."[24]

It is in the famous scene of indirect communication between Wentworth and Anne leading to the renewal of his suit that she demonstrates this mastery. Through a supple interplay of assertion and accommodation in her conversation with Captain Harville about the nature of men's emotions and women's, she manages to avoid violation of her proper reticence while at the same time conveying to the overhearing Wentworth the truth of her own capacity for "'loving longest, when existence or when hope is gone'" (5:235). To do so requires the greatest skill and alertness. Simply hearing Wentworth drop his pen at a telling moment in the conversation (when she has mentioned the strength of "woman's feelings" and the unlikely possibility that such feelings might coexist with man's boldness), she is able to realize in an instant that he must have been overhearing the conversation, that he must have been emotionally responsive to what she had said, and that she may, with care, be able to speak to Harville in such a way as to convey enriched meanings to Wentworth. This she manages to do, by calling attention to the fact that decorum may prevent her from speaking freely ("'circumstances ... such as cannot be brought forward without ... in some respect saying what should not be said'"—5:234) and then claiming for her own sex the distinction of persevering in apparently hopeless love. Wentworth, who has at the same time been contriving his own indirect communication, understands. Anne manages at once to observe decorum and to convey her state of feeling. It is a triumph of achievement within constraint.

Austen's large-scale withholdings, then, like her heroines' social maneuverings, are evidence both of her society's constraints and of her own successful evasion of those constraints. The fires she cannot light in her text smoulder beneath it. Sex, economic insecurity, gender injustice—these are not omitted but masked, submerged, conveyed in reticent indirection. When Edward, in *Sense and Sensibility,* admits that Lucy, his first infatuation, was pretty and he was naive and foolish at nineteen, we know that he was also carried away by raging hormones, though Austen does not say so. When Emma is pierced by the realization that Mr. Knightley must marry no one but herself, she is in fact "pierced by sexual desire."[25] When Darcy indicates his awareness of Elizabeth's fine eyes, then her walk, her dancing, her speech, the movement of her hands over the piano keyboard, and when he renews his suit, we know that he is not feeling simply regard for Elizabeth but sexual fascination. His "passion" is "the subtextual force behind much of the action" of *Pride and Prejudice*.[26] It is a shadow plot in the book.

The expression of such passion, however, must always be indirect if it is to be acceptable within Austen's fictional structure. As Mary Lascelles so gracefully puts it, until *Persuasion* Austen never gave an actual love scene, that is, the scene in which the "spark and conflagration" occurs. Instead, during these "most private moments" her lovers "walk away into a friendly cloud."[27] Austen's characteristic practice, employed, I would say, in all six novels, not excepting *Persuasion,* is to suspend the dramatized presentation of events leading up to the romantic climax, a presentation developed largely through close-grained dialogue, and to shift instead to indirect discourse or, more often, to a somewhat abstracted narrative summary.[28] At the same time, she renews her characteristic reliance on generalization, a practice which stresses the shared, common qualities of the characters' experience and which engages our participation or assent as readers while disengaging us from highly charged particulars.[29] The practice is thematically right, conveying as it does both Jane Austen's faith in the continuity between the individual's personal interests and those of society and her stress on the moral value of a widened perspective, even as it is dramatically disappointing to the emotionally involved reader. After all, the proposal scene would seem to be crucial in novels patterned, as Austen's are, on the love-and-marriage plot, and readers have in every case followed, with considerable perseverance (to be sure, with considerable pleasure as well), a series of lengthy "verbatim" conversations only to arrive at the culminating moment and find very nearly a blank. This blank—that is, the reticence evident at the obligatory proposal scene—is, I take it, the most concentrated indication of an overall reticence in emotional matters.

In *Northanger Abbey*, the first (by one mode of reckoning) of the completed novels, the culminating event is distanced both by being given in a narrator's account, rather than direct rendering, and by the narrator's gently amused tone as she summarizes Catherine's reaction to the unseen proposal. Such phrasing as "explain himself" for declaring his love, "so well" for his ardency in addressing her, and "could ever be repeated too often" for her love of being made love to, smiles at the ecstasies of youth without derogating them. Further, the proposal scene is distanced and weighted by passive verbs, which put the emphasis on the action itself, as an idea, rather than the doing of it or the agents of the action as individuals. "Some explanation on his father's account he had to give; but his first purpose was to explain himself, and before they reached Mr. Allen's grounds he had done it so well, that Catherine did not think it could ever be repeated too often. She was assured of his affection; and that heart in return was solicited, which, perhaps, they pretty equally knew was already entirely his own" (5:243). That is all.

In *Northanger Abbey* the abbreviation of the proposal scene is not likely to be so bothersome to readers as it is in the other novels, since the tone of that novel throughout is parodic and its characters, as a result, are generally distanced anyway. Further, the theme, misinterpretation of appearances, is more directly insistent in this work than is any abstract theme in any of the other works. Thus the mildly comic use of "explain" and "explanation" in the proposal scene—comic both because of its dry understatement and because of the disparity of meanings between explaining his father's actions and explaining himself—continues that theme, even as it continues the amused, parodic treatment of the lovers themselves. For both effects, it is necessary that the proposal be presented in indirect statement. Thus the reticence of the proposal scene here can plausibly be viewed as being not only appropriate but even essential to the design of the novel.

The same cannot well be argued of *Sense and Sensibility,* yet the proposal scene here is very similar. What might be expected to be the romantic climax of the book, Edward's proposal to Elinor, is not a "scene," properly speaking, at all. It is merely an event that is acknowledged to have occurred. "How soon he had walked himself into the proper resolution, however, how soon an opportunity of exercising it occurred, in what manner he expressed himself, and how he was received, need not be particularly told. This only need be said;—that when they all sat down to table at four o'clock, about three hours after his arrival, he had secured his lady, engaged her mother's consent, and was not only in the rapturous profession of the lover, but in the reality of reason and truth, one of the happiest of men" (1:361). Not only the tone of disavowal and the absence of direct depiction, but the formally balanced syntax and the play of light mockery ("the rapturous profession of the lover," "the happiest of men") distance the reader, as well as the author, from the experience of a proposal of marriage. Even less attention is given to Marianne's engagement. Colonel Brandon's proposal to her is not even mentioned. We are simply informed, in the general winding up, that she has married him. One might well regard the amatory dismissal of Marianne as one of those "over-determinations" which Kermode sees as invitations to the reader to discover latent sense.[30] It is one of the most peremptorily foreclosed of all Austen's marriage plots.

It is *Pride and Prejudice,* of course, that affords the most familiar and most frequently noted example of Austen's reticence in presenting love scenes. Here, at the climax of the romantic plot, Darcy's second proposal to Elizabeth, we are shut out. We hear him ask permission to speak again, but we do not hear him speak. This is all the more interesting, as well as the more frustrating, because we have already seen, or heard, the first proposal at so great—and such indicting—length. That occasion, of course, was not (except, perhaps, for Darcy's opening outburst) a romantically emotional scene. Indeed, it was more an exercise in self-deception and aggressive appropriation (and therefore, for Austen, an occasion to be fully reported). In the first proposal, Darcy summoned Elizabeth to be his wife. In the second, when he had learned to love her properly, he came to ask her. The reader, naturally enough, is eager to witness the second scene. But at the crucial moment the narrator interposes, telling us only that Darcy "expressed himself on the occasion as sensibly and as warmly as a man violently in love can be supposed to do" (2:366). Similarly, when the secondary love plot culminates in Bingley's proposal to Jane, we glimpse the lovers moments afterward, and we hear Jane's expression of happiness, but we are denied the actual proposal.

In much the same fashion as *Pride and Prejudice, Mansfield Park* offers a heavily evaluative pair of contrasting proposals. The contrast is not so crisp as in the earlier novel, but its import is much the same. Henry Crawford, one of Austen's stock characters, the insincere young man, is "quite determined to marry Fanny Price" (3:291) and approaches her with a "sanguine and pre-assured mind" (3:302). Like Collins, though without Collins's ridiculousness, he speaks at length, not once, but twice. Edmund's proposal to Fanny, however, is, like Austen's other worthy proposals, shielded from the derisive effects of lengthy reporting. Indeed, Edmund's proposal, like Edward's in *Sense and Sensibility,* is scanted altogether. It is shunted aside in favor of commentary on the naturalness of his coming to want Fanny for his wife. The emphasis is on the motivation, not the act. "Edmund did cease to care about Miss Crawford, and became as anxious to marry Fanny, as Fanny herself could desire" (3:470). Recalling the brother-sister quality of their relationship, it would be tempting to read this as meaning, in other words, that he did not want it very much, or at least very passionately. Such a meaning, however, is certainly foreign to Jane Austen's intentions. Her irony is not so surreptitious as that, and Fanny remains, after all, the moral center of the novel. Nevertheless, the report of their feelings is so subdued that the actual proposal, as an occurrence, gets lost. Two paragraphs after the assurance that Edmund's feeling came to equal Fanny's, the reader discovers that the engagement is an accomplished fact: "Their own inclinations ascertained, there were no difficulties" (3:471). The nearest thing we have to the proposal is thrown into a participial phrase!

The proposal motif in *Mansfield Park* is actually considerably more complex, and bears considerably wider implications, than this summary of Edmund and Fanny's engagement indicates. We will return to a consideration of those complexities and their similarity to the structures of *Pride and Prejudice* later.

A very different situation is presented in *Emma,* in that the proposal scene is extended for some pages with close attention to the fluctuating emotions of both Emma and Mr. Knightley. Again, though, the words of the actual proposal are omitted. Solicited to give her assurance that she will at least hear him, Emma says "just what she ought" as a lady "always does" (4:431). Beyond this the reader is given no indication of the words or gestures in which they pledge themselves. For this reason, *Emma* is generally included in the prevailing critical indictment of Austen's proposal scenes as being "frigid exercise[s]."[31] To be sure, Austen retains in great measure the decorum we expect of her. Much of the proposal sequence is given in something between indirect discourse and narrative account, summarizing a retrospective view of Emma's and Mr. Knightley's emotional development toward the sharing of love. Even in the indirect discourse, however, the pressure of emotion is conveyed in a brokenness of phrasing, with sharp interruptions by dashes and exclamation points.

Emma actually offers considerably more of the direct discourse of the love scene than do the other novels. Mr. Knightley's apology for his verbal inadequacies—"If I loved you less, I might be able to talk about it more" (4:430)—is given directly. We are provided a more minute account than in other novels of the surging of emotions as the scene progresses. Even so, even in the passages of direct quotation, much of the deepest feeling is conveyed not so much by what is said and done as by what is omitted. When Mr. Knightley speaks of how fortunate Frank Churchill is in finding and engaging his love so early in life, what he does not say is what he most feels, how he wishes that he were so fortunate with Emma. Once again, as she had most successfully in *Pride and Prejudice,* Austen uses, in Chandler's phrase, "the language of speechlessness" to convey her characters' deepest feelings.[32] Naturally, the "reading" of such a language requires the greatest care and sensitivity to nuance. To some degree, in fact, Austen's reticence in delineating highly emotional scenes can be seen as an expression of her demand for an intelligent, participating audience. Moreover, the demands made on the reader for perceiving the unstated are another form of decorum or distancing. It is possible (though incorrect) to conclude, as Lloyd Brown does, that Mr. Knightley and Emma talk "at cross purposes" in an "irony of errors."[33] These very errors, however, are the means by which Austen lets the reader see her hero's and heroine's hopes and fears, and are the means by which they arrive at an understanding. Babb is both more correct and much more helpful here in his tracing of the ways in which indirection in the dialogue conveys the "intense private emotions" of both.[34]

In *Emma,* then, Austen offers a fuller rendering of the emotional evolution of her characters toward a commitment to marry. But it is still a subdued revelation of that commitment, and one which avoids a direct rendering of the pledges of love.

In *Persuasion,* too, Austen manages to give a sense of the emotional pitch of Wentworth's and Anne's declarations of continuing love, yet to retain, finally, the overall decorum and concealment that have so often been pointed to as evidence of her supposed incapacity for or fear of strong emotion. (Again, I would disagree with Lascelles as to whether she does, in fact, *give* an actual love scene.) She conveys the emotional tenor of the proposal by means of Wentworth's impulsive, urgent letter, which conveys the intensity of his feelings in such language as, "You pierce my soul. I am half agony, half hope" (5:237). At the same time, it *is* a letter. Recourse to presenting a declaration of love in writing is a way of avoiding the confrontation, interaction, and sharing of a face-to-face love scene. Later, when Anne and Captain Wentworth do meet and talk, their arrival at an understanding is not only offered through the convention of indirect discourse (a perfectly legitimate device for maintaining pace and for avoiding effects of bathos) but is marked by brevity, passive verbs, generalization, and formal syntax, all of which are means of dissipating the immediacy and the emotional impact of the proposal scene itself.

> There they exchanged again those feelings and those promises which had once before seemed to secure every thing, but which had been followed by so many, many years of division and estrangement. There they returned again into the past, more exquisitely happy, perhaps, in their re-union, than when it had been first projected; more tender, more tried, more fixed in a knowledge of each other's

character, truth, and attachment; more equal to act, more justified in acting. . . . they could indulge in those retrospections and acknowledgments, and especially in those explanations of what had directly preceded the present moment, which were so poignant and so ceaseless in interest. All the little variations of the last week were gone through; and of yesterday and to-day there could scarcely be an end.

(5:240–41)

In spite of the greater openness to intuitive or emotional values evident in *Persuasion,* which many readers have noticed, Austen maintains her practice of subduing the most intensely emotional moment of the novel.

In all of the proposal scenes of her heroes and heroines, then, Jane Austen avoids fullness or directness. In part, this restraint in presenting what is, in terms of plot at least, the climactic point of her novels, is a function of her concept of novelistic tact. She meant to avoid the bathetic and trivial effects of a preoccupation with private details. In *Persuasion,* she censures such a preoccupation, in connection with everyday gossip about an upcoming wedding, as "minutiae which, even with every advantage of taste and delicacy which good Mrs. Musgrove could not give, could be properly interesting only to the principals" (5:230). We may disagree; we may protest that we would be very interested indeed in such minutiae. But we do not live in an age committed to decorum. Austen did. At any rate, her tastes and convictions were formed in such an age. Further, it is clear that Austen's reluctance to give her characters' emotional lives—and for the modern reader this means to a great degree the physical aspects of their emotional lives—a fully rendered immediacy is partly determined by her purpose of keeping the thematic dimension central to her fiction. She appears to see a full depiction of powerful private emotions as a detraction from that emphasis.[35] The bareness of her proposal scenes, then, is a result of a deliberate aesthetic choice, not simply the manifestation of Austen's own anxieties or emotional limitations.

But beyond these factors, what I want to suggest is that the quietness, the virtual negativeness, of Jane Austen's proposal scenes arises not only from a theory of the novel but from a theory of language. Even an eagerness to avoid the breaking of decorum does not explain the verbal absence of her proposals. Not only is the language of love moderated, it is for the most part passed over. Her reason for doing this, finally, is a belief that language is in itself inadequate to the expression of strong emotion, or, in other words, that certain kinds of emotions have a quality of ineffability, putting them beyond the representation afforded by everyday speech. James Thompson, in a 1986 essay entitled "Jane Austen and the Limits of Language," points out that such distrust of "'worn' language" is a quality which Austen "shares with Romanticism" and that, specifically, novelists of the very late eighteenth and the early nineteenth centuries often invoked ineffability in the narration of proposal scenes.[36] To be sure, as Thompson points out, Austen had "no fully articulated language theory,"[37] but her numerous specific references to the capacities and the limits of human language (in *Mansfield Park*, in particular, where by Thompson's count the narrator refers to the inexpressibility of various characters' feelings twenty-four times) as well as the texture of her art in itself demonstrates that she did have a strong conscious interest in language.

Austen's problem, then, as a novelist working with plot conventions centering on romantic emotion was how to render in a verbal medium a quality of experience beyond words. In life, the inadequate words might be supplemented by gesture, intonation, eye contact, and, most emphatically, body contact. But these forms of expression are, for the most part, unavailable to Austen, for the reasons (decorum, emphasis on general themes rather than individual events) that we have already seen. Only the smallest gestures—gestures, though, which are very highly charged with emotional significance—might be delineated. We have, for instance, Elizabeth's and Darcy's walking together in the scene of his second proposal, an almost balletic movement conveying their joy in being together and their success in accommodating their previous excesses of personality to the corrective of each other and of their love: "They walked on, without knowing in what direction: (2:366). Elizabeth's excited anticipation and her awareness of the overwhelming emotional import of the moment are conveyed in the mere phrase, "had Elizabeth been able to encounter his eye" (2:366). Similarly freighted physical details are, from *Emma*, Emma's turning away from the door in order to walk further with Mr. Knightley and, from *Persuasion*, the view of Anne and Captain Wentworth as they "slowly paced the gradual ascent, heedless of every group around them" as he now walks "by her side" (5:240–41).

These are very significant patterns of motion. Yet they are undeniably, on the surface at least, subdued, even minimal. With no further notation of the various lovers' physical responses and gestures, and with only a minimal indication of what they said to each other, we are left to "supply from our own imaginations," as Chandler summarizes it, "the potency and force" of the characters' emotion. Austen presents the reader with a nearly empty space and invites the reader to fill it in out of the reader's own wishes, memories, and shared feelings.

That this can work—can make even a few of Austen's readers (those who are willing to allow her her own methods and standards) feel that the culminating scenes of the love plots are satisfying—is largely a matter of her understanding how to use techniques of large contrast. It is a matter, too, of her allegiance to a theory of language and her alertness to the possibilities of making that theory work positively in the dramatic structures of the novels.

First, and more generally, the proposal scenes do stand in strong contrast to the earlier scenes in all the novels, which are typically developed in reliance on elaborated discourse. That is, Austen gains the impact of strong difference by poising her nearly speechless love and proposal scenes against the sheer spokenness of sequences involving all other matters. In *Pride and Prejudice*, she takes us through those wonderful, witty dialogues of Elizabeth and Darcy and the vapid or deadly prolixity of Collins and Lady Catherine de Bourgh, building our expectation that all of the relationships between characters will be dealt with in speech, only to have the lovers fall speechless at the time of their revelation. This scene, Austen's practice tells us, is different and special. Words, she implies, cannot possibly fill the need—either the characters' words or her own. This time, we must consider "the implications of silence" and conceive of a state of anticipation, as well as "confusion and intensity of feelings," which are "beyond mere statement."[38] Much the same thing happens in *Emma*. After experiencing in chapter after chapter an Emma who brightly and confidently pronounces her playful caveats and a Mr. Knightley who does not hesitate to enunciate his settled judgments to Emma and to his acquaintances in general in weighty, well-rounded cadences, we find a Mr. Knightley who must rely on "looking the question" and whose speech rhythms are nervous and broken: "'As a friend! . . . Emma, that I fear is a word—No, I have no wish—Stay, yes, why should I hesitate?—I have gone too far already for concealment.—Emma, I accept your offer—Extraordinary as it may seem, I accept it'" (4:429–30). The difference in his speech patterns and his loss of confidence in his own saying—"'I cannot make speeches, Emma'"—make us realize the greatness of his emotional stress. A somewhat different contrast between speech and tacitness occurs to great effect in *Persuasion*. After the lengthy and often empty speech of the populous social situations with which she surrounds her lovers, Austen poises them in their crucial hour walking quietly and without reported dialogue among the "sauntering politicians, bustling house-keepers, flirting girls, . . . nursery-maids and children" (5:241) of busy ordinary life.

It is largely because of this contrast between the relative speechlessness of her lovers at the moment of their revelations and their talkativeness on other occasions that we believe the scenes involved are very special and worth our imaginative filling in. They *must* be presented indirectly and filled in by the imagination, not provided in the characters' own speech, precisely because they are so important. Conversation, Austen believes, always to some degree falsifies. People exaggerate, or they fall into embarrassment, or they misremember the actual truth they are reporting and resort to imaginative embellishment, but at any rate they are never able to communicate to others the precise state of their views and feelings. Even when they believe that they are being most candid, they are likely to misunderstand what it is that they are conveying to others. Thus Elizabeth, in *Pride and Prejudice,* means to be honest when she is, in fact, needlessly bold and pridefully opinionated. She means to be a thorn in Darcy's side, but so intrigues him that he falls in love.

Conversation, then, is necessarily imprecise. From the vagaries of the speaker's intentions and abilities and the predilections of the listener, as well as from the nature of language itself, it inevitably misses the mark. As Emma herself remarks, expressing her concern that Mr. Knightley might not have caught Robert Martin's meaning regarding his engagement to Harriet Smith, "'Did you not misunderstand him?—You were both talking of other things; of business, shows of cattle, or new drills—and might not you, in the confusion of so many subjects, mistake him?'" (4:473). If conversation is so inadequate on ordinary occasions, how much more so when the emotions are strained! It is on these occasions that people most need to express themselves, yet such occasions are too important, to the principals involved, to be entrusted to discourse. Through a very delicate irony, then, when Austen's characters most need to communicate with one another, they dare not place their confidence in the primary medium of communication, conversation. After the scene of Mr. Knightley's proposal to Emma, Austen as narrator steps in to observe, "Seldom, very seldom, does complete truth belong to any human disclosure; seldom can it happen that something is not a little disguised, or a little mistaken; but where, as in this case, though the conduct is mistaken, the feelings are not, it may not be very material" (4:431). Her heroes and heroines must hope to convey their meaning despite the inadequacies of language. Accordingly, Austen hopes to convey the sense of their avowal scenes in other ways than by reporting their speech.

But Austen goes further, even, than this. She not only doubts the adequacy of language to strong emotion, she doubts as well the integrity of language when used in situations where there ought to be strong emotion. More accurately, as we have seen, she doubts the integrity of those who are able to remain fluent, flowery, or verbose in such situations. The reticence of her good or worthy people, in contrast to the fulsomeness or glibness of the unworthy, demonstrates the value and authenticity of what they say.

Plainly, working with such a set of contrasting associations, Austen could not give verbally rich proposal scenes to her authentic heroes and heroines, who number among their virtues a becoming diffidence naturally at war with glib speechifying. We believe them and esteem them all the more for this trace of reticence, with its hint of their being slightly overwhelmed by the experience of loving and hoping to be loved in return. Denying herself the recording of their direct expressions, then, Austen also denies herself the author's prerogative of speaking for them, very fully at any rate, through narration. Here her commitment to decorum and to an emphasis on general truth, rather than details of private experience, precludes any very detailed account of her characters' approaches to each other. The result, in her proposal scenes, is the bareness that so many readers, especially in the "open" twentieth century, have seen as being insipid, timid, or priggish. Perhaps those elements were present in Austen's personality, though the letters do not seem to indicate that they were, and they may have become embodied to an extent in her fiction. But it is clear that a biographical explanation of the point is by itself insufficient.[39]

Austen was working out of a conscious theory of her medium and her form. There is considerable irony in the fact that a novelist who worked so much in dialogue and who believed so firmly in conversation as a social bond, should also demonstrate a belief in the failure, the ultimate inadequacy, of language for the expression of strong feeling. There is also considerable intellectual honesty in her willingness to admit this inconsistency into the structure of her fiction.

Jane Austen has been a powerful and motivating presence for women writers of the twentieth century. Indeed, it is scarcely conceivable that for a woman writer of our time, employing a reserved or silenced style, Austen would not have been of influence. But we do not have to rely on reasoning from inconceivability; her importance has been abundantly demonstrated. Virginia Woolf testifies to Austen's importance in various essays and in *A Room of One's Own,* where she speaks of Austen as a kind of absolute measure of the way a woman can write, and write well, and as one of those incandescent minds, like Shakespeare, that draw al things into clarity and balance. "Arrange the great English novelists as one will," she writes, "it does not seem possible to bring them out in any order where she is not first, or second, or third, whoever her companions may be." We can see the influence of Austen in the absences and voids of Woolf's novels. For Willa Cather and for Katherine Anne Porter, too, she was an admired, central presence. Cather, as we know, wrote of Austen as "in some respects the greatest of . . . all" her foremothers in the novel. Porter named Austen, with Woolf, as one of those few writers who gave her a "sense of some mysterious revelation of truth."[40] It is to Cather and to Porter that we will turn next.

CHAPTER THREE

The Duplicitous Art
of Willa Cather

*You must tell it in such a way that they don't know
you're telling it, and that they don't know they're
hearing it.*

———————— WILLA CATHER, *The Song of the Lark* ————————

Katherine Anne Porter writes of Willa Cather's reserve, "I remember well my deeper impression of reserve—a reserve that
was personal because it was a matter of temperament, the grain
of the mind; yet conscious too, and practiced deliberately: almost
a method, a technique, but not assumed." Porter's somewhat tortuous comment not only puts its verbal finger on the puzzling
duality, even duplicity, of that reserve, but enacts in its uncertain
juggling of terms—"a matter of temperament," "the grain of
the mind," "conscious," "deliberat[e]," "almost a method," "technique"—the reader's plight in confronting Cather's bare style.
What is a behavioral quality, a trait, that is all these things? How
can a quality of reserve be "conscious" and "practiced deliberately," yet be only *almost* but not quite a "method"? Does the
"almost" apply to "a technique" as well as "method" or is Cather's
deliberately practiced reserve, in Porter's view, a technique indeed? If the latter, does Porter's sense of Cather shift between
"almost a method" and "a technique," becoming more assured on
that point? or does Porter in fact see a difference between
"method" and "technique," so that something can be fully the one

66

but not fully the other? And what is the meaning of the final nervous qualifier, "but not assumed"? Does it mean something like not faked or put-on; that is, inevitable and natural, fully expressive of Cather's personal self, not assumed as a disguise even though "practiced deliberately"?[1]

Porter's statement is curious. It is a striking departure from her usual precise delineation even of ambiguity. Moreover, it reveals a deep uncertainty, as if in confronting Cather she loses her own assurance. She recognizes a pervasive quality of reserve in the writing of another famous American women writer, only some twenty years older than herself though far more prolific, but she seems not to know what to make of that reserve. Is it a personally compelled, that is, involuntary, reticence, a conscious withholding, or an aesthetic discipline? or all three? The syntax of the great writer's sentence betrays her inability to say—perhaps because she could not have said clearly what her own reticent style meant.

The problem so evident in Katherine Anne Porter's assessment of Cather's reserve is one encountered (or evaded) by every critic of Willa Cather. In my view, it is a problem and an interest inherent in Cather's work. Those critics who view her as a virtuoso of the classic style, practicing an art of discipline and selectivity,[2] are surely correct. The bare forms and "laconic style"[3] of her fiction are based on an aesthetic commitment to the idea of the "novel demeuble" (7:235–41)—the unfurnished or, probably better, disfurnished novel. At the same time, those critics who view her work as the expression of a need to suppress and conceal very profound personal anxieties[4] are also correct. Neither view, by itself, is complete. The aesthetic principle that Cather consciously and capably defended and that she followed in so craftly a fashion was chosen, at least in part, because it accorded so well with her need to find a strategy of avoidance and suppression. The need fueled the theoretical affiliation that gave it aesthetic respectability. This does not mean that the two are coterminous, as if Cather's aesthetic discipline were only a disguise or a rationalization of her neurotic need: they are not; each element has its interest, its importance, and its validity as an explanatory rationale for her fiction. But they do overlap. And that, in essence, is why Cather is so difficult—much more difficult than she has generally been regarded. Her narrative is deeply, elusively duplicitous.

In its duplicitousness, Cather's work (as recent criticism has demonstrated) is of great interest to feminist scholars, both in its grounding in issues of sexuality and social construction of gender and in the verbal strategies Cather devised for dealing with these issues. But the import of those verbal strategies, and in particular of her strategies of reticence and omission, is even more difficult to assess in Cather's case than it is for Austen, Porter, or Didion. Her silences are so profoundly determined by her own need to disguise and evade issues of discomfort, and they speak so eloquently as exempla, that the extent to which they are also a rhetoric, a purposed communication, is uncertain. It will be our task here to assess and, insofar as possible, to resolve that uncertainty.

Cather is not often called a feminist,[5] but it is clear that she admired and affirmed freedom, independence, and individual achievement by women. She lived freely and independently herself, outside the normal societal expectations of how women live, and achieved distinction on her own terms. At the same time, she affirmed or felt a need to affirm the fulfillment of the most traditional of female roles.[6] Yet when she does so, in the overt celebrations of maternity in My Ántonia, for example, counterelements in the text—verbally *in* the text, as well as counterelements suppressed *from* the text—undermine those celebrations of transcendence through self-denial and mothering. In the dual thrusts of their intentionality, then, Cather's fictions become feminist texts, sometimes proclaiming a feminist vision, sometimes depicting the perniciousness or merely the invalidity of the varying forces arrayed against a feminist vision, or, more simply, arrayed against women. The fact that she could not state, and perhaps could not acknowledge, some concerns whose absence leaves silences in her texts illustrates the debilitating effects of her position in a patriarchal heterosexual society.[7] But beyond this, she is able to use silences subversively to invite questioning of assurances that come too easily. The careful reader can no longer rest comfortably in a belief that Cather's fiction, late or early, is centered on "sunny" assurances.[8]

Critics have long recognized that *My Ántonia,* for instance, is not the happy bucolic idyl it was once read as being and that Jim Burden is not so transparent a narrator as he may seem.[9] If the "first wave" of critical readings of the novel highlighted its glorification of America's heartland and her sturdy pioneers, the "second wave," in venerable New Critical fashion, stressed narrative point of view. For this reading, the key comes in the last sentences of the framing "Introduction" when Jim Burden puts a title to his ostensibly naive narrative: "He went into the next room, sat down at my desk and wrote across the face of the portfolio the word 'Ántonia.' He frowned at this a moment, then prefixed another word, making it 'My Ántonia.' That seemed to satisfy him." The subject of the book, then, is not simply Ántonia herself or the world she seems to represent, but her meaning and that world's meaning *to Jim Burden.* The act of knowing, of appropriating Ántonia for himself, becomes, in this reading, the central act of the book.

Such a reading proves very fruitful. It is still based, however, on a view of the text as a relatively complete, impermeable construct. A reading emphasizing Jim's act of narration, and thus his relationship to Ántonia and the life she represents, may take passing cognizance of what he does not say, but the overwhelming emphasis—understandably enough—is on what he does say. Jim's vision, to be sure, is limited and particularized, but so long as the critic's vision is larger and more perspicacious than Jim's, his narration adequately comprises the tale.

In recent years, a third wave of critical readings has more radically questioned Jim Burden's act of narration, sometimes invoking the presence of Cather herself as a controlling narrator who purposely undercuts and exposes to question the narrator positioned between herself and Ántonia, but more often exploring ways in which Jim Burden's limited consciousness has reference to and is shaped by Cather's life and her own emotional complexities. Such readings have crossed between the text and a better informed awareness of Cather herself to identify ways in which she, too, like Jim, is a limited narrator, unable to speak consistently or fully. In readings of this sort, which typically confront

Cather's lesbianism more candidly than those of the past, *My Án-tonia* becomes a new book, and an unsettling one. It takes on a new, less comfortable, vitality.

My own reading assumes the viewpoints of these recent bio-graphical-deconstructive readings, such as those of Deborah Lambert and Sharon O'Brien (and not so recently, Blanche Gel-fant and Leon Edel).[10] I am somewhat concerned that in our zeal to illuminate the elaborate and obscure connections between Cather's living and the constraints on her writing, we may have come to present her as a victim of her own neuroses and society's imposition of relatively rigid expectations relating to gender, and to treat the book, as well as Cather's other works, as the record of that victimization, a record pocked by all she could not say. But beyond those pockmarks—and they are surely there—Cath-er's text is marked by an intentionality of silence. Jim Burden's inadequacy as a narrator is not our discovery alone. Cather was there before us, *leading* us, by her silences as well as by her words, to question him.[11]

Indeed, she did give us, as the point-of-view analysts have in-sisted, an interpretive key in the Introduction that frames the novel—but not just the obvious one of Jim's act of entitling and self-entitlement. That act, we recall, is Jim's alone. It is Jim who asserts, by his title, that Ántonia is his, and that his is the view of her that matters. Earlier, however, the reader—who is expected to be more perspicacious than Jim is—has been given a key that is validated by being, not Jim's alone, but the product of the in-terchange between Jim and the encompassing narrator, the "I" to whom he presents his portfolio about Ántonia and the frontier world of his childhood. As the two of them talk, they agree that the key to understanding their early way of life, the way of life Ántonia epitomizes and which both narrators have shared, is ex-periencing *both* the "stimulating extremes" of the Nebraska cli-mate: "burning summers when the world lies green and billowy beneath a brilliant sky, when one is fairly stifled in vegetation, in the colour and smell of strong weeds and heavy harvests; blustery winters with little snow, when the whole country is stripped bare and grey as sheet-iron" (6:ix). Neither view, they agree, is adequate alone; neither will do without the other. Yet when Jim Burden comes to write out his story of Ántonia, in what he insists is a spontaneous, unshaped way, he will present only one view at a time, first the sunny view, then the "stripped bare and grey" view of Ántonia's ruination and hardship, then at the end the sunny one again of Ántonia's rich fecundity (the view that Susan Rosowski has called an achievement and an affirmation). But Jim's omission of the gray side, the side that acknowledges how worn down Ántonia is by her role, is *his* omission, not Cather's. In the Introduction's reference to the necessary duality, she gives us the key that helps us see the deficiency of Jim's view, and uses his omissions to convey more than his self-consciously romanticized narrative can accommodate.

The familiar opening of Jim's narrative, the train ride from Virginia to Black Hawk, Nebraska, illustrates splendidly the artistry of Cather's compression, which has led to critical celebration of her classically limpid style. A thousand details might have accrued around such a train trip; it might have become a panorama of America, with a foreground cluster of train passengers, all with their own baggage, literal and figurative. Instead, what we get is focus: on Jim's shyness and his traveling companion's inexperience, on his first hearing and then first glimpse of the still nameless Shimerda family, on the wearying and disorienting effects of the long trip across open plains. These few significant features are surrounded by verbal empty space, just as the train and then the platform are surrounded by the geographic empty space of the Midwest.[12] "The only thing very noticeable about Nebraska was that it was still, all day long, Nebraska. . . . I couldn't see any town, or even distant lights; we were surrounded by utter darkness" (4:5). This kind of effect, an immersion of narrative in an object or a quality of experience of deepest concern which is set against an utterly uncluttered field, is characteristic of Cather's work.

Structurally as well, she builds her novels through an episodic accretion of focused and compressed, apparently simple scenes,[13] displayed against contextual vacancy. The connections, the narrative or expository sequences that would link scene to scene or episode to episode, are omitted from the text. Moreover, the principle of selection among scenes or episodes seems to be determined by no very rigorous plan. Unlike Jane Austen, whose densely social novels are put together on a principle of close-knit cause and effect, Cather builds hers pictorially, working toward something like pictorial "composition."[14] But the individual scenes, themselves typically spare in presentation, are surrounded by vacancy. They are not, as Austen's would be, embedded in a fully developed social context. As Eudora Welty so perceptively observed, Cather's novels are vacant in the middle distance,[15] at precisely the narrative depth that occupies so much space (page space) and attention in Austen's work, for all its compression and ellipsis at moments of crisis. Just as the middle distance drops away, so the connections between episodes are omitted. Episodes, stripped, focused scenes, are placed in positional relationships that we must infer as we contemplate the similarities and contrasts, the small hints and great silences, of the individual designs.

In *My Ántonia*, for example, a two-year gap lies between book 1, "The Shimerdas," and book 2, "The Hired Girls," another gap of time between books 2 and 3, and a much longer one between 3 and 4, when a Jim Burden diminished by all that has happened during the intervening blank time returns to fix on Ántonia as a sustaining ideal—and in the process to complete his denial of her personhood. Similarly, in *O Pioneers!* Cather moves without transition from the beginning of Alexandra's struggle to fulfill her father's injunction by establishing the family's land holdings to the culmination of that struggle—an interval of sixteen years. In *The Professor's House* varying amounts of time pass in the intervals between one chapter and another, each giving its single dispiriting incident or picture, or sometimes two or three, not to mention the enormous gap of time and of space and of narrative connection surrounding Tom Outland's tale, interpolated as book 2. A gap of two years, during which both the narrator and social conditions change, occurs in the middle of *A Lost Lady*. *My Mortal Enemy* is structured around two great gaps, one of twenty years between Myra's elopement (occurring before the novel begins but glimpsed in remembrance) and Nellie's first meeting with the storied Myra and a second gap of ten years between Nellie's first extended observation of Myra and her husband (occurring some months after the first glimpse) and her second period of acquaintance with them. In *Death Comes for the Archbishop* the pattern is even more prevalent than in these other novels, with books and chapters within books appearing like emblems set against a flat, blank surface and taken up into narrative attention in an order that moves around in time, without explanation of the intervening times and their events.

One effect of Cather's episodic technique is to sharpen contrasts. By setting the fulfilled and gratified Alexandra beside the aspiring Alexandra, with nothing between, she causes us to experience very sharply the great difference between them. By moving from scene to scene in Bishop Latour's long ministry in the wilderness, without summarizing the intervening periods, she brings us to feel not only that what we see can be taken as typifying the whole but that what we see is of great spiritual significance and the omitted daily struggles, with their inevitable clutter and their probable urgencies, do not matter. We have a sense that we understand the essence of Father Latour and the great panorama of spiritual conquest he represents. Because some emblematic scenes are outwardly minor while others are outwardly momentous, we also develop a sense of understanding that in the spiritual dimension importance is not determined by outward measures. The effect is precisely that of the selectivity and emphasis Cather espoused as an aesthetic principle and achieved over the course of a prolonged discipline in her art.

At the same time, the artful omissions and gaps in narrative such as the ones I have referred to are also a means of evading or suppressing what Cather (or her narrative persona) does not want to confront directly. Her reticence is expressed in the spaces between the episodes or "pictures," as she places them in an array which is the novel, as well as in the stripping of the "pictures" themselves. My interest here is not so much in the artfulness of that selective stripping and positioning per se as in the evasiveness and disguise that accompany and, to a great extent, determine the art and in the rhetorical use to which she is sometimes able to put her reticent and evasive art.

Cather is, paradoxically, one of the most frank and one of the most hidden of writers. We have many photographs of her, showing a square, plain, forthright face, but her letters, the few that survived her systematic efforts at destruction, are, by the terms of her will, screened from quotation. Her biographer James Woodress, always eager to quiet speculation on questions of sexuality, insists that Cather's desire not to publish her letters came from the artistic principle of wishing to be represented only by her best, most carefully revised work.[16] His argument, it seems to me, does not hold water. Novelists are not "represented" by their letters, but by their novels. Other artists of equal perfectionism—Henry James, for instance—have realized that letters belong to a different category altogether, one not valued by the same aesthetic standards as their fiction. Cather's insistence on privacy, on eradicating the personal record, seems to me more compulsive than Woodress allows it to be.[17] It is a part of what Bernice Slote refers to as her secretiveness,[18] a part of the same pattern of concealment that caused her to dress in men's clothes, call herself by a masculine name, and adopt male narrative voices.

Her purpose in adopting a male persona is not, I believe, to deny her female identity but to deny or evade the conventional femininity that went with it. Here I agree with Woodress, who attributes her adoption of "male values and attitudes" in her youth to her sense that the options in life that interested her were not available to her because of her sex.[19] That is, he attributes it to frustration at society's construction of gender. Susan Gubar, in an article on cross-dressing as practiced by several modernist women, including Cather, amplifies this idea. Since clothing "plays a crucial symbolic role in the response of women to their confinement within patriarchal structures," the assumption of male clothing, seen as a "costume of freedom," became for these women a way of appropriating masculine "potency." Cather, Gubar argues, realized that "male dress could alienate her from conventionally female roles and activities."[20] Those conventional roles and activities were precisely the ones that stood to hamper her in her bid for professional stature in literature and letters.

And so, as an adolescent, Cather cut her hair short, wore male clothes and caps, flaunted her enthusiasm for pastimes conventionally more boyish than girlish,[21] spoke and walked in a mannish way, took male parts in plays, and sporadically called herself William. It is interesting that these behaviors disappeared in her later college years, when she was achieving a reassuring measure of success in newspaper writing. Perhaps by then she no longer needed to borrow the outwardly male "trappings of authority,"[22] or perhaps she realized that she needed to enter the professional world in a guise less calculated to startle. O'Brien says simply, she reached a "reconciliation of gender and vocation."[23] But she would later borrow male trappings of a different kind, the male narrator that Gubar calls "a kind of mask."[24]

Behind the mask her own presence was elusive, shifting. Sometimes the narrator has features closely resembling Cather's own, sometimes not. It is not altogether one way or the other, any more than her early male persona was clearly a disguise or was not: she called herself Willie, but then, her family had done so, as a pet name, from infancy. Surely there is no oddity in a person's continuing a name used by parents, and if Willie sometimes became William, wasn't it an easy and natural shift? And so her "cross-dressing" in narration, as in personal presence, was shifting, occasional, inconclusive.

In *My Ántonia,* which has more often been examined for its narrative strategy than any other of her works, Cather's use of Jim Burden as narrative persona means, most obviously, that Ántonia's own expressions and interpretations will be silenced except as they are reported to him, submitted to the filtering of his remembrance and interpretation. Jim then reports to the reader his construct of Ántonia, his own experience or remembered experience of her. Jim's narration becomes an act of expropriation, of taking her away from herself and appending her to his own self. Accordingly, in book 1, "The Shimerdas," he censures Ántonia's unguarded generosity in the offer of the ring (4:27) and disapproves of her (surely unavoidable) crudeness, arrogating to himself the right to decide when she is acceptably "nice" and when she is not. If she is not conciliatory and submissive, he reserves the right to cast her out of his regard, just as Napoleon casts out Josephine in the frontispiece Jim chooses for his homemade gift book for Ántonia's little sister. Ántonia's own views of their differing social behavior, like her views of being rejected by Jim, are effaced by the first-person narrative strategy. On the one occasion when her own emphatic rejection of him—"no friends any more"—is quoted (4:130), Ántonia and her family are "silenced" by being shown to be utterly, even laughably, in the wrong (in the wonderful picture of Mrs. Shimerda trying to shove her cow into hiding).

Jim's assumption of the power of approval or disapproval reaches its peak in the incident of Wick Cutter's attempted rape, in book 2, when Jim has swapped sleeping places with Ántonia for the night. When Ántonia cries outside his door the next day, after he is beaten up by Cutter, Jim has her sent away. She is not allowed even an expression of regret for the incident—certainly not of anger at Cutter. In much the same way, the monstrous (to Jim's eyes) Mrs. Cutter can do little more than tremble and sputter with rage at her husband's devious behavior. Mrs. Cutter's humanness is as effectually barred from the novel as the sexuality or the interpretive viewpoint of Ántonia.

If the savagery of Jim's rejection of Ántonia for her role as unwitting victim of another's depravity—"I hated her almost as much as I hated Cutter" (4:250)—is shocking, it is not entirely unanticipated. It is signaled, in fact, by the haunting interpolated tale of the bride thrown to wolves. This traditional Russian folktale, sometimes called extraneous or pointless,[25] is a nightmare version (even to the awakening monastery bell which signals the return to the daylight world) of Jim's preparedness to throw Ántonia's friendship overboard when exigencies require it. Those exigencies are, to be sure, considerably less deadly than Pavel and Peter's wolves. They include the tainting, by association, of Jim's genteel social image, reminders of the possible inadequacy of his masculinity (he has admired tales of Jesse James and idealized the safe maleness of Otto, the hired man), and all manifestations of physicality. That the tale of the bride thrown to the wolves is to be seen as a nightmare parallel to Jim's own behavior or potential is indicated by his fantasizing response to the story and by the incident that immediately follows the story of Pavel and Peter's horrible ride: "At night before I went to sleep, I often found myself in a sledge drawn by three horses, dashing through a country that looked something like Nebraska and something like Virginia" (4:61). Then Cather accents the connection structurally by bringing in, in the next chapter, the incident of Jim's taking Ántonia and her sister riding in "a clumsy sleigh" (4:63). The hint of a connection remains, of course, tacit. And Jim does not throw anyone out of his "clumsy sleigh." It is only later that he throws Ántonia out of his friendship (that is, throws her to the wolves) and then, when he needs to hold on to his idealized version of her, throws out her sexuality and her hardships in arriving at his version of the truth.

The question arises whether Cather intentionally exposes the inadequacy of her male persona or whether the viewpoint presented as his is also her own. That, of course, is a difficult question to answer. Cather's novelistic presence is not simple or unitary. But the undercutting of Burden's views seems to me too frequent and too insistent to be inadvertent. Jim manages to report the entire Wick Cutter incident without a single acknowledgment of Ántonia's possible motivation. He does not point out, for instance, that if Ántonia had had any life of her own to look forward to she might not have staked her happiness entirely on dancing in a tent—the pastime that led to her losing her job with the Harlings and going to work for the notorious Cutters. He adopts, even while piously disavowing, the prevailing class-bound condescension toward the foreign-born hired girls of Black Hawk, as a group, reporting sympathetically the "plight" of the upper-class young men sexually tempted by the hired girls' vitality and presenting a comic view of the temptress image by which the girls themselves are scapegoated. When Lena, Tiny, and the other girls talk about the hardships of women on the raw frontier

(4:239–41), Jim neither agrees nor disagrees but offers tribute to his conspicuously male heroes, the appropriating Coronado and the aggressively phallic plow (4:244–45).

Later, as a student at the university, Jim effectively silences Lena's real humanity by viewing her merely as a representative of a social class (though we see her as being singularly individualized) and then by making her into an archetype, a muse. He continues to arrogate to himself the right to judge and forgive Ántonia's sexual adventure (an adventure in victimization). Returning from school after she has borne her first child, he heartlessly but sentimentally tells her that he would have liked to "have" her for "anything that a woman can be to a man." "Have" her—as if he could simply appropriate and possess her; "would have"—as if her life were over, as if he no longer would like to do so since she is ruined. After this piling up of blatant insensitivity to Ántonia's being-for-herself and to the hardships and goals of women in general, we can scarcely accept his idealization at the end, with its blithe ignoring of the physical evidence of how life has battered the heroically loving Ántonia, as Cather's own view of the matter.[26]

Cather again assumed a male narrative center, this time adopting a variable third-person form, in *A Lost Lady*. Again the narrator betrays a lack of understanding of the woman he observes and, in his own limited way, loves. Like Jim Burden, who belongs nowhere—not on the raw prairie, not in Black Hawk, not in New York with his haughty wife—Niel Herbert is caught between generations, belonging to neither. Despising the sharp dealers who are his contemporaries, the younger generation of the novel, he respects and admires the older generation of early railroad builders. Motherless, like Jim, Niel is driven to idealize an older woman, Marian Forrester, the charming and gracious wife of the town's leading citizen. Responsive as he is to her sexual charm, he is determined to see her as a pure woman, despite ample evidence of her frustration with the impotent Captain and her need to fulfill a very real sexuality. In bringing us to understand that Marian Forrester's story is in large measure the story of a frustrated sexuality finding sporadic expression in illicit affairs with unworthy partners, Cather comes very close to open treatment of active sexual involvement. Even here, of course, the theme is approached largely through innuendo—which, as Gelfant points out, is "hardly surprising" since she was working "within a prohibitive genteel tradition" that prescribed reticence if not outright avoidance.[27]

In Marian Forrester, Cather creates for the reader a woman who possesses not only elegance and perfect hospitality but liveliness, passion, and a not inconsiderable gallantry. After Captain Forrester loses his money, she struggles to maintain her charm and gracious good humor while carrying the full weight of unaccustomed household drudgery. Niel, who gives only lip-service sympathy to her hard work, has no conception of the unhappiness and frustration that drive her to first one and then another affair with men unworthy of her. Never really knowing her, he can esteem only his own idealization of her. When she betrays that idealization, he shuts her out from his friendship as surely as Jim Burden does Ántonia.

Once again, as in *My Ántonia,* the male narrator is troubled both by sexuality and by social class. So long as he can suppress his growing adolescent awareness of the source of Marian Forrester's charm, Niel can make her his ideal of all that femininity that makes life pleasant. So long as his recognition of her sexual allure can be comfortably indirect—experienced in glimpses of her lace underwear and meditations on "that something in [her] glance that made one's blood tingle" (7:37) and expressed in tributes of wild roses[28]—he can refuse to "name" that "something.'" He is able to believe that the reason he leaves her company in a "high sense of elation" has something to do with her natural interest in people (7:66). When faced with the realization that she is a sexually active woman as well as a titillatingly flirtatious one, he makes more and more desperate efforts at denial until at last, in a blatantly symbolic act, he attempts to silence her embarrassingly authentic expression of self by cutting the telephone cord when she begins to pour out her passion to a former lover. No longer able to make that denial, but instead having to face the fact that she is not only sexually active but sexually active with "common" men, he feels only a "weary contempt" for her and wishes she had died along with her much older husband (7:168). That way, she would have remained safely shut off in a realm of the ideal.

It becomes clear, as the book proceeds, that Niel's disillusionment with Mrs. Forrester stems partly from a perception that she fails to maintain standards of social class. And indeed she does "fall" from associating only with the leaders of society's commercial development to associating with a brasher sort of man on the make to, at last, an offensively crass shyster lawyer and the unrefined sons of the local lower middle class. She "falls" from having servants who clean and polish and cook for her, with a formally dressed butler to serve dinner parties, to seating the kitchen help at the table along with the guests. Indeed, by this time her kitchen help and her guests are of indistinguishable social standing. All of this bothers Niel inordinately; it is inconsistent with his ideal of the patrician lady. But we need to ask why it bothers him so. To be sure, the conversational tone of Mrs. Forrester's later guests is not elevated or clever, but then, the conversational tone of some of her earlier guests, the Ogden mother and daughter, for example, was scarcely even civil, and Niel did not find them socially unacceptable, only disagreeable.

The problem arises largely from Niel himself. Worried about his own social standing from the outset (his socially proud mother had died, his father had "an air of failure and defeat" about him, and the cousin who kept house for them preferred reading to keeping the place presentable in case of company), he takes the Forresters to represent the ideal parents he lacked and identifies himself with their style. To be sure, Marian Forrester is not solely a mother figure to the boy; particularly as he grows older, she becomes also the embodiment of a glamorous but discreetly diffuse sexual appeal. Later, as she begins to betray the standard Niel expects of her as his ideal mother substitute and sweetheart substitute in one, he worries more about the impression townfolk will have of her than he does about her actual problems, such as her unaccustomed hard work and her drinking. If she tarnishes the dream by which he has defined himself, how can he go on believing he is better than others?

Again, it is hard to be sure how much of Niel's distaste is his as a character, shown up by Cather for the wistful snobbery it is, and how much is her own. Certainly Cather herself enjoyed beautiful clothes, as Mrs. Forrester does, and good conversation and a well-run household. Her French cook was for years one of the most important people in her life. The style of living Niel so admires is one she liked to maintain herself. Moreover, the distaste for crass moneygrubbing that Niel expresses was certainly her own, appearing in more than one novel and in her personal pronouncements Even so, Niel cannot be taken as a Willa Cather in trousers.

The undercutting of Niel's position, sly as it is, is clear enough to distance him from his author.[29] In his worry over Mrs. Forrester's associating with a commoner sort of young man, he forgets that she had been friendly to the working-class boys he played with as a child, when he adored her, and discounts her statement that she wants to give these young men a little polish. Of course, we do not need to take *that* statement at face value either. Marian Forrester has quite evidently been lonely; we can believe that she badly wants a bit of company. But that is a possibility Niel does not even consider. In the dinner party scene, the reader notices that these young men stand up when Mrs. Forrester enters the room; Niel notices only that their standing up is not done gracefully. The reader notices that Niel worries a great deal about the impropriety of her appearing *en déshabillé* to "her inferiors" but not much about the fact that she has to work so hard at keeping house after having been accustomed to having servants. When Captain Forrester is dying and the care of him is very demanding, Niel worries more about the fact that the neighbor women will see Mrs. Forrester's shabbiness and the bubble of popular envy will be burst than about her need for help with the lifting and bathing and other work of caring for a gravely ill person. He worries about people's noticing that she drinks, not about the reasons for her drinking. In short, there is a great deal that Niel does not notice but that Cather leads us to notice. The conclusion is inevitable that Niel is, to some indeterminate extent, deliberately distanced and undercut. It is the lady of his distorted and unrealistic conception that is lost, not necessarily the lady, the person, herself.

Why, then, did Cather adopt these male personas? To say that they are a way of claiming literary authority does not take us far, since she did not adopt masculine personas in her earliest novels, when presumably she would have been more in need of that sense of authority. David Stouck's view that she used the masculine point of view in order to achieve the distancing and impersonality that were a standard of the French impressionist and symbolist writers Cather admired is plausible.[30] She had been dissatisfied with two of her first three novels, finding *Alexander's Bridge* inauthentic and *The Song of the Lark* cluttered. She knew, as an admirer of Henry James, the importance of a defined and elaborated narrative point of view. It seems natural that the adoption of a masculine voice might occur to her as a likely technical experiment. But this explanation, I believe, is inadequate; there are more factors at work here than one. We might just as plausibly point out that Cather's male personas in the two novels are in several ways much like herself. They show her distaste for moneygrubbing, her urge toward a simpler and more integral past, her fascination with strong, beautiful women. She had enjoyed expressing herself in masculine guises before. Why not now? The idea may well have been appealing in its own right, and it allowed her to express her ardor toward the two women characters, both based on real women who had exerted some sort of emotional pull on her in the past, without raising the complication of an emotional cast that she surely knew, by now, would be regarded as deviant.

Though that last may carry a ring of simplicity or convenience, it is really, I think, an expression of her urge to duality. Employing the vantage of a Jim Burden or a Niel Herbert allowed Cather both to express the ardor that she felt toward Ántonia and toward Marian Forrester (or their prototypes) and to avoid crude *telling*. She could maintain her allegiance to the method of conveying "the thing not said." At the same time, to put it within a slightly different frame of reference, it allowed her to convey her emotional response to the presences at the center of the two books and also to undercut an uncritical idealism (that of her two narrative personas) by revealing its distortions and inadequacies. Certainly, as O'Brien points out, her adoption of a male point of view does not indicate "subservience to patriarchal values."[31] By adopting the male persona she could evade some of the discontents she herself felt with female experience—such as heterosexual romance—while placing on the male centers of consciousness the onus of failing to confront the full truth. Or, to shift the frame of reference yet again, her choice of an imperceptive male narrator allowed her to point tacitly to those problems and emotional nuances of female life he fails to see, without obviously belaboring them.

This is not to say that Cather's aim in employing the male persona was simply to invalidate the male perspective. Not only does she invest the male persona with much of her sense of self (in *The Professor's House,* for example), but she also develops similar kinds of duplicitous evasions and multiplications of interpretive possibilities in novels employing impersonal narrative modes or female centers of consciousness. As we have seen, the ironic distance between the controlling vision and the depicted vision is particularly clear in *Ántonia* and *A Lost Lady,* where the obvious distinction between male characters and female author can underscore and mark off differences in vision as it obscures the full and confusing extent of the identification we sense in the warmth of the narrative tone.

Cather's narrative irony, however, is by no means dependent on distinction of sex. In *My Mortal Enemy* an almost equally clear ironic gap is developed between the perceptions of the narrator/reader and those of the young, naive, and extremely romantic *female* narrative center, Nellie.[32] Meeting the main character, Myra Henshawe, after having heard for years the story of Myra's romantic elopement, a fifteen-year-old Nellie regards Myra and her husband as the embodiments of charm and sophistication. When Nellie accompanies her Aunt Lydia on a Christmastime visit to the Henshawes in New York, she glimpses some cracks in the veneer of their romantic life, but partly because she does not fully understand what she sees, she continues to cling to her earlier illusion. In the last third of the novel, after a gap of ten years (it is characteristic of Cather to end her novels with a later view), Nellie runs across the Henshawes again in a very different place and in drastically reduced circumstances. Older and more experienced, Nellie now carries her own burden of disillusionment, which moves her closer to the larger narrator/reader perspective. Even so, her vision of the Henshawes is clouded by a wish to maintain some shred of the romantic view she had clung to as an adolescent. Thus even her enlightened view is distanced and, to a degree, undercut.

The technique of playing between a fallible center and a tacit larger vision allows frequent ambiguities as well as unspoken "statements" implied by the inadequacy of Nellie's vision. In the opening paragraph, when Nellie gushes that Myra Henshawe's life "had been as exciting and varied as ours was monotonous" (11:237), she shows no awareness that her judgment of the one may be issuing from her experience of the other. Recalling the splendid funeral mass of Myra's uncle, she imagines that there had been "no dark conclusion to the pageant," that he had escaped the "dark . . . night" of death itself (11:251). Plainly, he did not; no one escapes that night. By analogy, it is scarcely more likely that Myra has, as Nellie's imagination would have it, escaped the grimness of a life lived solely as a long, acquisitive denouement to the marriage vow. When Nellie imagines the dead uncle better off than his poor niece, having to live on in an unromantic world of "shirts and railway trains, and getting a double chin" (11:252), she is missing the point. The real sadness of Myra Henshawe is not the necessity of dealing with everyday reality instead of a lifelong fairy tale, but the disaster of never having found a locus of satisfaction in reality. As a consequence, Myra has lived as a spiteful, envious, unfocused person. When Nellie goes to visit the Henshawes with her aunt, she is so "moonstruck" by the spectacle of New York that she can suppose "winter brought no desolation" here. She sees Myra's display of charity to a coatless child on the snow-piled street only as one more evidence of her spontaneous nature. The reader, however, sees not only the inadequacy but the actual self-indulgence of the empty gesture: Myra enjoys purchasing the illusion of being softhearted as the price of merely "a coin." Caught up in a round of parties and carriage rides, Nellie believes, much longer than the reader does, that Myra dislikes and disapproves of the rich people whom, in fact, she merely envies (11:270–71).

In these details and many others Cather shows us that Nellie's view is not an entirely reliable one. But she never tells us so directly. By this stage in her career, Cather was wondrously adept in the use of an observer-narrator who both defines and misinterprets what is seen. To illustrate: when Nellie and her aunt arrive with Myra at the Henshawes' apartment, Oswald is drinking a whiskey and soda, which he put down as they entered and "forgot all about it" (11:258). It is Nellie, of course, who believes he forgot his drink. Yet the reader knows, without Cather's having to say so, that Nellie's interpretation is naive and that the business with the drink is laden with concealment. Through small details such as this Cather builds up her narrative irony, silently opening the door to other views than Nellie's.

Some questions, however, are created, not by narrative irony, but by Cather's own reticence or tact. Again and again she brings the alert reader to the point of asking, but does not raise the question directly or, of course, provide an answer. Why was Nellie's family's life so monotonous? Why was an elopement of twenty years ago, however dramatic, still the dominant topic of conversation, especially by Nellie's aunt, a person well beyond the years of adolescent melodrama? Why, for that matter, did Aunt Lydia take such a great interest in a niece? Why not in her own sons? One wonders if Aunt Lydia bore some grudge against the male sex and, if so, what its origin was. Why does Myra have to be so sarcastic to people? Because, we judge, her only distinction in life has been her love story, and with that failing she has no secure sense of self-worth. The bitterness of that lack is not told in words, however, but yawns in the abyss lurking under Aunt Lydia's comment that Myra and Oswald Henshawe have been about "as happy as most people." Nellie thinks at the time only that couples who launch their marriage so romantically should have *more* happiness than others, not just about as much. Later, during her visit to the Henshawes in New York, she sees, though she does not entirely understand, that their lives are marred by squabbling and an odor of adultery. But in this light Aunt Lydia's estimate of their happiness takes on a new tinge. What sort of unhappiness would lead Aunt Lydia to judge so inharmonious a life as being "as happy as most"? What has she known that Nellie has not known? A grim view indeed of the quality of most people's lives is tacitly conveyed.

Like *A Lost Lady, My Mortal Enemy,* Cather's shortest novel and one of her most cryptic, turns on the reference of the title phrase. On her deathbed Myra laments having to die "like this, alone with my mortal enemy" (11:321). Is that "mortal enemy" her husband or, as some readers have thought, her divided self? There is no easy way of telling. After all, Myra is not alone with Oswald when she speaks the line; Nellie is there too. Bitter as it is if the statement refers to herself, as Nellie interprets it, it is more bitter yet as a complaint against her supposed love and a slight of her young friend, who simply gets ignored if that is the meaning. If anything, the fact that Nellie sees it one way might incline us toward the other, since irony has played around the first-person point of view throughout. But Nellie's view has not by any means been totally invalidated, and in any event we do not, I believe, have to decide. It is enough to see Myra's bitter frame of mind and Nellie's horror of it. The question is still debated in criticism of the novel, despite the assurance with which partisans on both sides have asserted their views. Those who believe that the mortal enemy is the husband cite a comment made by Cather herself in a letter to George Seibel, which seems to affirm that reading.[33] Unfortunately (or not, perhaps), it is an extremely ambiguous comment, in that the phrasing of the letter is itself open to interpretation. The point is not really as significant as it has been made out to be. More interesting, I think, is the consideration of how Cather manages to raise so many questions, throughout the novel, without voicing them, in a book so terse that readers have sometimes called it incomplete.

We have glimpsed the silences and the teasing dualities lurking beneath the apparently direct surfaces of two novels and the somewhat more obviously ambiguous surface of another. In fact, such silences and dualities are evident, to varying degrees, in all of Cather's novels. In none—unless it is *The Song of the Lark*—does she present a fiction of fullness and plot elaboration or connectedness. Even *Death Comes for the Archbishop,* where the conspicuous gaps and silences can plausibly be seen as the essential features of a saint's legend modeled on a fresco, can equally well be seen as a novel of evasion.[34] *Sapphira and the Slave Girl,* giving what appears to be a detailed rendering of the texture of a society—down to introducing into the fiction, in a kind of essayistic gloss on the story, a direct version of Cather's own recollections of an incident from her childhood—nevertheless leaves great vacancies of mystery as to the motivations of the grand dame, Sapphira, and her adult daughter.

Perhaps the most evasive of all, however, as it is the most experimental of Cather's novels, is *The Professor's House.* Here she centers on a male perspective but does not actually assume it as her persona except here and there, momentarily. For the most part the ungendered narrator focuses on Godfrey St. Peter, sometimes showing us his shortcomings and anxieties, sometimes letting us into his thoughts. The vantage is one that catches us up just short of knowing to what degree St. Peter approximates "Cather," the narrating voice, and to what degree he is judged from a close scrutiny. Because St. Peter is himself demoralized and confused, the identification of the narrative perspective with his own, to the extent that identification occurs, leads inexorably to an effect of uncertainty, which Cather does not choose to dispel except through the greatest indirection. She does manage to accommodate within her laconic account of St. Peter's long depression hints and tacit pointers toward meaning, often through the silent language of symbolic action. Though the novel may not be one of full "showing," it is emphatically not a book of telling.

Most notably, the novel does not explain to us St. Peter's motivation. It does, however, raise questions about his motivation and the nature of his needs by making clear his singularity, his oddity. We wonder, for instance, why he has put up with the inconveniences of the old house for so long. For reasons of finances, surely. But he wouldn't have had to go the extent of opulence that his new house affords in order to find an improvement over the old, and we have no indication that he could not have afforded a modest improvement. Whatever the reason, why does he now regard those inconveniences "thoughtfully"? And why do his neighbors hold his garden against him? Perhaps because they see it as pretentious, as an implied rebuke of their own laissez faire approach to domestic landscaping. The book does not say. It is clear, though, that the garden is an obstacle to St. Peter's social interactions, since the implication that he has used the garden in the past as a means of evading change is unmistakably made by the narrator's insistence that he could not use it that way *now*. These and many other obscurities pervade the narrative.

In part, Cather does not explain the source and nature of St. Peter's gloomy detachment because she does not know. Or rather, she knows only in the disguised sense that the novel knows. As Sharon O'Brien cogently argues, Cather's work drew its impelling force from a profound tension between concealment and revelation. Insistently protective of her personal life and emotions, she struggled, at the same time, toward self-definition and an accommodation of her past. By the time she began *The Professor's House* she had largely worked through the tearing uncertainties over gender identity that had marked her youth and early career. But a new crisis in her emotional life, the crisis referred to in her frequently quoted comment that the world "broke in two" around 1922, fueled a more urgent need than she had felt in many years to sort through her personal feelings and allegiances. She began *The Professor's House* in 1923 and worked her way out of her personal crisis by working on the book. It is a profoundly autobiographical novel.[35]

The crisis that fed *The Professor's House* is well expounded by O'Brien. In 1923 Cather visited Isabelle McClung and McClung's husband Jan Hambourg in France, where they had established what was apparently a permanent home. The Hambourgs had then been married for six years, and Cather's initial devastation over her beloved Isabelle's desertion had abated. But when she visited them in the country that had long seemed to Cather the very home of art and of elegant and mature culture, she must have seen that their relationship was loving, stable, and almost certainly promising to last. In O'Brien's words, Cather "experienced the permanence of her loss most fully" during that visit.[36] Beginning *The Professor's House* that same year, and drawing on material already done for the Tom Outland section, she poured her sense of loss and gloom into St. Peter, who also has tried to avoid giving up a lost beloved—by treasuring and then trying to edit Tom Outland's diary—and who also feels disturbed by the spectacle of people close to him settling into new homes. Like Cather, St. Peter cannot bring himself to share their migration. Feeling emotionally cut off from the homemaking of others, who are at once near and strange to him, he shuts himself up with his memories, turning his face so firmly toward the past that he very nearly chooses death over life.

Yet St. Peter knows that his intense feelings for Outland, and through him for a whole quality of life now lost, would not be acceptable or even comprehensible to others. They are, indeed, not expressible; they are a very powerful "thing not said." And so the stifling of emotional expression, the impossibility of understanding or being understood, occupies the center of the novel. It is not a passing or a recent problem. Just as St. Peter has apparently resorted to his garden in order to evade contact, so he made a habit of "sending his wife and daughters to escape the humid prairie heat" (8:8), at which time he became "a bachelor again." One wonders: did he send them *so that* he could be a bachelor again? All the "delightful excursions and digressions" that fed his research for fifteen years (8:19) were made without family. His feelings toward family entanglements (including sexual entanglements) are so anxiety-ridden that he cannot bring himself to understand the faithful seamstress Augusta's reference to a life she might have had, but did not, apart from sewing for other people's families. "What other future could Augusta possibly have expected?" he wonders, ignoring the obvious answer that she might have expected to get married.

None of this regret and anxiety is ever expressed to others, even, or least of all, to his own wife. When Mrs. St. Peter tries to elicit some expression of his state of mind more direct than "an ironical turn" in his conversational tone (8:27), he fends her off. "'It's a nice idea, reserve about one's deepest feelings,'" he tells her (8:43). But his quiet amounts to more than reserve; it is a kind of deceit. Explaining to his daughter Rosamond that he doesn't want to take money from Tom Outland's invention, the proceeds of which Tom had willed to Rosamond, he says that would "make that episode in my life commonplace like everything else" (8:57)—everything, that is, including his very successful career and his apparently close family life. (Cather, too, often feared that she was commonplace and was intent on proving that she was not.) When St. Peter glimpses his wife's deep unhappiness during a moving performance of the opera *Mignon,* he is astonished. It is as if he had supposed only he were capable of hidden feelings. The moment seems to offer a breakthrough to new understanding between them. But instead of pursuing that opportunity when they return to their hotel, the professor turns his thoughts back to a perfect day from his past—significantly, a day without his wife. But Cather, too, had lived her best days, her most creative days, in a fictive world of her own, shut off certainly from her family and shut off as well, to the extent that the writer must be shut off, from the person who was more than family, Isabelle. At times, indeed, shut off in an attic populated by inanimate representations of people—the sewing forms that reappear in St. Peter's attic room and her own characters. She must have felt much of the guilt that drives St. Peter to perverse crankiness, but at the same time she must have known that she too, like him, would choose her attic, her art, over all human bonds.

Why did she project these complex feelings in the form of a male, rather than a female, character? It is impossible to know, of course, but I believe the answer has a great deal to do with her old feelings about the masculinity of art and something to do, as well, with her sense of France as the home of a great but essentially masculine artistic culture. Traditionally, men have been the scholars, men have been the writers, shutting themselves off in an austere but (at the same time) paradisal world above (more highly respected than) the warm human entanglements represented by women and children. The haunting guilt of that isolation is, of course, the fear of dehumanization. If she had chosen art over life, books over Isabelle, was she not assuming too male a role? taking on the guilts of the man of letters along with his exaltation? Isabelle and her artist husband had occupied the holy ground of art, France. But she had her own holy ground—an upper room, indeed; and an American upper room at that. Because her retreat to this "France" of her own was guilt-laden, she could not simply adopt Godfrey St. Peter as her own; she must also show the faults of his way. Hence his crotchets and his coldness. The narrator regards him sympathetically but also astringently. And Cather cannot explain because the conflicts are too profound, even as she will not, because it is fiction she is writing, art, art worthy of the French masters' example, not a personal essay.

At the end St. Peter prepares to come down, rescued by the sturdy and practical Augusta, even as Cather prepared to come down to a comfortable, well-ordered life, rescued and tended by the faithful Edith Lewis. Augusta represents woman as sustainer, as caretaker. She answers to St. Peter's deepest need, his will to live: her arrival coincides with his all but unconscious lunge toward the door of the gas-filled attic to escape a quasi-suicidal death by suffocation. Her rescue of St. Peter indeed, as James Maxfield comments, provides "for the first time in the novel a feminine influence . . . recognized as positive."[37] But I would add, recognized as positive, that is, by the Professor himself. If the presence of Augusta saves *The Professor's House* from being, in Maxfield's words, "one of the most misogynist works ever composed by a female author," it does so only insofar as we are willing to identify St. Peter's vision totally with Cather's. That we cannot do—even though he is not clearly separated either.

Though Cather invests St. Peter with much of her own presence—much more fully, indeed, than she does with the male observers of *A Lost Lady* or *My Ántonia,*—we do see glimpses of a narrative vision distinct from his.[38] In general, these glimpses lead us to doubt that the professor is altogether blameless in having arrived at the isolated condition in his family that we see in the novel. If Mrs. St. Peter flirts with her sons-in-law and schemes for their career advancement, we can see a reason in Godfrey's neglect and her own lack of an independent interest of her own. If she appears small-minded in her wish that he would not pour out his strongest convictions to mere students, we understand her sense that he has never shared them in that same way with her. Her momentary revelation of deep sadness at the opera is not the only glimpse we have of feelings starved by Godfrey's detachment. When she asks him "gravely" if he would rather have spent his book prize money on something other than the house, he replies condescendingly and rather chillingly, emphasizing the disjunction between *her* house and *his* delight in his work. These small indications that she may be more sensitive and caring than he, for all his self-pity, culminate in one of the few brief entries into her point of view. We see her filled with concern for her husband's "unusual weariness . . . , the bitter taste on his tongue," and his disappointment in their daughter. "Her heart ached for Godfrey" (8:151). But when she tries to share his mood by asking, later, why he had smiled so "agreeably" at something (it must be unusual!), he shuts her out with a misogynist witticism.

Augusta is, to be sure, a strong positive presence in the novel, conveying values that St. Peter might do well to emulate. But she is a positive presence *to Godfrey* largely because she is not a threatening one. She makes no emotional demands on him and does not raise the disturbing issue of erotic sexuality, an issue he prefers to avoid. Her very real strengths of character—her persistence, her practical service to others, her willingness to face such exigencies as illness and death—are strongly linked to St. Peter's renewed sense of reality and ongoing life at the end, after his rescue from death by suffocation. At that point he expresses an inward allegiance to "a world full of Augustas, with whom one was outward bound" (8:280). But we have no reason to think he will ever adequately appreciate her sense of her self (he has considered her life "bloomless" merely because it did not include conventional satisfactions) or that he will ever let go of his regressive self-pity. His rebirth is an oddly dispassionate one, to a life "without delight" (8:280).

Like Cather herself, Godfrey St. Peter has had to relinquish a prolonged emotional attachment that had given him delight. O'Brien and others who have worked with Cather's closely guarded surviving correspondence note that her tone when speaking of the somewhat Augusta-like Edith Lewis was reliant and calm, even matter-of-fact, while her tone when speaking of Isabelle was always ardent. St. Peter, too, has cherished his sense of joyful love for Tom Outland, the student with whom he spent hours of intent conversation in his garden and in his attic study (where his wife was never welcome). By clinging to his memories and to work that he associated with Tom—his eight-volume history as well as the editing of Tom's diary—St. Peter could cling to the illusion that the great emotion which had once fired his life still remained alive. But when he is forced to see that he must relinquish his attic retreat and reengage with everyday reality, he faces, as well, the fact that that phase of his life is over and he will be continuing on a comparatively less exalted emotional plane. In much the same way Cather herself prolonged her centering on Isabelle until the visit to the Hambourgs in 1923, when she had to face the absoluteness of a change to an emotional climate that was not bleak, but certainly less intense.

The fullness of St. Peter's emotional response to Tom Outland is left unspoken. It is the frame around the open window of book two in the novel, Tom's own story. It is the unacknowledged reason he will not go to Europe with his wife and the Marselluses: having wanted to make that trip with Tom, he will settle for going with no one else. But that absence, that tacit reason, is at the source of the strangely unexplained depression that pervades the book. Cather realized, perhaps, that her own exaltation of her love for Isabelle over her love for her faithful and supportive friend Edith was not reasonable and not even fair. If that is true, then we can see the tones in which she presents Godfrey St. Peter, making him out to be so curiously distant and prickly, as being in part traceable to self-judgment.

In part, too, they are traceable to her criticism of that male world of art and scholarship that made her *feel* so inadequate and excluded, even when she was no longer excluded at all but highly respected. She knew too well the male assumption of loftiness in the house of literature, where women occupied a domestic and sentimental ground floor. She knew the proclivity of the Henry Jameses of her world for keeping, not women, but devitalized imitations of women as accessories in their studious retreats— women headless, like St. Peter's dress forms, so that they cannot think, and armless, so that they cannot act effectively. St. Peter's determination to keep "my ladies ... right there in their own place" where he is accustomed to having them (8:14) expresses, in effect, his preference for effigies over real women. He fears being lured into a reliance on women because he suspects they will betray him just as the apparently soft-bosomed dress forms actually "presented the most unsympathetic surface imaginable" (8:11). If he is to learn Tom's lesson of human allegiance, the lesson that "anyone who requites faith and friendship as I did," in turning his back on his friend Roddy, "will have to pay for it" (8:252), he will have to give up this misogynist suspicion and exchange the effigies for real people. But he has never heard that lesson, despite his supposed attachment to Tom. Instead he believes only that for Tom to have lived and married—married St. Peter's own daughter, at that—would have reduced him to being "the instrument of a woman who would grow always more exacting" (8:259). Repeating, in effect, the error Tom made and repented of, St. Peter persists in his view of women as being hard and rejecting despite their forms. At the end he turns his face only grudgingly toward life.

The women's side of the story in *The Professor's House* remains untold, merely glimpsed. But we can safely assume that when Cather writes that "with her sons-in-law" Mrs. St. Peter "had begun the game of being a woman all over again" and "lived in their careers as she had once done in his" (8:73) she recognized fully the banefulness of a system that forces its women to live through men's careers because they are effectively denied careers of their own. Cather herself lived through her own career, pouring her life into her art; we cannot even imagine her living vicariously, through the art of someone else, some man. And when we glimpse, with Godfrey, a hint that the St. Peters' younger daughter may have been in love with Tom Outland too (as she speaks so warmly of him that St. Peter, presumably for the first time, hears her love like a melody in the air), we understand the bitterness of being a less attractive sister in a world that esteems appearance. That is not to say that Tom fell in love on the basis of the older sister's better looks, but that Kathleen, who is so conscious of the beauty and the fashionable clothes of the sister with whom he did fall in love, might well think so. The hinted subtext of the novel speaks of the inadequacy of the lives customarily lived by women. Cather distances herself from those lives by her sympathetic centering on Godfrey St. Peter and Tom Outland, but speaks of and for them by the tacit arguments of St. Peter's shortcomings and the almost silenced countervoice of the subtext.

In much the same way, in the interstices and the subdued murmurings we encounter throughout her work, Cather speaks of the difficulties and inequities of women's lives. Never one to use fiction as a forum from which to address pubic issues, she nevertheless leads her readers, through a submerged or tacit argument, to an awakened realization of the problems of gender roles—the problems that so unsettled her own youth and, to a lesser degree, her mature years. Just as the Benda illustrations provide (as Jean Schwind argues so cogently) a silent subtext to the text of *My Ántonia,* giving a "separate account" of Ántonia and iconographically empowering both Ántonia and Lena, so the glimpsed but unstated possibilities of Cather's novels provide a tacit amplification and counterstatement. Her restrained and laconic style, in which so many elements are skirted or suppressed, becomes a medium of communication and tacit persuasion. In managing to communicate what she does not state (the "thing not named"), Cather makes of her reticent style not only a medium of evocation but a rhetorical strategy.

In a recent review essay, Frederick Crews has mocked critical arguments from silence, the kind of method that "points an accusing finger at precisely what the text has 'repressed.'"[39] It is very much that kind of argument that I am making here in reading Cather's pictorial, "descriptive and reflective"[40] fiction as a rhetorical fiction, though I am not accusing but rather affirming her powerful submersions. I agree with Crews that such a method is inherently indefinite and easily prone to unfounded invention if one is not cautious. Fortunately, the evidence in Cather's novels is, for the most part, considerably more palpable than the absences Crews calls, sarcastically, repressions.

The readiest evidence of the rhetorical dimension of Cather's work, perhaps, is in *My Ántonia*. We have already considered the narrative irony of the work, the way in which Jim Burden's reality is distinguished from Cather's own. Considering his presentation of Ántonia across that gap of disapproval, we can see that Cather uses the inadequacy of his sense of reality as a tacit feminist argument.

From the time Ántonia first begins to work in the fields for her brother Ambrosch, Jim ignores both the necessity for her working and the hardships involved. It is a pattern that continues throughout his narrative: he shows inadequate comprehension of the circumstances of her life, as distinct from those of his own. In celebrating her personal magnetism, generosity, and vitality as he fixes her firmly in the role of earth mother, then, he scants his estimate of what this role has cost her. He thereby underestimates her courage and strength in standing up against all those battering difficulties. We see the missing teeth and shapelessness; Ántonia is visibly worn down by the trials of being a woman in a harsh society that expects endless rounds of childbearing and housework (as well as farmwork). But Jim sees only the part he wants to see—the evidence of her flowing maternity.

Jim ignores, too, the evidence that in fulfilling his ideal for her, Ántonia may not have been able to fulfill her own ideals. Her vision is greater than his, and different. She wants her daughter to have a different life from her own: "I'm going to see that my little girl has a better chance than ever I had" (4:321). Too, we see that Ántonia's children regard Frances Harling as a "heroine in the family legend" (4:350).[41] Certainly this can have happened only through Ántonia's representing her as a hero. But Frances, we remember, was a woman very different from the woman Ántonia seems to have become. She had "unusual business ability"

and excelled in such traditionally masculine activities as managing her father's office and watching "the markets" (4:149). Moreover, she at one time emphatically approved of Lena's avowal
never to marry. These details hinting at Ántonia's view of gender—her aspirations for her daughter and her presentation of an
"unwomanly" woman as hero—are planted for us by Cather but
ignored by Jim very much as he ignores Ántonia's daughters
when he sums up his praise of her mothering: "it was no wonder
that her sons stood tall and straight. She was a rich mine of life,
like the founders of early races" (4:353). Boys and their mothers,
so long as mothers confine themselves to mothering, are the
people who matter.

It is possible, of course, to argue that Cather's complex narrative strategy is not a generalizable rhetoric; that the textural
achievement of rendering the emotional coloring and the emotional limitations of a character's perceptions and interpretations
is a sufficient whole, and need not—some would say should
not—act as part of an argument or a persuasive view of a class
of such observers and interpreters. But Cather herself generalizes
her argument and in so doing clearly legitimizes the view that
her narrative strategies were also part of a rhetorical strategy. We
can see the evidence of a broadened argumentation in *My Ántonia*
and also in other novels, where an intentionality of challenging
accepted views of gender manifests itself as a subtext to other
narrative and rhetorical concerns. That this intentionality appears
at times to be intertwined with anxieties and allegiances which
seem to run counter to it (for instance, a general anxiety about
sex) is not a reason to doubt the real presence of the rhetorical
purpose, but evidence of the real humanity of Willa Cather, who
no more than the rest of us, or perhaps rather less, was able to
gather all her experiences and emotional needs into clear and
conscious consistency.

It has often been noted that marriages in Cather's fiction generally appear to be unhappy and inequitable. The marriage of the
Harlings, in *My Ántonia,* is especially interesting. Mrs. Harling,
the central force in the family, is a vital, energetic woman who
balances her own interests (her pleasure in playing the piano)

with the needs of the family. Mrs. Harling makes life a joy for all—except when her husband is on hand. When he comes home from his business trips, he domineers over everyone; he is a spoiler of their good times. He "not only demanded a quiet house" but "demanded all his wife's attention" as well, monopolizing her time, imposing his interests on her attention, and expecting her to cater to his whims to the extent of getting up to make coffee for him "at any hour of the night he happened to want it" (4:157). In the presence of her husband, Mrs. Harling is reduced from being a forthright and magnetic person to being a virtual servant. Implications that Cather saw a sexual dimension to her servanthood are raised by the pointed location of all this servitude in the Harlings' bedroom. In the case of the Harlings, Jim sees the injustice of the relationship quite clearly; he finds Mr. Harling's "shadow on the blind" of that upstairs bedroom an "arrogant shadow" (4:157). But his realization does not extend to reforming the system. His own wish for subservient affection would perpetuate the same system of dominant males and subservient wives / mothers. He is keenly jealous of Charley Harling, Ántonia's favorite among the youngsters, not because he disapproves of her catering to the boy in principle, but because he would rather get all that attention himself.

It is clear to us, but not to Jim, that women abase themselves to men, who demand sexual and household services, treat women as either amusements or property (a town boy who enjoys toying with one of the hired girls finally marries an older widow with half a section of land), blame women for men's sexual interest, and assert their sole dominion (Mr. Harling refers to "my back yard" and Mrs. Harling agrees that "this is his house"). Whether Mrs. Harling resents her husband's domineering or feels frustrated we can't say; her feelings are securely hidden. We can say, however, that the wife of the philandering, financially unscrupulous, and finally murderous Wick Cutter is very frustrated indeed. She is deliberately tormented by her husband, who enjoys her outrage at his behavior as much as a "last powerful liqueur after dinner" (4:253). And she is not alone, either in her rage or, apparently, in her victimization. Jim mentions in an offhand way, after confessing to finding the Cutters' grievous relationship "interesting and stimulating," that he has "found Mrs. Cutters all over the world" (4:213). It is an appalling spectacle: a worldful of women domineered over, thwarted, sometimes force fed (apparently to overcome their passive aggression), held in seething but ineffectual resistance. Cather does not press the idea; characteristically, she only affords us a glimpse of it; but in combination with the many other glimpses in the book it provides powerful implicit argument for social change.

In *The Professor's House,* as we have seen, a countertext of small glimpses and structured silences expresses Cather's urge to protest the social roles customarily assigned to women. Godfrey St. Peter, the dourly misogynist professor, clearly serves as a projection both of Cather's urge to a life of words, the discipline of the writing desk, and of her response to landscape images of starkness bounded by heights. At the same time, his exclusion of real, living females from the world of study and books projects Cather's own conflicted nature, her sense that in achieving success in that world she had to masculinize herself, shut out her more "feminine" aspects. Her depiction of St. Peter as being so querulous and so condescending to his wife and daughters constitutes, I believe, a rhetoric of protest against the exclusion of women from the masculine bastions of professional letters. Those who would exclude women are sour and insecure. She disapproves of them, as she disapproves of St. Peter's egocentric withdrawal—even as she sympathizes and identifies with him. And she shows us, as well, that the exclusion of women from significant intellectual and professional pursuits results in a trivializing of women's lives. It is true enough, as critics have been quick to point out, that the women who surround St. Peter, all except Amanda, are grasping and disagreeable. But it is also true, I believe, that Cather supplies elements of a plausible explanation of why they are that way. Their lives are stunted by their confinement to cramped gender roles.

We have seen an implicit rhetoric of protest in *A Lost Lady* as well, both in the grinding work that wears Marian Forrester down after she can no longer afford household servants and in the limited social horizons that cause her to define herself in terms of appearance, dancing partners, and being a charming hostess. Marian is a woman of vitality and presence whose life is deplorably constricted by social conceptions of gender. At the end, when Niel hears a report that she has been in South America, still laughing, still vibrant, we scarcely know how to balance our conflicting feelings. Yes, she has landed on her feet; she has demonstrated once again her powers of survival. To Niel Herbert, that is enough. But we see, because Cather leads us to see, that this victory, if it is one, has been won strictly within the social scheme of things, which prescribes that women gain power through attracting powerful men. The detail of Marian's dyed hair is Cather's indication of the cost: a person like Marian has to play the prostituting game if she is to win within this system. And that is wrong. She should have the choice of other ways to win.

In *My Mortal Enemy,* as well, the narrative indirection we have already examined serves rhetorical ends of argument against the established system of restraints on women's lives. The mere fact that the imaginations of Nellie and her Aunt Lydia would have been so wholly taken up by vicarious participation in a story of infatuation and elopement demonstrates the paucity of more autonomous sources of interest in these women's lives. The sad fact, of course, is that women like Myra Henshawe perpetuate this impoverishment of possibility even as they chafe under it. In the first scene in which Myra appears, she makes a show of having "mournful arithmetic" and cautions Nellie not to be "solemn" about being "clever," since "nothing is more tiresome" (11:240). That cleverness is, we surmise, one reason for Nellie's feeling so inadequate in the presence of this romantic woman: she senses that her very nature debars her from the kind of success she has been conditioned to admire in a woman. Later, as Nellie and her aunt are leaving New York at the end of their visit, Myra spitefully tells Lydia she knows Lydia had lied for Oswald to help him find a way of wearing an illicit gift of jeweled cufflinks without having Myra know that they were the gift of an admirer. "'I was sure to find out, I always do. I don't hold it against you, but it's disgusting in a man to lie for personal decorations. A woman

might do it, now ... for pearls!'" (11:283). The comment illustrates Myra's scheming for possessions within the limited range
of activity open to her; she would lie for pearls. We are not sur-
prised at that; Cather has clearly shown her as a person of distasteful materialism as well as frustrated energies. But it shows as
well a different standard of truthfulness for men, as if they are
superior creatures and therefore can be held to a higher standard.
Aunt Lydia's response would seem to corroborate Myra's view
that less is to be expected of women: "'I'm sick of Myra's dra-
matics.... I've done with them. A man never *is* justified, but if
ever a man was ...'" (11:283). A woman may indeed be justified
in lying, she seems to say, but more is to be expected of a man.

Cather, we know, does not endorse such a view. Her women,
at their best and freest, are not weak vessels, nor did she hold
herself any less capable of adherence to a high standard of art
than any man. (Not to a high standard of truth, perhaps, but that
was not because of her sex!) But she does not directly indicate a
disavowal of Aunt Lydia's view. We are left to infer it—and to
understand how Aunt Lydia would hold such a view, given her
society's construction of gender. Women have more need to lie.

At the end of *My Mortal Enemy,* Myra Henshawe stages her
death as she has staged everything else, dramatizing and drawing
attention to herself. It is a powerful expression of her drivenness
to find artificial sources of value for her life, where no more gen-
uine values were available to her. But the fact that the effect of
the death scene is not altogether sad, that Cather presents it as a
kind of victory, shows not only Cather's tact but also her duality.
She was herself caught up in the countercurrents of a changing
situation in which her own emotional and intellectual commit-
ments were torn by the tension between old ways and new. The
book is not only complicated by layers of irony and a tacit questioning that must remain tacit for both aesthetic and rhetorical
reasons, but in addition it is deconstructed by Cather's own profoundly divided sense of self and society.

Her rhetorical undermining of patriarchy did not always pro-
ceed by the negative means of showing (however tacitly) what was
wrong with the circumstances of women's lives. It also proceeded

by the positive display of strong women who demonstrate, through their achievements and their very selves, the injustice of a system based on the disenfranchisement (in the fullest sense) of women. Her Thea Kronborg, in *The Song of the Lark*, and Alexandra Bergson, in *O Pioneers!*, are women who challenge any theory of weak vessels. They achieve success in difficult, competitive enterprises generally regarded as precincts of male leadership—artistic performance and the agricultural transformation of the frontier; and they do so through their own strength, in spite of overwhelming hardships.

Both Thea and Alexandra achieve their successes through a fusing of conventionally masculine and conventionally feminine qualities. If Alexandra's conduct of affairs seems bold, like that of an explorer or adventurer, and if she demonstrates in her handling of affairs a "masculine" directness and assertiveness and hardheaded business sense, her farming methods nevertheless draw on a "feminine" spirit of cooperation with the land and intuitive understanding of her animals' needs, quite different from her father's method of trying to master or "tame" his "wild land" (1:18). One of her most treasured images of the spirit of the land is the peaceable image of a female wild duck she and Emil had once seen on the river, which she holds in her imagination as "a kind of enchanted bird that did not know age or change" (1:175). Subliminating her sexuality into her active love of the land, she feels at times so "close to the flat, fallow land" that she can feel "in her own body the joyous germination in the soil" (1:173)—a strikingly female, strikingly traditional image. Further, strong and resolute as she is, comfortable as she is in a man's coat (1:6), she values the "feminine" quality of being "tender-hearted" (1:47). It is this quality that she loves in her friend and finally her husband, Carl. Alexandra has, then, a kind of totality in which her masculine strength does not deny her feminine attributes but uses them toward reaching her goals.[42]

Thea, too, in *The Song of the Lark*, draws on her femaleness even as she rejects conventional feminine roles in her drive to success as an artist. Intensely female images dominate the text: Thea's bowllike throat, the hollow cave in Panther Canyon where she retreats to think, the Indian women's jars that give her a new vision of her art. She is a woman strong "like a horse, like a tree" (2:256) whose body becomes "absolutely the instrument of her idea" so that, through discipline, her "deep-rooted vitality flowered ... like a tree bursting into bloom" (2:571). As O'Brien rightly argues, the operatic soprano voice provides Cather a "powerful symbol to counter her earlier identification of creativity with masculinity" and a plausible occasion to show "authority and power" in a richly feminine artist.[43]

But Cather is relentlessly clear about the cost of this blossoming of Alexandra's as well as Thea's. For both, their triumphs have meant absolute commitment, exhausting work, and a redirection of sexuality to make its great energies serve a larger discipline. In the process of denying the satisfaction of their instinctual selves, they have suffered emotional impoverishment. As Alexandra says of herself, she is like a vine (surely a feminine plant image) cut back repeatedly until "it grows hard, like a tree" (1:145). Thea, too, we remember, is likened to a tree. For both Alexandra and Thea, the sexual, emotional self is not killed, but driven into deep submersion, where it cannot easily and directly be expressed. Both characters find the vision that will sustain their efforts in a time of solitude and silence, as they look out over a western landscape. For both, silence is a gathering of the self and an emptying of the self's more superficial clamorings. Thea goes to Panther Canyon, a place of "inexorable reserve" (2:367), to find herself. What she actually finds there, in the relics of a dead culture, is a vision both of the hardness of life and of the insistent need of the long-dead cliff dwellers to find aesthetic satisfaction nevertheless. Catching sight of a golden eagle soaring through the canyon and then up past the rim, she catches, as well, a vision of heroism and the "glorious striving of human art" (2:399). The image of flying conveys solitary endeavor and achievement. After leaving Panther Canyon, she goes on to become a successful, artistically powerful operatic performer for whom romantic love and sex can only be subordinate experiences, not the directing commitment of her life. She can add a husband to her autonomous achievements, but she could not have added those to a husband.

After Alexandra's quiet pondering of the advice of old Ivar, a crazy old man intuitively joined to the animals he heals, she goes on to become a great landowner and farmer, the head of her family. But she does so not only at the cost of foregoing that "freedom" that she later says she would rather have had than her land (1:105) but at the cost of isolation, suppression of her emotions, and an inability to recognize, acknowledge, and express sexual love. She channels her sexual passion entirely into her drive for land ownership and successful farming.[44] She succeeds at the cost, too, of conflict with her brothers, who speak with the voice of a sullen and mindless patriarchy. Even though their father had designated her as the leader of the family and enjoined his sons to "be guided by your sister" (1:23, 24), they rebel once their fortunes are secure, when she shows signs of asserting not only her ownership of her own farm, but also her sexuality. "'The property of a family really belongs to the men of the family,'" they argue, "'no matter about the title'" (1:143). It is a traditional argument and, in the context of Alexandra's vision, hard work, and practical leadership, a conspicuously unjust one. When Alexandra dares them to "'go to the county clerk and ask him who owns my land, and whether my titles are good,'" they lament that "'this is what comes of letting a woman meddle in business'"—as if they had merely indulged her in some whim (1:142). Yet the entire story of their adoption of successful farm methods and their economic rise has demonstrated that it was Alexandra who was able to see ahead and direct their efforts, and her own, toward success. It is obvious that her brothers are, in comparison, dense, inept, and unfair. Their ineffectual mouthing of male supremacist notions is a ploy in a strong rhetoric of feminism.

Cather found, in developing these two victorious women characters, Thea and Alexandra, a way to reconcile vocation (the "masculine" side of her self) with human feeling (the "feminine"). But it is a reconciliation in which marriage, the institution within which she saw women's lives being enfeebled and impoverished, is reduced to a secondary, nonthreatening relationship of friends. As Rosowski says, references to Thea's marriage are "perfunctory."[45] Significantly, no children accompany these unions.

Significantly, too, both Thea and Alexandra have resolved their goals and formed their own patterns of life before they take husbands. They have achieved autonomy and are not, in fact, as Alexandra repeatedly daydreams, carried off by a powerful man. Neither are they likely to be malleable to the domestic expectations of new husbands. Instead of subservience to a masculine head of the household, they direct their own lives and choose to share them with men whose qualities include none of the bluster and bullying of Alexandra's brothers.

It is often noted that Cather's strong women characters, those who achieve heroic stature, were created early in her career, and that her later novels celebrate women characters who are more conventional in their aspirations. This view of the shape of her work is accurate in its reflection of the stature of Thea and Alexandra, but it is oversimplified, in at least two ways. First, as Motley correctly argues, it "too easily" overlooks Cather's "prolonged, if sometimes veiled, examination of the psychic cost a woman's success exacts" in both these two early novels.[46] Second, it does not adequately reflect the subtleties of narrative point of view in so late a work as *The Professor's House,* for example, or *My Mortal Enemy,* in both of which Cather questions, through the buried rhetoric of her subtext, the view of women's lives that seems to be propounded on the surface. Even so, it is true that Cather was uncomfortable with change, in a time when women's roles were changing drastically, and that in her own insecurity she yearned toward the traditional comfort of a maternal presence. It appears true, as well, that her own defiance of traditional roles was attended with considerable anxiety and guilt. The commonplace view of Cather's work, then, is largely true, that as she became increasingly troubled by change, she reached ever further into the past for the subjects of her fiction. This meant removing her characters from the changes in gender roles that could more plausibly be explored in more nearly contemporary settings.

Certainly, in her later work especially, Cather was capable of affirming the traditional structures of society, including traditional home-ordering roles for women. This is particularly so in *Shadows on the Rock,* where Cecile finds deep fulfillment and reassurance in an almost ritualistic enactment of domestic routine. The creation of domestic order becomes, indeed, an art. In *Sapphira and the Slave Girl* as well, both the domineering Sapphira and her staunchly resistant daughter fulfill very traditional roles as domestic rulers and workers. Rachel, the daughter, may assert her moral resistance by helping a slave girl escape persecution, but she does not challenge the social system in other respects. When her two children fall ill with diphtheria, she follows the instructions of the (male) doctor even when they go against her intuition and are, in fact, wrong. Only the authority of another man, a loving father figure of a doctor from town, can turn her from the treatment that is killing her children. In none of this does Cather seem to question the privileging of masculine authority.[47] Moreover, the reactionary vision of women's lives that seems to be conveyed in these two late novels can clearly be traced, in large measure, to crises in Cather's own life and her need to enact what Merrill Skaggs calls an act of "ritual penance" by giving "idealized parents the perfect firstborn female her own parents never had."[48]

Even as she affirms social tradition, however, Cather provides reasons to doubt its fairness. Thus even her later works, which seem so conservative in their social vision, at times speak a subdued rhetoric that questions the social construction of gender. In both *Death Comes for the Archbishop* (an extremely institutional, as it is an extremely male, book) and "Old Mrs. Harris" (one of the three stories that make up *Obscure Destinies*) we catch glimpses of the repressed woman, even the abused woman.

In *Death Comes for the Archbishop*, the wife who has been beaten into acquiescence with crime and the wife who has been trivialized into preferring poverty to telling her true age (much as Godfrey St. Peter's wife and daughters have been trivialized into compulsive and disagreeable acquisitiveness) are only two of the "repressed social problems" that haunt the tranquil surface of the novel. They haunted, we may assume, Cather's tranquillity as well. Ever more committed, as she grew older, to a stable social order she could only posit far in the past, she continued to be troubled by the lives of women in such an order.

In "Old Mrs. Harris," it is the system itself that pushes the older woman into a cramped corner and demands that she fill her days with cooking and child care and efface her own personality, all for the benefit of the family. Mrs. Harris herself does not complain; she welcomes her straitened circumstances as a kind of security; but we can scarcely suppose that Cather, who so relished her freedom of movement and self-determination, meant to endorse what seems so obviously wrong in this treatment of the older woman.

It is sometimes argued that responses to the story that center on the plight of Mrs. Harris, seeing her as a mistreated person, ignore her own sense of her position. To be sure, the story emphasizes the discomfort of her life—relegated to a curtained corner of a common room, sleeping on a thin mattress, thanklessly carrying the burden of virtually all the housework even when she is no longer physically able, and deprived of social contact except under the daughter's watchful eye. But, it is argued, women such as Mrs. Harris were content with their lot because it fulfilled their ideas of propriety. Their proper role in young adulthood had been to bear children and be the center of the family stage, and now their lot as older women is to provide the support efforts that enable their daughter to move to the center. They may be marginalized in the household, shoved to the "background," but at least "it was their own background." Occupying that niche, they held a kind of power over a defined realm, and they "ruled it jealously" (12:111). Cather, such an argument goes, was a social realist who understood the society of which she wrote, and not only understood it, but accepted it.

Such a reading has much to recommend it—primarily, its clarification of an interpretive vision that might be clouded by sentimentality. But it is not fully adequate to the story. In my view, "Old Mrs. Harris" does emphasize the plight of the old woman and does operate to create reader sympathy for her. Disregarding that sympathy, even as we acknowledge the larger social structures that mitigate it, is not appropriate. But regarding the old woman simply as a victim is not appropriate either. The story explores both her motivation and her surprising assertiveness in a much fuller way than readings of Mrs. Harris as pathetic victim would allow. In doing so, the story actually broadens its scope in subtle ways so that it becomes a protest, not merely of the harsh treatment of one old woman but of the condition of women generally. It becomes an appeal for change.

Like Ántonia, Mrs. Harris is determined to give the younger generation a better chance than she ever had. In the case of her daughter, Victoria, that determination had taken the form merely of pampering the young woman and catering to her whims out of sympathy for the domestic life that lay ahead of her. Victoria is now a mature woman who expects others to work hard while she goes to card parties or takes her afternoon rest and who hopes to attract attention and friendships by wearing pretty dresses. She is, in short, a kind of grown child. Such behavior is acceptable to her mother, however, because Mrs. Harris realizes that Victoria is caught in the only pattern of life either of them has ever known, a pattern of life that includes sexual servitude to a husband and the resulting bearing of children. But the granddaughter, Vickie (we might read, Willa) shows an aptitude for learning; she wants to go away to college. And Mrs. Harris is determined she shall go.

The problem is money: the shortage of it in general, and women's total lack of control over it in particular. Even the money realized from the sale of Mrs. Harris's own home has been given over (as women's property once was, by law) to the control of her daughter's husband, who has invested it as he sees fit and now cannot or will not call it in for Vickie's college expenses. Invested: "that was a word men always held over women, Mrs. Harris thought, and it always meant they could have none of their own money" (12:138). She absorbs that realization in silence, merely "sigh[ing] deeply."

For the women in this story, silence is, indeed, a refuge. Unlike Thea or Alexandra, who summoned their strength in silent communion with the land and with birds, emblems of freedom, Mrs. Harris and the neighbor who becomes her friend remain silent because they are unable to speak up. They feel discontented, but for the most part, they shut their discontent up inside themselves and try merely to fulfill more perfectly the roles they know. Victoria, for instance, withdraws to her bedroom and complains of headache when actually she is suffering the realization that once again she must pay the price of her position in the social order by bearing a baby. She cannot defy the dominance of a husband; perhaps she cannot even think of doing so. But her silence is merely a period of sulking and self-pity, not a gathering of the power to speak.

For Mrs. Harris, however, the silent realization that life is not fair operates somewhat differently. Mrs. Harris's role is in fact one to which she would have felt resigned, if economic pressure had not made circumstances so uncomfortable and if the family had not moved to the frontier, where old patterns were yielding to new ones and the old sharing with others in like circumstances was cut off. There, however, without the sustaining social network of other marginalized older women, it becomes clear that something is wrong. That something is most obviously the fact that the old woman is exploited and undervalued. But her exploitation is only a symptom of a larger problem. The entire set of roles played by mother and married daughter and grandchildren is built on one fact: the hardship of women's lives. Marriage and childbearing are so hard on women that their mothers are willing to enslave themselves in order to postpone the inevitable hardship as long as possible for girls and to relieve the trials of household management as much as possible for the younger married women. That is the reality Mrs. Harris has accepted. In a stable society, one where generations of families remained in one place and roles could be passed on, it is a reality that could have provided her a certain sense of security. But in a changing society she perceives what is wrong and moves to change it.

Mrs. Harris's silence, then, becomes a time of awareness for her. Her motivation for continuing in her present hardship has been her realization of the harshness of women's lives and her determination to relieve that harshness, as much as possible, for her own daughter. Now, however, she determines that the cycle will not go on forever. Deprived of apparent power, deprived even of her own money, she determines to find a way of securing the means for her granddaughter to go to college. It is a powerful, if unspoken, indictment of the system.

For all her nostalgia for secure, orderly patterns of social life and for the material and emotional sustaining provided by a mother, Cather saw and protested the unfairness of the past. In the mindless masculine rhetoric of Alexandra's brothers, in the callous escapism of Mrs. Harris's son-in-law, who goes off for a few days when his wife realizes she is pregnant, and in the snide inconsiderateness of Godfrey St. Peter she presents an indictment of men under the old dispensation. For all her dislike of change, she offers in her fiction a powerful rhetoric arguing for precisely that. Caught in toils of anxiety over "concealment and disclosure" which were "in part connected with the lesbianism she could not name," so that she feared the openness of the "creative process" even as she devoted herself to it,[49] she developed a hidden rhetoric which relied on implication and reader response. Disliking the muckraking journalism of social exposure with which she worked as editor of *McClure's Magazine,* she nevertheless, even as she turned to a pure art of disciplined fiction, worked toward social exposure of the system with which she could never be personally comfortable. Her novels repeatedly display the plight of women caught in toils of propriety and biased judgment. But within those novels we see images of free-flying birds, such as the eagle with which Thea identifies herself during her silent communion with self in the canyon or the wild duck (pointedly a female duck) which for Alexandra represents both the land and freedom, the two together. These are Cather's positive images for herself and her women characters. They constitute a powerful silent rhetoric of change.

In the last chapter of the "Kronborg" section of *The Song of the Lark,* when Thea sings the perfect part for her voice, Wagner's Sieglinde, and sings it triumphantly, "shining like a Victory" (2:568), the "closed roads opened, the gates dropped" (2:571). In part, that is because her "inhibitions chanced to be fewer than usual" (2:571)—that is, because she is precisely not reserved or restrained. But her achievement of that state of art with "everything working together" is based, even more, on years of preparatory restraint. It is only that long discipline that makes possible the illusion of absolute freedom. Even in the moment of transcendence, however, the truth of Thea's self and her commitment are conveyed indirectly, hidden within a role. Her powerful demonstration of female heroism is a wordless message spoken as "the thing not named" through the language of music and dramatic image. Thea, a "close one" with "ulterior motives" (2:391), is thus, as readers have observed for a great variety of reasons, a splendidly idealized representation of Cather herself, even to her achievement of the single, unsexed stage name by which the closing section of the novel is called, "Kronborg."

In a more unabashedly inspirational way than Cather's subdued late fiction would allow, Thea's story argues for, by demonstrating, the necessity of letting girls become women on their own terms so that they may achieve their own uncommon successes, even though the preponderance of a masculinist world, in the person of what Thea's lover calls "most fellows," won't like their sense of bulletlike "direction" (2:392). Cather "dramatizes but does not resolve" such issues as the capacity of women to achieve great things when they are given the freedom to do so.[50] Through its silences and through its nondiscursive images, her fiction tells things in such a way that, unless we are very attentive, we won't know we're hearing them.

CHAPTER FOUR

Katherine Anne Porter
and the Reticent Style

*I loved that silence which means freedom from the
constant pressure of other minds and other opinions
and other feelings, that freedom to fold up in quiet
and go back to my own center.*

——————— KATHERINE ANNE PORTER, "HOLIDAY" ———————

Virtually every critic who has written on Katherine Anne Porter
has spoken in terms of precision, compression, a prevailing economy of style and overall strategy. Robert Penn Warren, in an early
essay that remains the fountainhead of Porter criticism, notes "the
exceptional precision of her language." Eudora Welty—like Warren, a friend as well as a reader of Porter—comments on the
"distilled" quality of her imagery. Robert Heilman praises her gift
for the "succinct summarizing sentence" and notes her use, like
Austen's, of "pithy," or compressed, "geometrical arrangements."
Debra Moddelmog regards "He"—rightly; it is a masterpiece—
as an "economical" story in which "not a word is wasted and
much is implied." Harold Bloom, in his usual cryptic way, compares Porter's style to Hart Crane's in that, like Crane, she "concentrated her gift, and her stories match his lyrics in their
economy and in their sublime eloquence."[1]

If Porter has suffered from too much praise as a stylist, as if
with the implication of mere stylist (she said once, "I've been
called a stylist until I really could tear my hair out"[2]), the reason

may be that her work is difficult to get hold of, once the point about purity, compression, or integrity of style has been made. Heilman, attempting to define the "certain elusiveness" that makes her style "not quite easy to account for," suggests that it is hard to describe because it is "a style without mannerisms, crotchets, or even characteristic brilliances or unique excellences."[3] His insight is, I think, useful, indicating as it does a kind of full achievement unmarked by distortion or peculiarity. But accounting for the effect of Porter's style is not, finally, one's goal, even if it could be done. Darlene Harbour Unrue indicates a more fruitful line of inquiry when she views Porter's style as something more than manner, and links the style to perceived themes. In Unrue's words, Porter's "pure" style is at once "the medium of the honest vision and also the symbol of it."[4]

Porter's manner and her matter are indeed closely integrated—so closely that their weld is almost too smooth to see, let alone break open. My interest here is not to try to disengage them, but to indicate how style does, in fact, become the symbol of Porter's vision, and how that vision that is also a style is related to a pervasive quality of reticence. Within Porter's relatively slight canon, my focus is on "Noon Wine" and on the Miranda stories, defining that category to include "Hacienda" and "Flowering Judas."[5] My reason for this focus is that these works, if given the closest possible reading, provide a clear understanding of the method in her work as a whole. Further, despite the valiant efforts of Unrue and of Robert Heilman in arguing the merits of *Ship of Fools,* I believe with the greater number of her critics that Porter's really fine work is in shorter forms.

Questions of generic affinity—why Emerson wrote essays while Hawthorne write stories, why Eliot wrote novels and Barrett Browning poetry—are elusive at best and conjectural to the point of uselessness at worst. In the case of Porter, Joan Givner's argument that her clear preference for short forms derives from a demonstrably short attention span is very convincing. Cause, however, is of less interest than effect. It seems clear that the brevity of Porter's forms is related to the economy of her language. Both are expressions of that unembellished precision, at once comely and incisive, that was her artistic credo. Art should not, she said, "imitate the shapelessness of life."[6] And indeed her art did not. Life is there, but shaped into comprehensibility—if one accepts that the shaped presentation of insoluble questions is a kind of comprehensibility. The work is detailed; in shaping, she does not merely generalize; but the details are the telling ones. The mental underbrush has been cleared away, by a process of judicious aesthetic consideration and pruning, so that we can see, in all their twigged completion, the plants that are of interest. Welty calls it, in her essay "The Eye of the Story," a "re-formed imagery" giving not so much the experience itself as experience "from memory's remove."[7] The phrase puts its finger, so to speak, on a major vein in the life of Porter's fiction—the sense of a doubling back and a brooding over lived experience until its fine network of essentials is revealed, held up finally to just the right light.

It is no clearer in the case of Porter than in the case of Austen (or Cather or Didion) precisely how the sense of reticence in the work—which is not necessarily the same thing as brevity, though in this instance it is certainly related to brevity—may be implicated in the social expectations placed on women or in the artist's own sense of some constraint because of her sex. Certainly Porter, raised in the South at a time when Southern ideas of womanhood formed a mystique even more restrictive than those of American society generally, brings to her work a complex and very powerful sense of what is or is not acceptable behavior for a woman. The combination of defiance and adherence to these standards in her own life and in her direct comments is often puzzling. That she felt the presence of constraints which were not brought to bear on men and chafed against them is clear. But it is equally clear that she adopted and even avowed certain conventionally feminine patterns—she dressed stylishly, and never in trousers; she advised serving one's husband cocktails and being charming. That she extended ideas of propriety or constraint to include the matter of language is clear from, among other things, her remark on Hart Crane's use of "words so foul there is no question of repeating them."[8]

But the question is not so much one of timidity or finickiness, refusal to confront certain issues directly (a trait commonly associated with women writers until very recent years), as it is one of both purposeful artistic discipline and a pervasive sense of constraint on her being-in-the-world from the fact that she is a woman. It is impossible to assess adequately the effects of Porter's characteristic economy without giving full regard to the centrality of women in her fiction.[9] Reticence is, to be sure, an expression of her deepest sense of artistic rightness. In arguing that it is also a rhetorical strategy for bringing the work to bear on questions of the status and intentions of women, I will want to stress that this rhetoric is employed in very subtle ways.

"Noon Wine" provides the clearest paradigm of Porter's ability at once to employ verbal style as a manifestation of values and to enact those values, with great subtlety, through her own style. Verbal style is for her an issue of the utmost seriousness, not only aesthetically and as a matter of decorum (very much in the Austenian sense), but morally as well. In "Noon Wine," speech is character, or at any rate, the primary index to character. Within the context of Porter's own concise narrative style, the dialogue of "Noon Wine" takes us to the heart of her elusive artistic and moral vision.

In its outlines, it is a simple, direct story. Mr. Thompson, a farmer in Texas, hires a handyman, Mr. Helton, who proves to be oddly taciturn (perhaps because his English is limited) but capable and hardworking. Helton's only activity outside his work on the farm is playing a single repetitious tune on the harmonica. After nine years, during which Helton brings the farm from bare subsistence to prosperity, a stranger calling himself Homer T. Hatch comes looking for him and says that Helton is an escaped mental patient who once killed his own brother. When Hatch tells Mr. Thompson that he intends to take Helton back to North Dakota and collect a reward, Thompson kills Hatch with an ax. After this, although he is acquitted of murder, Mr. Thompson spends his time driving around the countryside explaining his innocence to his neighbors. At last, despairing of ever fully exonerating himself, he commits suicide.

Almost deceptively simple, the story well illustrates that quality of limpidness and verbal perfection that has both established Porter's reputation as a stylist, a "classical writer,"[10] and made her work so resistant to definition. It is as if the actual verbal structure of the story were simply a transparency laid over a set of real objects and scenes that had first been meticulously stripped bare and arranged. The images of the story themselves shine through in what Robert Penn Warren has called "a kind of indicative poetry."[11] The author seems to step aside and let her rigorously selected details establish themselves autonomously. That is, the style of "Noon Wine" is not at all an external decoration draped over the skeleton of a story. Indeed, part of the difficulty of determining what the story is "about" is that its style and its substance are so inseparable. For Porter, manner is matter. As she put it herself, "the style is you."[12] It is this interrelatedness of manner and meaning that is the key to "Noon Wine" and the reason the story occupies such a central position in Porter's work.

The frequently noted economy of Porter's style is particularly evident here in the way she establishes an aura of mystery surrounding Mr. Helton. By avoiding omniscience, limiting herself instead to what Helton tells the Thompsons—very little—and what they can observe of him, Porter forces the reader to share the Thompsons' ignorance and their puzzlement, or what should be their puzzlement. Surprisingly enough, though, for the Thompsons the mystery is not pressing. Helton is so unobtrusive that they easily become accustomed to his presence, and so useful that they are glad to accept the benefits of his work without wondering about him as a person. Indeed, the ease with which the Thompsons dismiss the mystery of Helton's character is one of the story's judgments on them. For the reader, the mystery is very real, primarily because it is so sharply particularized in Helton's peculiar and slightly ominous fixation on his collection of harmonicas.

This peculiarity is established in few words, chiefly in two main incidents. When Mrs. Thompson goes out to the hired man's shack on his first day to meet him, she notices his harmonicas and intimates that they may attract the attention of her two little boys. Her husband, she mentions, used to play an old accordion until the boys broke it. At this, Helton "stood up rather suddenly, the chair clattered under him, his knees straightened though his shoulders did not, and he looked at the floor as if he were listening carefully" (p. 245). The reader is tantalized by the intensity of his reaction, but Mrs. Thompson goes imperturbably on, politely ignoring his oddity, which apparently is no worse than the "quirks and crotchets" of hired men she has seen before, and advises Helton to take protective measures. Whereupon Helton, "in one wide gesture of his long arms, swept his harmonicas up against his chest, and from there transferred them in a row to the ledge where the roof joined the wall. He pushed them back almost out of sight" (p. 228). In the quickness and the absoluteness of the "one wide gesture," the protectiveness of his gathering them "against his chest," and his care to push them "back almost out of sight," Porter conveys how overwhelmingly concerned Helton is for the safekeeping of the harmonicas and creates a mystery as to why he feels so strongly.

Some two years later, a second incident jars the story with its unexpected intensity. Walking back from the garden one spring day, Mrs. Thompson catches sight of Helton wordlessly shaking the two boys, first one and then the other, by the shoulders. His face is "terribly fixed and pale" in a look of "hatred," and the action is performed "ferociously" (pp. 237–38). This brief glimpse of the man's silent fury, which has been evoked by the children's meddling with his harmonicas, fixes him in a dense aura of mystery that is never dissipated. As Thomas Walsh observes, "however he is atomized," the quiet Helton "remains, like Melville's Bartleby, a mystery."[13] He is last seen, at his moment of capture, trying to retrieve two harmonicas that have fallen out of his jumper pocket. The reader is left with the unanswered question of why the harmonicas were so important to him.

As the motif of Helton's mystery demonstrates, Porter's concise, disciplined style achieves not only spareness but also a clear focus on the telling detail. It achieves also a sense of unspoken depth. In this, perhaps more than in any other way, Porter resembles Jane Austen. For both writers, what is unsaid is as important as what is said. We are invited to speculate about the unsaid, and that act of speculation in itself lends weight to the said. This weightiness, this sense that something has been kept in reserve, makes Porter's style indeed "compact with meaning."[14] Like Austen, she is able to achieve the great in the small.

The standards of conciseness and reserve demonstrated in Porter's narrative style are elaborated in the contrasting speech styles of the characters. As we have noted, Helton is a man of extreme reticence, who never says two words if one will do. On first approaching Mr. Thompson, he announces bluntly, "'I need work ... You need a man here?'" (p. 223). In response to Mr. Thompson's roundabout questioning, he gives only the barest facts: his origin (North Dakota), his name, and a terse summary of his qualifications: "'I can do everything on farm ... cheap. I need work'" (p. 223). Later, when Mrs. Thompson comes out to introduce herself, he says even less, a total of ten words to her two hundred and sixteen. His silence is emphasized by narrative comment: "Not a word from Mr. Helton" (p. 229). Mr. Thompson finds him "'the closest mouthed fellow I ever met up with'" (p. 229).

Mr. Thompson himself is not close-mouthed at all. We see from the start that he is given to empty talk, filling conversational space just for the sake of filling it. When Helton approaches him asking for work, he replies with extraneous chat about his previous two hired hands. When Helton says where he is from, Thompson muses vacantly, "'North Dakota ... That's a right smart distance off, seems to me'" (p. 223). Sensing a bargain at hand, he warms to a forced geniality, saying "in his most carrying voice" that he guesses they had better "'talk turkey'" (p. 223). Porter adds that in business dealings Thompson "grew very hearty and jovial" to disguise his dislike of spending money (p. 224). It is more an amusing fault than a vicious one, but it indicates, to his discredit, Mr. Thompson's willingness to use a friendly manner and a stream of talk for purposes of dissembling. The point is especially worth noting since it will contribute to the pattern of doubling developed later in the story. In sum, Mr. Thompson is a "hearty good fellow among men" (p. 234) or as

Frederick Hoffman says,[15] a man of "broad, self-sustained" speech who cares greatly for "his dignity and his reputation" among his neighbors (p. 233). Each aspect of Mr. Thompson established here in such brief terms will come to bear on the ending of the story.

The contrast between Helton and Thompson is particularly evident in their different disciplinary approaches to the two Thompson boys. Mr. Thompson is all bluster, making dire threats and working himself up into rages (p. 240) with little effect. By contrast, the one time Helton is seen chastising the boys he does so without a word, and they remember it. Indeed, when we see them after Helton has been on the farm nine years, they are no longer disorderly but "good solid boys" (p. 242). Helton's effect on the boys is typical of his effectiveness in general. He gets things done. By contrast, Mr. Thompson is generally ineffectual, as much in his farming as in his child rearing. He is harmless and well-intentioned, but full of false pride and excuses for not getting things done, and under his management, before Helton arrives, the farm is generally run down. We cannot say that there is any cause-and-effect relationship, but the story firmly associates Mr. Thompson's kind of talkativeness with shiftlessness or shallowness and, positively, associates reserve with dignity and conscientious, competent performance. The person with a reserved demeanor is accorded more respect than the big talker. Still waters, Porter seems to indicate, do indeed run deep.

It is no wonder, then, that when Mr. Homer T. Hatch walks onto the Thompsons' farm and into the world of "Noon Wine" we know at once, by his roar of false joviality and his unfunny joke, that he is a shabby character. We see immediately that his waters, which are far from still, do not run deep. Yet, in a sense, they do; Mr. Hatch is "deep" in the sense of "devious." He roils his waters to keep the bottom hidden. Not only does he talk too much, but his talk manages to be at once loose and calculated. If Helton is taciturn almost to the point of surliness and Mr. Thompson is garrulous, Hatch is voluble. Almost as soon as we decide he is not deep, we decide that we do not trust him.

Mr. Hatch has, as Porter says, a "free manner" (p. 243). And for her this is no small matter. He introduces himself senselessly by saying he has come about buying a horse, then explains wordily that he didn't mean it, he only says that to draw people into conversation. This small ploy warns us, here is a man not entirely to be trusted. Hatch's boisterous laughter elicits an echoing laugh from Mr. Thompson but, significantly, a limited one ("haw haw" rather than Mr. Hatch's own "haw haw haw"). Mr. Thompson, too, is on the alert. He has noticed that the "expression in the man's eyes didn't match the sound he was making" (p. 243). Later, when Mr. Thompson laughs at his own witticism about youth breaking out like measles all over a person but leaving "no ill effects" (p. 245), Mr. Hatch's laugh is again the louder and longer, "a kind of fit." And once again Mr. Thompson notices that it doesn't ring true, that Hatch "was laughing for reasons of his own" (p. 245).

Hatch's talk is shot through with simple untruth. He claims to be from Georgia and to have family "up the country a ways" (p. 244), but later refers to things "back home in North Dakota" (p. 251). He claims he wants to have "a little talk" with Mr. Helton, but actually wants to capture him. Worse than that, though, his talk is purposely, deviously false; it is used for ulterior motives, false in a calculating sense. His opening gambit about the horse, which he calls "an old joke of mine" (p. 243), is admittedly a ploy, a calculated use of language to ingratiate himself so he can pursue other motives. When he later says that a reference to Mr. Helton's having been in an asylum "just slipped out" (p. 247), we know it was no slip, even though it is precisely the kind of careless mischief that might be worked by a voluble man. Indeed, he counts on Mr. Thompson's thinking so. He has played on his own volubility to set up his "slip." Hatch is more than a loose talker; he is a man practiced in devious talk.

Hatch's effect on Mr. Thompson is not only to evoke irritation and profound dis-ease, but, at the same time, to evoke echoing behavior, like the echoing "haw haw." Indeed, it is partly because he does evoke echoing behavior in Mr. Thompson that he evokes Mr. Thompson's dis-ease. Hatch sets off a series of false conversational leads that take Mr. Thompson down branching byways of empty talk. Hatch's explanation of why he uses the ploy about the horse leads Thompson to explain needlessly that he always trusts a person until he has reason not to, an explanation that clouds the conversational air by raising the possibility of untrustworthiness. Hatch's reference to family origins leads to Mr. Thompson's defensive claim to a long family history in this part of Texas, provoking Hatch to ask if they first came from Ireland, provoking Mr. Thompson to ask why he thinks so. And so it goes. The simple cutting of tobacco plugs leads to a page-long exchange on types and prices of chewing tobacco, with mounting overtones of mutual disparagement and hostility. Hatch's volubility evokes even more needless talk than Thompson would usually indulge in. In this respect, Hatch is Thompson writ large, the enlarged mirror image of Thompson's backslapping "public" self.[16]

Hatch becomes Mr. Thompson's double, a "grotesque parody of Thompson's own nature,"[17] reflecting and magnifying his accustomed patterns of behavior and his latent feelings. Hatch has the same glad-handed volubility, but raised to a pitch that provokes Thompson's, and the reader's, distrust. When Mr. Thompson defends Helton for his steady, sober behavior, mentioning in passing that he "'never got married'" and concluding that "'if he's crazy . . . I think I'll go crazy myself for a change,'" Hatch laughs uproariously and picks up on that wish in a surprising way: "'Yeah, that's right! Let's all go crazy and get rid of our wives and save our money, hey?'" Dismayed at the twist of the conversational line, Thompson feels he is "being misunderstood" (p. 247). Again, when Mr. Thompson remarks on his wife's poor health and their high medical bills, Hatch takes him up vigorously: "'I never had much use for a woman always complainin'. I'd get rid of her mighty quick'" (p. 248). Poor Mr. Thompson had not meant to wish himself rid of his wife, or at any rate he has not thought he meant that. But his situation does make it plausible that he might harbor the repressed urges that Hatch expressed so baldly. Mr. Thompson thinks to himself that Hatch "certainly did remind" him of "somebody" (p. 244) but, stifling the realization that it is himself he is reminded of, decides he must be mistaken.

More surprisingly, Helton, too, becomes Mr. Thompson's double. As we have seen, Mr. Thompson is given to empty talk, while Helton is taciturn. The two are opposites. Yet Hatch takes Mr. Thompson for an Irishman, just as Mr. Thompson earlier took Helton for an Irishman. Helton kills his brother abruptly and apparently without warning on a hot day; Mr. Thompson suddenly and without thought kills Hatch on a day of "almost unbearable" heat (pp. 242, 252). Helton is a stranger in the land; Mr. Thompson, for all his family roots and his familiarity, becomes a stranger after his act of murder.[18] Helton is never able to express himself in words to anyone; Mr. Thompson is never able, either during his trial or afterward, to convey to anyone his sense of what has happened.

Indeed, in the last section of the story, when Mr. Thompson drives from one neighbor's farm to another trying to justify himself to them, he acts out his relation of doubling both to Helton and to Hatch. We have seen that Mr. Thompson is very anxious about the esteem of his neighbors, his good name among them. He cannot live with the suspicion that they no longer consider him respectable, particularly since he himself can no longer feel absolutely certain of his own rectitude. Compulsively, he goes over and over it in his own mind, and over and over it to his neighbors. Like Helton he is isolated by his inability to explain himself, but like Hatch he is voluble in the attempt. It is a painful sequence; we share Mrs. Thompson's embarrassment, sitting "with her hands knotted together" and listening to her husband repeat his story, and we share Mr. Thompson's chagrin as he sees "something in all their faces that disheartened him" (p. 262).

At the end of the story, writing his suicide note, Mr. Thompson makes one more attempt to explain his motives and his view of what happened. But when he writes the words "my wife" he stops, thinks a while, and obliterates the two words before finishing with a concise summary statement: "It was Mr. Homer T. Hatch who came to do wrong to a harmless man. He caused all this trouble and he deserved to die but I am sorry it was me who had to kill him" (p. 268). He has recognized both the futility and the indignity of continuing with lengthy pleas that would throw into public view more and more of his private life and feelings. That he recognizes this, that he chooses instead to cut off his plea with the most direct, unembellished statement he can make is a measure of his increased stature. Both in its conciseness—its avoidance of wordy groveling before an unsympathetic, but very curious, public—and in its honesty, his suicide note is also a measure of his distance from Mr. Hatch.

The kind of lesson Mr. Thompson learns in "Noon Wine" is for Porter the key to real dignity. Here and elsewhere (for instance, in "He," where the mother protests too much), her characters are measured personally by the adequacy, the honesty, and the economy of their language. Not that she holds Mr. Helton up as a standard. His limited, halting speech is clearly shown to be a deficiency and an impediment. Even so, it is clear that in the ambiguous world of "Noon Wine," Helton occupies a much higher position in the reader's and the author's esteem than does the voluble and disagreeable Hatch. If we must choose, we take honest deficiency over devious excess. Indeed, for most of the story Helton occupies a higher position, despite his limitation and his oddity, than Mr. Thompson, who is simply an ineffectual babbler until he learns to maintain the dignity of reticence.

Within this structure of contrasts among Helton, Hatch, and Thompson, the role of Mrs. Thompson is more elusive yet. Not a strong woman, she stays in the background, where her observance of the proprieties would keep her anyway. Moments of decisive conflict and of decision, such as the hiring of Helton, belong to the men. All the same, Mrs. Thompson is by no means a stick figure. Porter eases us toward an understanding of her individuality as well as her place in the social order with great sensitivity.

As we have seen, when Mrs. Thompson first encounters Helton she is relatively talkative, but even so, there is much that she refrains from saying. For the most part, here as elsewhere, this consists of her apprehensions and dissatisfactions to do with men, her fear that this "lazy and worthless" looking hired man will prove as "no-count" as his predecessor and her wish that her husband would "be more considerate, and take a little trouble with his business" so she could "believe in" him (pp. 226, 228). But she also reins in her conversation with Helton out of courtesy, thinking it is "a shame to keep at him" with questions and small talk when, as she judges, his English isn't good enough to let him make conversation easily (p. 229).

With her husband, of course, Mrs. Thompson is more open, but by no means fully so. Her tone is somewhat querulous; she complains, apparently habitually, of feeling poorly, though not, early in the story at any rate, about having to fulfill her basic duties, such as having to cook supper even though she is unwell. She speaks to him directly on the subject of his drinking in the saloon, urging him before he goes to town not to "go to the hotel" (p. 226) and reproving him after he comes back because he "smell[s] like a toper" (p. 229). She can say these things freely and "with perfect dignity," that is, without any onus of inappropriate or ill-tempered behavior, because she is speaking within her rights as a woman, and therefore, in this rather straitlaced society, a guardian of public morality in such matters. Notably, however, she does not reprove him for his big talk or his carelessness in running the farm. These are matters proper to his masculine role, and therefore beyond her rightful scope; she thinks but does not comment. The limitation is accepted—by Mrs. Thompson herself, by Porter. The story does not openly chafe against customary limits.

The catastrophe that brings three men to death subjects Mrs. Thompson to a ruin that she has had no part in causing. In this, she fulfills her character as Porter has outlined it, as a person of passive suffering and weakness, a "little frail woman" with a "suffering patient mouth and diseased eyes which cried easily" (p. 227). Victimized by being caught up in the actions of men, she is too weak to outface that victimization. After the trail, as her husband insists upon their driving about the countryside to explain what happened, she can see nothing to do but to "bear it somehow" (p. 257). She has apparently not resisted his determination to make these miserably uncomfortable calls, during which she has been called on to support his story far beyond the point of strict truth, even though she thought "they should never have gone at all" (p. 257). It is clear that these virtually enforced testimonials deprive her of her sense of self. But instead of confronting and resisting him, she is glad to hide behind darkness and her smoked glasses, where she is "safer, hidden away" (p. 257).

Even after they return from the last terrible visit, she will not hear to his being challenged or criticized by their sons. But inside she thinks with the "bitterness" of a lifetime that the whole misery has come about because of men: "of course they had to be rough. They always have to be rough" (p. 259). If she will not criticize him, however, neither will she say "anything to comfort him" (p. 262). After a lifetime of constricted expression, she can scarcely do otherwise, but the accumulated tension makes her more than ever subject to her own weakness. She lapses into groundless fear of her poor husband, who is at least as hard pressed as she, and her unwitting revelation of distrust drives him to suicide. Porter regards them both, husband and wife, with a restrained and astringent pity. The plight of the woman as hapless victim is deplored, but not denounced. This is not a story of anger, but of combined acceptance and regret.

The use of reticence as an ethical standard that we see in "Noon Wine" also characterizes the Miranda stories—and indeed, Porter's work as a whole. Just as Mr. Hatch and Porter's lesser villains and clowns define themselves by their garrulous, unreliable speech, so Miranda defines herself by her reserve. Indeed, reticence is perhaps the single most characteristic trait we would associate with Miranda. Like her namesake in *The Tempest*,[19] Miranda marvels at the sometimes brave but always profoundly interesting new world she observes around her. But she does not often follow Shakespeare's Miranda in responding with rapturous exclamation. Instead, it is largely in silence that she ponders the follies and the wonders of this world and attempts to puzzle out their hidden meanings. It is this silence, this reticence, as much as any demonstrated astuteness in her understandings themselves, that Porter offers as evidence of Miranda's wisdom.

Following Miranda's growth from early childhood in "The Old Order" to fully formed adulthood in "Pale Horse, Pale Rider," we can see that in virtually all her appearances, including those as Laura in "Hacienda" and "Flowering Judas," Miranda is guarded

in expressing her own feelings. Perhaps her single most unguarded expression of private emotion in any of the stories is the
eager, almost urgent declaration in "The Grave," "Oh, I want to
see" (p. 366). Paradoxically enough, however, that exclamation
conveys very little beyond her wish to discover for herself the
world and her own feelings about life. Like the brother to whom
she speaks, we are left with very little direct knowledge of what
those feelings are—only guesses, inferences. To be sure, from
Porter's well-crafted construction of this quiet story of discovery
and remembrance, we can infer quite a lot. In other stories, we
. are given considerably greater insight into Miranda's thoughts,
while her outward expression remains guarded, so that we
understand a great deal more than the characters in the story.

In "The Old Order," a group of seven stories and sketches, we
see Miranda as a child who is peculiarly observant, peculiarly
thoughtful. In "The Witness," however, the third of the seven but
the first in which Miranda appears, she is identified by the narrator as "a quick flighty little girl" (p. 341). It is a surprising
description—the Miranda we come to know later scarcely seems
flighty—but an instructive one. "The Witness" centers, not on
Miranda, but on Uncle Jimbilly. The children, Miranda and her
brother and sister, seem to be little more than incidental; their
reactions to Uncle Jimbilly are scarcely even hinted. Accordingly,
with great narrative tact, Porter accords this mere child of six only
a passing judgment. Here we deal in first impressions. The child
is lively and inquisitive; such qualities in a small child, inade-
quately understood by her elders, might well convey flightiness.
Thus, the word *flighty,* though it is not the truth of Miranda, is
at least related to the truth, to her inquisitiveness and intensity.
While the other children are cautious in their approach to Uncle
Jimbilly, Miranda questions him without hesitation. She is impulsive in going after answers. As "the little quick one" she
"wanted to know the worst" (p. 342). Her impulsiveness and inquisitiveness are confirmed in other stories, where she is again a
questioner and a listener, wanting to see for herself, to learn all
she can, and, always, to make up her own mind.

"The Witness," then, is a more crucial story than it appears.

Not only does it establish the social milieu within which Miranda comes to awareness, but it adumbrates her inquisitive, pondering nature and teases us with a characterization of her which is not quite accurate but not altogether off target.

In both "The Circus" and "The Fig Tree," the fourth and the sixth of the "Old Order" stories, we see the child Miranda's inability to express the emotional turmoil with which she is beset as she encounters experiences beyond her comprehension. Not unwillingness, note, but inability. Her fear both of and for the sake of the spectral circus clown, a fear that seems unreasonable to those around her, and her terror in "The Fig Tree" that she may have buried a baby chick alive, are intensely private, inchoate emotions. Not only are they unshared by those around her, but they separate her from others by causing her to behave in unaccountable and disruptive ways. In both instances the isolating emotions that grip Miranda can be traced to private discoveries and realizations about life and death. No one else in "The Circus" sees the clown as an image of death or the precariousness of life, and Miranda has no means of telling them or even of understanding, herself, what she sees in him. No one else in "The Fig Tree" worries over the chick's death-in-life or receives Great-Aunt Eliza's absolving lesson (the correct identification of the *weep weep* sound as tree frogs) that she is not guilty of mistaking a live creative for a dead one and that life and death are often closely related.

Miranda is established, then, as a person isolated by her own quickness and her own inwardness. She sees more than others see, and she feels more, and what she feels cannot be stated even if she wished to. But she is also, later, a person who *chooses* not to express her feelings. In the final story of the group, "The Grave," when Miranda is nine, she is not simply "agitated" but "quietly" agitated (p. 367). It is important to understand why she has learned to mask her agitation.

The grouping of the "Old Order" pieces as a presumably coherent whole implies that Miranda's reticence is in part an outgrowth of the family's reaction to her wild abandon of fear in "The Circus." There, and in "The Fig Tree," they mocked her for being afraid and crying. They had no comprehension of her emotion, and their reactions to her outcries, either cross or condescending, gave her no reason to think a fuller explanation would be sympathetically received even if she could give one. Now, even though the discovery of the unborn rabbits is a moment of intense realization for her, she will not tell her brother what she is feeling lest he, too, mock her for not knowing about birth before. Feigning knowledge just as she feigns self-possession, she conveys her agitation only by her deeply characteristic rejection of the pregnant rabbit's fur: "'I won't have it'" (p. 367).

She will not tell anyone else, either. Her brother Paul's insistence that she not tell is easier than he can guess for her to comply with. The impact of the discovery remains hers alone. Because it does indeed *remain,* stay with her and a part of her, the sight of brightly colored candy animals in a Mexican market years later summons, by her own process of association, the earlier experience. Again the moment is both isolated and isolating. In the midst of the teeming market, she alone knows of that earlier moment and she alone realizes the "mingled sweetness and corruption" (p. 367), the preciousness and the suggestion of death, of the life images held up before her. Like the buried chick of "The Fig Tree," they speak to her of death in life. Characteristically, she tells no one; the realization is unexpressed. Her vision of her smiling brother is only a vision. Even the ambiguous smile she remembers indicates an isolated, unexpressed feeling of his own. At the end of "The Grave," Miranda is left with her own memories and realizations, which she seems never to have communicated to anyone.

That Miranda is placed in Mexico at the end of "The Grave" (not Mexico by name, but certainly Mexico nonetheless) is one reason to identify her with both Laura of "Flowering Judas" and the unnamed protagonist of "Hacienda." In both stories, Laura (by name or by implication) is Miranda-like in her keen observation and in her reserve. The notably intense lyrical passage in "Hacienda" that begins, "Some day I shall make a poem to kittens washing themselves in the morning" and ends, after many ring-ing parallel phrases, "to all thriving creatures making themselves cleanly and comely to the greater glory of life" (p. 139) is a meditation. It is thought, not spoken. Within, Laura is intensely responsive and emotional; without, she is detached, inexpressive. She hardly speaks in the whole of either story. In part this is because Porter's interest, here as elsewhere, is in what Beverly Gross terms the "perceptual reality" of her character's life.[20] As Gross points out, it is also because of the isolating problem of having to speak in a language that is foreign to her. But there are other reasons as well.

Laura's reason for maintaining silence or near-silence is largely one of self-preservation. In both stories, she moves in an atmosphere of threat and senses that if she says too much she will evoke some terrible vengeance. The politically powerful Braggioni who serenades her so repulsively in "Flowering Judas" is not only corrupt but "cruel to everyone" so that "nobody" has the "courage . . . to offend him" (pp. 90–91). In "Hacienda" the implied danger is economic more than physical, but no less real. In both stories, she is threatened as well as revolted by the attitudes that the men around her display toward women, but she does not dare to reveal how deeply she despises them. At a more profound level, however, the danger she fears is loss of control. DeMouy's comment that "if a woman cannot control her body, she cannot control her life" is certainly applicable.[21] Clearly, in both stories, Laura fears sexual invasion, but her fear of giving free rein to her emotions is even greater. The detachment manifested as near-silence is a kind of discipline in stoicism, which she cultivates as a bulwark against the "disaster she fears, though she cannot name it" (p. 97). Thus her reticence is a sign of a deeply pessimistic view of life. She lives in a perpetual angst, not only about what is coming, but about the possibility that when it comes she will be emotionally devastated. If she can maintain her stoical reserve, she will have something of herself left.

Thus one motivation for Laura's extreme reticence appears to be self-preservation combined with neurotic dread of the seething id. But there is another dimension to it. In a faltering and perhaps finally self-defeating way, she is trying to learn the traditionally

Christian way of how, in T. S. Eliot's words, "to care and not to care." She is trying to reconcile involvement with detachment, to be in the world and yet not of it.[22] This paradox lies at the heart of many readers' sense that "Flowering Judas" is steeped in religious symbolism. That Laura's effort lacks balance is obvious; she learns the lesson of detachment more easily than the lesson of involvement. But evidence of her involvement is present as well, chiefly in her relation to the children at her school and to the political prisoners she visits.

Even more than the nameless "disaster" ahead or the possibility of emotional upheaval, Laura fears that she will become like those around her, the shallow moviemakers and the childish, doll-like Julia of "Hacienda," all of them utterly impervious to the real lives of the Mexican people, or the corrupt Braggioni of "Flowering Judas." It is this aspect of her fear that relates to Porter's use of reticence as a measure of ethical value. When Braggioni tells Laura that he and she "are more alike" than she realizes, she feels "a slow chill." Though this chill is associated, too, with her "purely physical sense of danger," she prefers "any kind of death" to being "as callous, as incomplete" as Braggioni (p.93). Her greatest fear, then, even greater than the fear of death, is that she will be unable to hold out against the corruption around her and will lose her very self. If there is a certain self-righteous egotism about this—and this is part of the reader's ambivalence toward Laura—there is also a real humility in that she sees and acknowledges her liability to the same weaknesses that have destroyed others.

It is in this respect that the two Laura stories relate most clearly to "Noon Wine." The representatives of the corrupt society around Laura run on in endless talk and deal continually in exaggeration, like the big talkers of "Noon Wine." Resisting their habit of lax, empty talk is a way of resisting their laxity of character. Through the "double vision" of Porter's supple narrative point of view,[23] we see how Laura reins in her speech as a means of self-definition. Her reticence is an effort at moral, as well as physical and emotional, self-preservation.

The fullest explorations of the character Miranda come in "Old

Mortality" and "Pale Horse, Pale Rider," two of Porter's indisputably finest works. If "Pale Horse, Pale Rider" provides our most intensive view of her as an adult, "Old Mortality" offers the most extensive tracing of how and why she becomes the person she is. In three emphatically separate parts, "Old Mortality" takes Miranda from the age of eight (one year younger than in the main action of "The Grave"), when she is deeply immersed in her family and its complex, highly romanticized past, to the age of eighteen, as she returns home for the funeral of one of the most notable avatars of that past and tries to come to grips with both her separation from the family and her continuing involvement with them. Emerging from this confrontation and the struggle to clarify her own feelings as a newly independent grown child, she will go on to endure the solitary loss and disillusionment that come in "Pale Horse, Pale Rider."

In the Miranda of "Old Mortality," part 1, we recognize the lively, inquisitive child of "The Witness." Once again she is quick to pursue information but reluctant to verbalize her feelings and judgments on what she learns. For example, in a frequently quoted passage on the disparity between their father's statement that "there were never any fat women in the family" and Maria and Miranda's certain knowledge of several women in the family who were fat (p. 174), we see Miranda's growing understanding of his tendency to romanticize the past. The very phrases reflect her mental groping toward such awareness: "Well, great-aunt Keziah was famous for her heft, and wasn't she in the family?" But it is a *mental* groping. Her citation of the great-aunt is not said aloud. She observes, she puts observations together, she reaches tentative conclusions, but she does not discuss her conclusions with anyone; she keeps them to herself. Or again, we hear the two girls' questions about Aunt Amy—a series of "Tell me again ..." "Why wouldn't she ..." "Was she really ..."—and we hear answers (p. 176), but the girls' cogitations about what they are told and what they observe, for instance in pictures of Amy, are given without quotation marks, as unspoken thoughts.

It is not entirely clear that the girls' restraint about voicing their reactions is altogether a matter of personality. Issues of decorum may be involved as well. Their elders would very likely have found it more acceptable for children to ask questions than to voice opinions. It is understood, for instance, that they may go with their grandmother to the attic and look through family keepsakes only so long as they "were very quiet and touched nothing until it was offered" and so long as they remembered that the grandmother's tears were not to be "noticed or mentioned" (p. 175). Assertiveness on the part of little girls was surely not encouraged. But decorum would not seem to account for Miranda's refraining from telling her grandmother that she, too, "felt melancholy" after these sessions (p. 175), or for her hoping "secretly" that she would grow up to look like Amy (p. 177). In this Amy-adulating family, such an aspiration, however contrary to probability, could only be met with approval.

Part 2 of "Old Mortality" does not at first seem concerned with the Amy-olotry that dominates part 1. The narrative shifts abruptly from the keepsakes of Amy, which "seemed to have no place in the world" (p.193), to the present situation of Maria and Miranda. The family past, it seems, is past—it was part 1; this is now—part 2. We notice, though, that parallels with the past keep turning up. The girls, now ten and fourteen, also seem to have "no place in the world." They are banished to a convent school, "immured," as they say, behind convent walls. And even there, in the discipline of their unworldly retreat, they are confronted with the problem that bothered them in part 1 and forms the broadest tension between 1 and 2, the problem of the disparity between romanticized legend and sober fact. In the melodramatic anti-Catholic fiction they enjoy reading, immurement in a convent is a lurid and direly perilous fate; in the fact of their experience, life at the convent school is simply dull. We must assume that it is to the former, the highly romanticized life, that Miranda aspires in avowing an "ambition to be a nun." At various other times, she hopes to be a tightrope walker (imaginatively conquering her fear of the tightrope-walking clown in "The Old Order"), a jockey (asserting her resistance to negative comparisons with Aunt Amy's Spanish-style riding), and a pilot (resisting constraint on her freedom of movement). Similarly, her momentary insistence that she wants to be a nun is a way of asserting dominion over the confinement of school, by claiming to choose what is in fact imposed on her. As the convent sisters correctly perceive, she has no vocation for so stringent a discipline as the life of a religious.

In the early pages of part 2, ten-year-old Miranda seems to be, not reticent at all, but highly demonstrative, vindicating her early image as a lively, even flighty child. She falls flat on the floor in "despair" over arithmetic. She announces her vocation. She shares with Maria the romanticizing fantasy of being "immured." She forthrightly complains to her father that he should announce his visits in advance so she could enjoy looking forward to them. But in fact her real reticence is being manifested and indeed reinforced even here. The things she is talkative about are all relatively shallow; the things that engage her more deeply she does not discuss. Even with Maria she does not share everything, since Maria, it seems, can't keep a secret and is at any rate a more tame, or "prissy" (p. 197) child, presumably liable to be shocked by Miranda's wilder ideas. When serious discoveries are made, as they are later in part 2, Miranda thinks her own thoughts, privately. As to her histrionics, they are merely a means of adding interest to her life during periods of boredom. Furthermore, when she does indulge in open displays, she encounters lessons in restraint. Her open avowal of her idea of being a nun evokes "barely veiled" (a fine pun!) disapproval. Her complaint to her father brings a reminder of past misbehavior and punishment. Unhappiness over being punished has to be a "secret mourning" because "if one mourned too noisily, it simply meant another bad mark against deportment" (p. 195). External pressures drive her more deeply into reserve. But it also through her own discoveries that Miranda's exuberant personality grows more toward inwardness.

The girls' excursion to the racetrack, where they at last meet the legendary Uncle Gabriel, is a great watershed of discovery for Miranda, allowing her to bring into focus a cluster of uncertainties intimated to the reader throughout parts 1 and 2. All during this enlightening event, she preserves her characteristic reticence in dealing with her important feelings, while continuing to play the impulsive "lively" child when lesser issues are at stake.

Gabriel, the girls see, is "a shabby fat man with bloodshot blue eyes" (p. 197). Wordlessly, staring, they ask each other if this can really be the man they have heard about for years. *Wordlessly*, yet the questions they ask with their eyes appear in quotation marks: "'Can that be our Uncle Gabriel? . . . Is that Aunt Amy's handsome romantic beau? Is that the man who wrote the poem about Aunt Amy?'" A fourth question, though, is not enclosed in quotation marks: "Oh, what did grown-up people *mean* when they talked, anyway?" The first three, though unspoken, are communications shared between the two. The last is Miranda's private wondering about the general and very serious problem of memory, fantasy, and truth. Preoccupied by the puzzle of Uncle Gabriel's disillusioning appearance and manner, the girls fall silent until the race begins. Then again they are demonstrative, both of them "screaming and clapping their hands" and shedding "tears of joy" (pp. 198–99). But when Miranda sees the brutal fact behind the victory, that Gabriel's filly has been run when she shouldn't and now pays the price in snoring breath and "two thick red rivulets" of blood "stiffening her tender mouth and chin" (p. 199), she is revolted by the cruelty of the race and by her own complicity in it, through having cheered. Her disgust and shame, a more serious and long-lasting emotion than her victory elation, she keeps to herself, without a word.

Miranda does risk asking her father one question about her multifaceted discovery—"'Uncle Gabriel's a drunkard, isn't he?'"—but is told harshly, and quite typically, "'Hush.'" At that rebuff, both girls feel "resentment," but rather than complain of their father's "obvious injustice" they merely "loosed their hands from his and moved away coldly, standing together in silence" (p. 200). Taken to meet Uncle Gabriel's wife, Miranda observes every detail of the shabby rooming house and Miss Honey's barely repressed anger. She sits in silence, making her own assessment of the situation. Back in the carriage, she pursues her earlier question about Gabriel's drinking, then abruptly bursts out with a rejection of the ambition she had never before admitted: "'I've decided I'm not going to be a jockey, after all'" (p. 205). But she says not a word about her disturbing awareness of the hatred and degradation glimpsed in her brief view of Uncle Gabriel and Miss Honey. Once again, she speaks what is less important and holds back what is more.[24]

At the start of part 3, the eighteen-year-old Miranda encounters Cousin Eva Parrington on a train en route to Gabriel's funeral. Cousin Eva recalls Miranda as "'a lively little girl ... and very opinionated'" (p. 207). It is a somewhat ironic comment, since if "opinionated" may be taken to mean having her own ideas, Eva can have no conception of how opinionated Miranda really is. Throughout the long conversation between the two cousins, Miranda's characteristically brief remarks are counterpointed to her considerably more elaborated thoughts, both memories and a running inner commentary on Cousin Eva and the issues she raises. Porter calls attention to the counterpointing of words and thoughts in a particular sequence that might otherwise seem rather pointless, though it also, perhaps, demonstrates how well Miranda understands this aging cousin of hers.

> "They didn't do you much good, those parties, dear Cousin Eva," thought Miranda.
> "They didn't do me much good, those parties," said Cousin Eva aloud as if she were a mind-reader.
>
> (p. 208)

The reader is put on notice: thinking and saying are being played off against each other. Miranda's reaction to the sequence is characteristic. Her "head swam for a moment with fear that she had herself spoken aloud." It is a natural enough fear; one would not wish to offend so touchy and pathetic a person as Cousin Eva. But it is a fear that reminds us of Laura's cautiousness in "Flowering Judas" and "Hacienda." To speak is to make oneself vulnerable.

While Miranda talks guardedly with Cousin Eva, her thoughts are busy with the things she cannot or will not say: that if she speaks meekly she may disarm this strange old lady's ferocity; that Cousin Eva looks very old for the age she must be; that she should try to make Cousin Eva feel valued by the younger generation, though something in her resists it; that the Parringtons were known for their love of money; and so on, as she compares her present impressions with her memories and the things she has been hearing all her life. At their most urgent, as if they were about to break the bonds of caution and burst into speech, her thoughts assume quotation marks: "'Oh, must I ever be like that'" (p. 208) and "'My mother was nothing of the sort'" (p. 217). These strongest thoughts, however, are precisely the ones she does not even come close to expressing, though she does venture to correct certain details of Eva's version of the story—that is, of the story of Aunt Amy.

Miranda's thinking throughout the long section that recounts her conversation with Aunt Eva brings her to three very important realizations, none of which she states. First, she realizes that Cousin Eva hates Amy, dead though Amy is. Miranda is not yet sufficiently free of the myth of beautiful womanhood to understand why, but she knows it is true. Second, she realizes that Cousin Eva's personal unpleasantness, or deformity, is somehow tied up with her very real strength of character and foresees a like duality in herself. And last, she realizes that Cousin Eva, who denounces the tyranny of the family, is not only a pitiable person but a kindred spirit, a sister. This last realization she conveys to Cousin Eva, not in speech, but with a spontaneous kiss.

Beyond even these realizations is the larger realization unifying the entire work. That, too, is never spoken by Miranda, not because she will not or dare not say it, but because she does not yet understand it well enough herself. Here we see the direct connection between the Miranda of "Old Mortality" and the Miranda of "Pale Horse, Pale Rider." "Old Mortality" has been concerned throughout with the disparity between romanticized legends and plain truths. The children have been puzzled by that seeming disparity, and as they grow older they have realized, at least in part, that they can and must rely on their own perceptions as correctives of the handed-down legend. It would appear at first reading that part 3, the encounter with Cousin Eva, at last presents a coherent summary of the plain truth as opposed to the romanticized falsehood. The one seems to be corrected by the other. But it is not that simple. We realize as Cousin Eva talks that her own version is also a romanticized distortion. Naturally, it differs from the version given by Miranda's father and the others. As Liberman says, she "substitutes one unacceptable myth for another."[25] Cousin Eva's motive, unconscious as it is, is to magnify the unhealthiness and the destructiveness of Amy's story, while theirs was to magnify its glamour. But it is a distortion and a dramatization, all the same.

This much Miranda understands. But that is not the whole wisdom of "Old Mortality." The Miranda of part 3 is not yet able to reach a genuinely realistic view, because she views experience from a vantage of insufficient maturity. At eighteen years of age, she is still excessively hopeful, excessively sure of her own freedom from the distorted vision of her elders. Watching the easy friendliness of Cousin Eva and her father, after they have gotten off the train, stung by his coldness to her now that she has asserted herself by getting married, she turns against Eva after all and walks behind them "in silence" (p. 219), wordlessly disavowing them both. Drawing into herself and her own thoughts, concealing from her heedless elders the turmoil of emotion she feels, she tells herself she will be rid of them, she will leave off worrying about "the legend of the past" and instead "know the truth" about her own experience. But her ability to do so is no more certain than Eva's ability to correct Harry or Gabriel's romanticized view. Promising herself "I won't have false hopes, I won't be romantic about myself" (p. 221), Miranda is sunk in a romanticism of her own, the Byronic exaltation of the solitary rebellious spirit.[26]

It is not, finally, a happy romanticism; she is shut in bitterness while Eva and Harry go on chatting comfortably. But Miranda's mistake is not the last word either. The voice of an older and wiser Miranda, looking back on the eighteen-year-old's romanticism masking itself as truth, pronounces on "her arrogance, her pride" and comments that her silent promise to herself to know her own truth has been made "in her hopefulness, her ignorance" (pp. 219, 221). The older narrator understands just how limited a young woman's freedom to live her own life and develop her own ideas really is. It is on this note of mingled triumph and poignance that the story ends.

"Old Mortality" neither fully vindicates not fully repudiates Miranda's withdrawal into her own counsel. If at the end she appears bitter and alienated, while the self-deluded Eva and Harry are secure in their places and free to be "precisely themselves" with "perfect naturalness" (p. 219), there is still no denying that their vision has been false. We prefer Miranda's eagerness to know things for what they are. The fullest vision of the story, fully affirmed in that it is at one with the voice of the narrator, is that of the older Miranda, looking back on her eighteen-year-old self and pronouncing herself mistaken. But the path to that older, affirmed self lies through the eighteen-year-old deluded self. The two are the same, and Miranda's habit of keeping her own counsel is part of her essential character, affirmed as the story's positive center.

The Miranda of "Pale Horse, Pale Rider" brings to fullness the stoical reserve we have seen developing from her early childhood, in "The Old Order" and "Old Mortality." Set near the end of World War I during the devastating flu epidemic of that period, the work opens with a dream of death and ends, or nearly ends, with a dreamlike hallucinatory experience of near-death. What follows, Miranda's reawakening to a life that seems to her scarcely worth living, shows us the end product of all her family background and experiences, the person she is and will be. Between the two death-dreams (the latter more than a dream, and very autobiographical on Porter's part) we are given the two-day period during which Miranda pursues her work as a newspaper reporter and suffers the onslaught of the flu, then the period of her illness. Intertwined with both, she experiences what is apparently the one real love of her life. Beset by a devastating combination of dire forces—the flu epidemic, the war, the forced patriotism all around her, shortage of money, her sense that her love is doomed—she has no refuge but style, her manner or way of suffering them. She becomes, in a sense, the Hemingway hero as woman.[27] The way she chooses, the only way she can choose, is the way of the stiff upper lip. By the same token, she does not dare to give open expression to her delight in her sweetheart, Adam, lest she tempt fate and call down the disasters that loom all around them. It is a futile caution, of course. The disasters fall anyway. The flu she has felt coming on is so serious she almost dies, and Adam does die—from flu caught while nursing her. At the end the only resource with which she faces the rest of her life is her long discipline in stoical repression.

It is because of the pervasive emphasis on style—style in the sense of overall manner—that "Pale Horse, Pale Rider" has such a quality of artifice or play. Porter regards the plight of her two beautiful young people, beset by both natural evil and social evil, with a hard edge of bitterness, which she contains by a fictive structure of taut and stringent beauty. Similarly, Miranda and Adam contain their bitterness and their hopelessness within a studied manner. There is a great disparity between the flip poses they adopt and the real emotions we know they feel. Their speech becomes a self-protective device or mask. As DeMouy notes, they "engage in ironic exchanges that force them to laugh—rather than cry—over the war. ... They cloak their despair under a patina of slick talk. Their careless conversational patter not only hides their serious feelings, it eliminates the possibility of their voicing them."[28] The comment is perceptive and well-founded; however, Adam and Miranda's patter is not at all careless, but very careful. It is a calculated strategy that works in several ways at once. By talking about relatively trivial matters, they hope to distract themselves and each other from their anxieties. By speaking in a light, ironic tone they manage to convey their anxieties without having to drag them out in distressing obviousness, knowing they are helpless to resolve them anyway. By mocking disaster they attempt to deaden themselves so they won't suffer so much when the worst blow, whatever that may be, comes. And most important, perhaps, by maintaining their flip tone and holding themselves to crisp understatement, they distance themselves from the falsifying cant all around them.

In all of these ways, Miranda's speech in "Pale Horse, Pale Rider" is an outgrowth and an intensification of the patterns of guardedness established from early childhood. The things that matter most she keeps inside. She tells no one about her death-dream and is very cautious—rightly so, given the political situation—about expressing her disaffection from the war effort and the entire war mentality. She contains and controls her anger. When she does once risk speaking to Adams about "what war does to the mind and heart" (p. 294) she comes up against a masculine chauvinism she can never share: "'If I didn't go,' said Adam, in a matter-of-fact voice, 'I couldn't look myself in the face'" (p. 295). At the end, she leaves unspoken her sense that she would just as soon have died. Most poignantly, when she reads the letter informing her that Adam is dead, she does not even mention the bad news but merely asks the nurse, "'I've been here a long time, haven't I?'" (p. 316). Porter never allows us to think that Miranda does not really care about these things. Rather, we see her caring so much that she fears she cannot tolerate the intensity of her caring if she once starts to let it surge forth. It is rather like keeping the finger in the dike.

Actually, Miranda does talk to Adam more openly than we might expect, given the character of her speech as we see it in the other stories. That she does so is one of the strongest evidences we have that Adam is indeed to be taken as the one real love she has ever had. Even so, she never tells him about her family ties and the web of family traditions within which she has struggled to find herself, which we know is one of the most important elements in her life. And she tells him directly that she loves him only when she is feverish and knows she may die. Moreover, when she does set aside her reticence so far as to tell Adam her fears and concerns, she greatly underplays them.

Examples of the ironic underplaying kept up by both Miranda and Adam are abundant: we need consider only a few. At breakfast, Miranda says she feels "'rotten'" and it can't be "'just the weather, and the war'"—as if the war were a minor point. Adam replies that the weather is "'perfect'"—by which we think it must be bad—and the war "'simply too good to be true'" (p. 282). When he tells her that the average life of a sapping party in combat is "'just nine minutes,'" she quips, "'Make it ten and I'll come along.'" They might almost be a vaudeville team, except that their snappy patter is too grim at the core. They laugh about the ludicrousness of someone's having computed such a statistic as the sappers' nine minutes until Miranda wipes her eyes and remarks, only too lightly, "'My, it's a funny war, isn't it? I laugh every time I think about it'" (p. 283).

The two carry their sense of style into Miranda's illness, when Adam has to cope with the unpretty chores of nursing. We know that Miranda must be not only miserable but embarrassed, yet they both maintain an elaborate, jocular politeness, as if her disordered bodily functions were little lapses of manners. After swallowing her pills, when she "instantly vomited them up," presumably on her bedclothes, she says, "'*Do* excuse me,' . . . beginning to laugh. 'I'm so sorry'" (p. 300). Making light of the hospital nun's refusal to admit her, because there is no room, she says, "'I think that's abominably rude and mean, don't you?'" When she then "sat up with a wild gesture of both arms, and began to retch again, violently," Adam jocularly misapplies military commands, "'Hold it, as you were'" (p. 301). It is hard to imagine conducting a bout of flu more elegantly. Later in the night Miranda gallantly suggests they "'tell each other what we meant to do'" (p. 302).

This tight-lipped irony sets Adam and Miranda apart as the only admirable people in a crowd of long-winded ranters. They speak ironically but tell the truth while the propagandists and unthinking war supporters around them speak flatly but falsely. The contrast is drawn in a series of four particularly telling instances, set in two balancing pairs. First, the two government men who pressure Miranda to buy bonds speak in prefabricated jingoistic phrases of "'the Huns overrunning martyred Belgium'" and "'our American boys fighting and dying in Belleau Wood'" without the least real care about the soldiers fighting and dying. Miranda, who does care, represses an urge to say what she "really thought," namely, "'to hell with this filthy war'" and confines herself to the unvarnished realities of what she can and can't afford. When she goes on an excursion to a military hospital with "loot" for the soldiers, the other girls chatter vapidly about there being "so many good-looking men . . . the cutest things you ever saw" and how "frightfully hard on them, the poor dears" it must be to be wounded and hospitalized when they are "all crazy to get overseas and into the trenches as quickly as possible" (pp. 275–

76). Miranda, embarrassed by the "idiocy" of the whole thing, finds their meaningless chatter enough to "freeze the blood." She will not pretend to a good cheer and affection she does not feel, but tells one of the girls straight out, "'I hate it'" (p. 277). We applaud her honesty.

The second pair of contrasting instances also involves first a government propagandist, then a chattering girl, a parody rendition of the stereotype of petty and mindless womanhood against which Miranda must define herself. At the theater, a between-acts Liberty Bond salesman brings out the same cant phrases as the two professional patriots of the morning. Porter presents his "same old musty speech" in blocks of disconnected phrases like prefabricated sections: "give till it hurts—our noble boys Over There—Big Berthas—the death of civilization—innocent babes hoisted on Boche bayonets—your child and my child" (p. 293). In contrast, Miranda and Adam comment tersely, "'He's getting into the home stretch.'" Miranda, seeing through the speaker's manipulative rhetoric, wishes she could demand, "Coal, oil, iron, gold, international finance, why don't you tell us about them, you little liar?" We remember that in her own journalism she will "never learn" to play the game of fakery but goes on "panning" performers when she believes they deserve it (pp. 287–89). She is a truthteller in a world of false speakers. After the play and the writing of Miranda's review, she and Adam go to a nightclub where they witness a second object lesson in true and false communication. While wishing she could tell Adam how fearful and in pain she is, she sees two couples at neighboring tables. One couple sits "without a word," the girl silently crying. At the other table the girl goes on and on with a long, shabby story all in current slang. The story breaks off in mid-sentence, so meaningless it doesn't deserve completion.

The two pairs of incidents, framing Miranda and Adam's day together, clearly distinguish them from both the carelessly chattering crowd and the manipulative falsifiers. It is this contrast that sets the stage for the scene of Miranda's illness, with its ironic, chipper gallantry. The two of them are appropriately shut off from the disordered world outside by the walls of Miranda's room, but are unable, for all their charm, to resist the forces of disease and death. When the ambulance comes to take her away, she is still the child of "The Witness," who "wanted to know the worst" without putting it off. That tough-mindedness commands respect and honesty in return. "'Well, Dr. Hildesheimer,'" she says, "'aren't we in a pretty mess?'" "'We certainly are,'" said Dr. Hildesheimer" (p. 306).

It is clear that Miranda is in some ways a deprived and incomplete person, largely negative in her impulses. Particularly in "Flowering Judas," the emotionally constricted Miranda-like Laura conveys a sense of sterility and stasis. At the same time, she provides the only value-center in the world of the story. At the end of "Pale Horse, Pale Rider," Miranda is still an ambiguous character. We wish that she could bring herself to confront what she feels more fully and to say what she means more directly. We sense a trace of Prufrock in the dandyism of her preparations for what appears to be a death-in-life existence. Indeed, in the final paragraph Porter underscores this Prufrockian quality with verbal echoes of Eliot's poem—the phrases "empty streets" and the concluding sentence, "Now there would be time for everything" (p. 317). One hears, at a distance, "There will be time, there will be time / To prepare a face to meet the faces that you meet." And Miranda, too, is concerned about preparing an acceptable face; she asks for cold cream and powder and wonders if she needs eye shadow.

Yet if Miranda is a less complete, less fully alive person than she might have been, we cannot, for all that, withhold our admiration. She and Laura are not offered as images of human perfection, but are affirmed as persons of integrity, of real character. We prefer them to anyone around them. In part, this is simply because we share their point of view; Porter's preferred narrative strategy is from inside a particular character's perceptions. But in part, too, it is precisely because they do hold themselves so aloof, because they do cry out with "the very cells of their flesh"— though not with their voices—the "one holy and talismanic word," no (p. 97). What they resist, what they say no to, is a corrupt society that deals in falsehood. Porter has drawn both

Miranda and Laura in the clearest possible counterpoise to that society.

Part of the falseness they repudiate is an unjust and distorted view of women. Though the reticence characterizing Porter's style can be seen as an essentially ungendered ethical framework, it gains added resonance when one recognizes that her work is in fact deeply gendered. Porter herself was not an overt feminist. Even so, her fiction is informed by a sense of female experience and a woman's perspective. The narrative centers of nearly all of her short fiction are female. Not surprisingly, perhaps, critics have almost uniformly ignored or masculinized the gendered essence of her work.[29] The current reassessment that takes into account its defined center in a female consciousness and its context of social inhibition is long overdue and altogether beneficial.

The Miranda stories very clearly depict a culture in which women grow up amid repressive standards and expectations. In large measure the story of Cousin Amy, dramatized as it is by a heavily paternalistic society, shows the conflict and frustration that result when an energetic, imaginative young woman has no acceptable opinions in life. There is nothing Amy can do with herself. If she rebels against the narrowly stereotyped course set out for her, she falls into another stereotype, the high-spirited belle or the wild woman. With no freedom to order her life, Amy can only resort to style, like the Miranda of "Pale Horse, Pale Rider," and finally, whether directly or not, elect to end it. Even then she is subjected to stereotyping, as family members romanticize her story out of all reality.

Confronted from an early age by the disheartening history of the beautiful and doomed Amy, Miranda adopts a series of "male" roles—the rambler of the fields in childhood, the jockey of her temporary aspiration. But pressures from her family and the larger society push her inexorably toward conventional, and surely limited, feminine patterns. Her father rejects her when she is not properly prettied up for him and responds with impatience or disregard when she tries to assert her intellectual curiosity. In every way, the family's ideals of womanhood are made clear, and she does not fit them. Her real self, the self that does not fit those conventionalized patterns, is unacceptable to the significant people in her life and must be repressed or disguised if she is to find her way into a responsive social structure.

Porter's fiction demonstrates that the idealization of women is severely alienating. Yet Miranda's urge, throughout the stories, is to define and authenticate herself. Discouraged from doing so openly, through verbal and behavioral assertion, she resorts to passive-aggression—a typical behavior adjustment of women in patriarchal society—through withdrawal and verbal suppression. In this way, Laura asserts her self by negation and nonparticipation, in "Flowering Judas," against the quasi-romantic pressuring of Braggioni. Reticence, even seeming passivity, becomes a strategy for asserting self-will in the face of a powerful and threatening male hegemony.

If this kind of passive aggression sounds ultimately detrimental to the self, one can only recognize that indeed it is. But that is nothing new or peculiar to Porter's work. Women have long asserted their resistance to male domination by their passive resistance (commonly called frigidity) in the marriage bed, as a way of preserving some core of self against invasion. It is scarcely surprising, then, that critics have noted sexual overtones in the reticence of Laura or Miranda. Their language and behavior imply a generalized emotional nonparticipation. Such behavior may well lead to emotional desiccation and a general impoverishment of personhood. But it is important to note that their passively resistant behavior, implying as it does a withholding of engagement at every level, possibly including an avoidance of sex, is motivated not merely by fear or inadequacy, but by a resolution to maintain personal identity.

Passive aggression, even at the cost of deprivation or damage to the self, is not an uncommon mode of resistance to be employed by oppressed social groups. It is well documented, for instance, that black slaves in the South resorted to self-maiming as a way of denying their masters the benefit of their unimpaired service.[30] Women, as Porter shows them, are oppressed by reproductive biology as well as social expectations.[31] Caught between basic needs that appear to be mutually exclusive, they find themselves faced with no-win choices. Many of Porter's men, of course—Helton, Mr. Thompson, Adam—are also trapped in no-win situations. Porter's vision is not selectively but generally bleak. But her women are subjected to devastating pressures of gender, as well as the general hardships. It is a deeply pessimistic view of the unequal relation between men and women.

Refusal to speak freely or to speak at all, like refusal to participate fully in sexual congress, is a means of withholding assent to such a situation. Confronted by a power structure that impinges on their power of self-determination and imposes a set of unacceptable choices, Porter's women refuse the role of willing collaborator. The reticence of their speech is a form of resistance to the gender inequities of their world. Porter's reticent style, then, is both an ethical-aesthetic statement in general and a strategy of noncompliance.

CHAPTER FIVE

Joan Didion and the Presence of Absence

"I didn't say anything."
"Very eloquent. Your silence."

───────────── JOAN DIDION, *Democracy* ─────────────

Every reader of Joan Didion's novels, especially *Play It As It Lays,* will be struck by their compression, by the paucity of words, the expanses of blank page.[1] Initially, perhaps, that blankness may seem to be merely a glib stylistic trick or gimmick, like the over-use of sentence fragments in magazine advertisements. And such an impression is not unrelated to what Didion is doing. Her social criticism draws much of its ironic pointedness from its echoing of the very tones of the rhetoric she judges to be specious. But there is more to it than that. The artistic seriousness of Didion's com-pression / withholding is indicated by her pronouncement, in *De-mocracy* (p. 162), that "the heart of narrative is a certain calculated ellipsis."[2]

Absence becomes a presence in Didion's work. Vacancy be-comes a force. It is not simply that Didion's style is economical, that she compresses much into little—though that is true. Nor is it simply that, like Austen and Porter, she uses absence as a device for reader involvement, leading the reader to guess at what she does not actually say—though this, too, is true. But beyond these effects of compression and tacitness, Didion makes a positive, even aggressive, use of blankness. She *wields* the spaces on the page in what is almost at times an assault on the reader. She carves out chunks of blank paper and poises them there as a meaning (that is, signifying) void in the spatial form of the novel.

Didion's curtailed style has been noted in the critical literature on *Play It As It Lays* (1970) chiefly as a device for characterizing the central character and sometime narrator, Maria Wyeth, but also as an expression of social criticism and an existentialist view. The "vacuum" of the abruptly ended brief chapters expresses Maria's "inability to empathize" or "lack of response."[3] The novel's blank spaces "reflect the emptiness Maria feels" and her "trouble interpreting experience."[4] Or, read as metaphors of a prevalent twentieth-century angst, the philosophical void, the absence of ultimate meaning, the blank spaces testify to "nothingness,"[5] the "abundance of white space" suggests an "image of the void."[6] The vacancy dispersed through the text conveys the impossibility of knowing—anything.[7]

If a strategy of vacancy has not been so abundantly noted in Didion's other novels, the reason is partly that the technique is not so utterly conspicuous in her other work. She carries it to its furthest realization in *Play It As It Lays*. Her first novel, *Run, River* (1963), gives little hint of the minimal style to come. Stylistically the fullest of her novels, *Run, River* has even been called "expansive" and a book that "tells all."[8] After the extreme minimalism of the second novel, *Play It As It Lays*, Didion's third, *A Book of Common Prayer* (1977), is again somewhat more abundant. There and in *Democracy* (1984) Didion's strategies of reticence are more subtle and more fully located in the narrator and her inability to fathom the fullness of her story. In all four novels, however, despite these variations, suppression and silence are at the center of the narrative act.

Critics and reviewers have been correct in viewing Didion's silences, the voids represented by abrupt disjunctions and by blank spaces on the page, as moral or philosophical statements as well as devices for characterization. Perceiving a world in disorder, morally bankrupt, aesthetically debased, relationally broken (the world anatomized in her essays), Didion has presented that perception in fiction not only by means of the depiction of disordered actions and emotional states but also by the absence of positive states—the blanks. Blanks serve as representations of negative moral assertions—assertions of hopelessness, of futility, of meanness, of the failure of meaning. As Maria says, near the end of *Play It As It Lays*, "I used to ask questions, and I got the answer: nothing. The answer is 'nothing'" (p. 209). Moreover, the blanks convey a sense of the uselessness of attempting to elaborate explanations of what only amounts to a zero, "nothing," in the end. It is as if the effort is too great, since it brings no payoff. Emotionally, the effect is a sense of futility combined with a great weariness (an effect sustained by the flattening of tone of virtually all interrogatives by ending them with periods rather than question marks). By constructing her fiction around blanks, Didion asserts that there is nothing worth putting there. It is clearly a statement about her world.

At the same time, and this is a slightly different matter, these visual voids in the text assert an epistemology of limitation. They imply the impossibility of knowing or understanding anything more than the minimum as stated. A scrupulous logic would, of course, tell us that Didion can't have it both ways; if she asserts the impossibility of knowing, she cannot also assert that what is there to be known is worthless.[9] But fiction does not operate through scrupulous logic. The symbol that is the total novel has its life as a multiple and multiplying signifier. The overall effect of Didion's work tends to the suggestion of a moral disaffection from the contemporary world, shading into a thoroughgoing, if not logically consistent, nihilism.

But beyond this general moral impetus to Didion's caustic fictive voice, which has been discussed with some fullness, what has not been sufficiently recognized is the extent to which Didion's silences and curtailments speak out of a specifically female quality of experience and with particular reference to femaleness. Discussions of her work that stress their nongendered philosophical or journalistic import deny the focused strength of her concern with women's being-in-the-world, just as emphasis on her expressed misgivings about active feminism blur the extent to which her fiction exposes the depersonalization that feminists have attempted to redress.

Didion's women are oppressed by their sexual identity. Indeed, they are oppressed by their sexuality. Raised on a myth of woman as romantic flame, a myth stressing allure and danger, but also on a set of conflicting myths emphasizing chastity and an idealization of marriage and mothering, they find themselves without any satisfying role that can unify these conflicting presumptions and provide an outlet for their sense of autonomy. Denied authenticity by the shallow stereotypes that constrain their socialization—the beauty queen, the society belle—they resort to sex, often to promiscuous sex, as a means of filling the emptiness of their lives. Yet in pursuing sex they not only destroy the possibility of achieving stable love relationships so as to satisfy their inbred ideal of wifely love, but bring on themselves an overwhelming guilt, even self-hate. Longing for the fulfilling relationships with a husband or lover that they can never achieve, especially in a world where men are often domineering and even physically abusive, they direct their emotional allegiance backward, to the love of their mothers or sometimes their fathers. Attempting to center their adult lives on their children, as a reenactment of the ideal parental love they yearn for, they are thwarted by failures of maternity.

In every novel she has published, Didion makes it clear, by doublings and parallels, that this grim scenario is not acted out by the central character alone, however extreme her experience may appear to be, but by women in general. In *Run, River,* Lily and Martha, though they are often at odds, share an obsessive promiscuousness and an inability to achieve, or even to conceive of, any satisfying career or work role. Lily's mother is equally at a loss for an identity; their acquaintance Francie is similarly trapped in an unfulfilling marriage with noplace to go; and other women glimpsed in the course of the novel appear compelled to beg for sexual attention as a reassurance of personal value. In *Play It As It Lays,* not only Maria's depression but her fixation on appearance, her frenetic sexual activity, and her inability to achieve a satisfying adult relationship are paralleled by her sometime friend Helene and glimpsed in other women she encounters. In *A Book of Common Prayer,* the narrator, Grace Strasser-Mendana, shares the experience of motherhood as grief that she sees in Charlotte Douglas, the character to whom she "witnesses." Every woman seen in the book is debased by her relationships with men. And in Didion's latest novel, *Democracy,* Inez Victor's disaffection from her husband is paralleled by the vacant or shattered marriages of her sister and her mother. In every book Didion is at pains, through a variety of devices as well as through direct assertion, to generalize her main character's griefs and to show that they are specifically female in quality.

Her women also share a reluctance to speak of their grief, to express it overtly. Their reticence takes many forms: an ingrained urge to protect their men from disturbances; a sense that full, easy conversation in the accepted manner betrays their selfhood; a wish to deny troubling realities by refusing to give them verbal acknowledgment; and a sense of futility, a hopelessness about ever being able to make sense of life or change it. For these various reasons Didion's women tend to be verbally inexpressive, to withhold words, though they may at times throw up a fountain of words as a diversionary tactic or engage in the kind of terse verbal aggression that characterizes Didion as narrator. It is the connection between their female identity and the reticence of her characters' speech and her own narrative style that interests me here.

Run, River, unlike Didion's other fiction as it is, provides an instructive opening into the later novels, in which she develops her minimalist style. It is indeed a novel of fullness, dense with relationships, with a sense of extended family and interactive social scene. Its physical setting is solidly realized, its evocation of emotional states ample. The emptinesses of the novel occur within that fullness—not in the shape of the sentences, their presence on the page, but within them. They are not narrative emptinesses but emptinesses in the communications of the characters as they are depicted. Therefore, these emptinesses are easier to "read" than the more striking absences of the other novels, in that the reliable narrator tells us, fully, that the emptiness is there. The text makes a less insistent demand on the reader to construct a presence by inference from absence. Both Martha McClellan and Lily Knight McClellan, the two chief characters, feel an acute and explicitly realized lack of meaning or purpose, and both are frequently reticent in their communications or simply their non-communication.

For Lily, the center of the story, reticence, particularly when dealing with men, is virtually innate. By adolescence she has learned to maintain a tactful silence to protect the male ego: after her father loses his bid for reelection to the California legislature, "neither she nor her mother ever mentioned politics to her father any more" (p. 46). She agrees to marry Everett, Martha's older brother, because she feels "as physically as she would a headache" the "weight" of his "vulnerability" (p. 60). In the same way, she refrains from telling Everett how unsatisfying she finds their first year of marriage and how she keeps thinking of their wedding week in Reno with "longing" and "nostalgia" because things had not yet gone wrong at that time (pp. 64–65). She wishes she could "go back to that country in time where no one made mistakes" (p. 83), a time she associates with the presence of her father. But she keeps this ache hidden away.

The presence of men is for Lily, as for Didion's women generally, a threat, an intrusion she alternately resists and, in an effort to fulfill what she perceives as her expected role, tries to love. During her one year at Berkeley she had been beset by "uncertainty" in her relations with boys. One young man told her roommate that taking Lily out was "like dating a deaf-mute" (p. 47). Rarely does she feel "safe enough" with a man to "say what she meant." On one occasion, when a date stops to buy condoms, she begins "shaking her head then, unable to think what to say" and "refused all invitations for three weeks afterward" (pp. 48–49). The problem is a conflict among universal but unspoken expectations of what a young woman should be and do. If she doesn't have dates, she is a failure, a woman lacking allure; but participating in the dating game implies a commitment to allow sex; but to allow sex would betray both her selfhood, vaguely associated with virginity, and her intense attachment to her father.

After she is safely home from school, when Everett, whom she has known all of her life, comes to visit and smiles at her, she again withdraws into protective self-absorption: she "extended one bare foot and contemplated it" (p. 46). When she goes out with Everett she is able to fall into the easy, flirtatious banter that had "eluded her at Berkeley" because he is part of the familiar world where her father is king. Inside, however, she is "struck by anxiety," though she gives no sign of her real feelings (p. 55). Initiating sex herself, to end the suspense, she then wonders whether she is "obliged to marry him simply because he had wanted her and taken her" (p. 57). But she hides that feeling, too, just as she tries to resist speaking the "only incantation which would satisfy them," namely, the words "I love you" (p. 58). For Lily, as for Didion's women generally, speaking that phrase means giving in to the "constant and incontrovertible presence" (p. 58) of men's power and their desire. At the same time, it is a phrase they must repeat as a part of their futile efforts to live up to the standard image of the loving woman, the helpmate.

Marriage and sex are an inevitability, "as fated as the exile from Eden" (p. 57), that takes Lily away from the inviolate state to which she longs to return. Yet she, like most of Didion's women, persists in promiscuous sexual activity despite feelings of guilt, despite the failure to achieve any sense of communion. Partly she derives excitement from playing with the forbidden, just as she adds frisson to her empty life by wearing expensive perfume around the house in the morning and by other mildly daring behaviors, but partly too, she uses sexual encounters as a way to punish men, particularly her husband. Her first affair is with a neighboring planter her husband knows well, whom she considers a "likeable fool" and with whom she "did not talk much" (p. 99). When he tries to recite the standard litany, claiming her as "his," calling her by her maiden name, she pointedly asserts her married state, as if to make it clear that in having sex with her he is affronting her husband. As a result, their relationship is "possibly sharper and better and more interesting than it had ever been before" (p. 100). But when their affair evolves into "the garrulous ambiguity of friendship" (p. 104), she loses interest. It is no longer a way of expressing disaffection. From this beginning Lily proceeds to a series of meaningless affairs, often one-night stands, which evoke repeated bouts of self-hate. Her infidelity is a tacit presence in her marriage; neither she nor Everett wants to discuss it because to do so would be to confront the whole unhappiness of their lives and the fact that they do not know how to change it.

Sex, like silence, is a way of evading the personal ramifications of Lily's belief that she is helplessly doomed by her gender. As she once says to Everett, "'Women don't ever win ... because winners have to believe they can affect the dice'" (p. 134). Faced with so hopeless a doom, she had best try to ignore and evade it: "things said out loud had for her an aura of danger so volatile that it could be controlled only in that dark province inhabited by those who share beds" (p. 105). Thus, after her abortion, she has no desire to talk about the experience, as her lover suggests. Early in her marriage, Lily had envied a cousin who became a nun, thereby avoiding the whole problem of pressuring and victimization by men. Later, Lily's self-hate is expressed in her compulsive reading of "a series of books on sacred architecture" (p. 126) as a way of avoiding Everett's presence. The cousin had taken orders after a trip to Europe during which she had toured cathedrals. Lily, too, is vicariously touring cathedrals, wishing for a return to virginity, a state that would allow her to make different choices.

Lily is keenly realized as a character with her own peculiarities. Unable to manage the simplest social situations without great excesses of anxiety, she can never engage in small talk. Trying to establish herself in a circle of women friends, she finds only a "vacuum" between them in which "overtures faded out, voices became inaudible, connections broke" (p. 70). Martha, her sister-in-law, shares none of this social awkwardness. They are very different. Yet at the profound level of sex, where women's roles are most crucially shaped by the complex of pressures that make up patriarchal society, Martha is as tormented and as withdrawn as Lily. They have in common the profound disturbances that characterize the lives of women in general and account for the fact that "women never win."

Just as Lily is fixated on her love for her father, which she never adequately expressed while he was alive and which never adequately sustained her against the griefs and mistakes of her life, so Martha is fixated on her love for her brother, Everett. In both cases, this love represents a deep urge to retreat to the security of the natal family, before the intrusion of the twin threats of sexuality and complex social expectations. Martha enters into an affair with an obvious ne'er-do-well, Ryder Channing, out of desperation at finding no acceptable role for herself after college and out of a deeply rooted need to shock Everett into giving her his full attention. When, after four and a half years of inconclusive romance, Ryder Channing marries someone else, Martha falls apart emotionally. Her behavior becomes stranger and more disruptive than ever. Still having found no defined role, nothing to do with her life, she begins sleeping around wantonly despite the self-loathing this behavior produces. When Ryder finds her alone at home, after his marriage, and forces sex on her, she insists that she doesn't want it, but her body responds. (We know this, despite narrative silence, because later in the day, when Lily and the children urge her to go to a parade with them, she consents with a bitter pun, "'Yes I can. I can come all right'"—p. 184.) Her sexuality is a trap, snaring her in self-betrayal.

Like Lily, Martha leaves unsaid the full extent of her frustration and unhappiness, only conveying them indirectly by her disruptive behavior and her terse, barbed sarcasms. After Martha's suicide, Lily finds a notebook where Martha had recorded all the torrents of hatred and tension she was not able to speak. The notebook contains lists of "reasons not to love Ryder" or Everett or "Daddy" (p. 192)—as if she were trying to redeem herself by perverse logic from the trap of loving. The entries for the last few days of her life are increasingly chaotic, finally becoming totally unreadable. Completely silenced, she gives up living. Lily, able to imagine no better way out of the dilemma of femaleness, muffles Martha's cry in an even deeper silence by keeping the discovery of the notebook to herself and burning it before Everett can find it. Once again she is protecting him from a knowledge too devastating, just as she had once protected her father from the fact of his own failure, by maintaining silence. When asked why Martha, who knew the river so well, would have gone out in a small boat during a flood, she can only answer, "I don't know" (p. 192). Plainly, she does know. Yet she, too, proceeds toward self-destruction, persisting in her own affair with the failed, failing Ryder Channing despite her realization of his worthlessness and her wish to maintain a relationship of loyalty and trust with her husband. What she does not know, truly, is why she persists in her self-destructive behavior. Late in her affair with Ryder Channing, when she becomes able to talk with him, it doesn't matter; he doesn't understand. At the end of the novel, after Everett has killed Ryder and killed himself, she is finally able to talk to her husband as she never could in life, lying down beside Everett's body and "telling him things for which there had never been any other words" (p. 222). It is a bleak view indeed of the possibility of understanding between the sexes.

Run, River, as a novel, is fully told. It is in the lives of the characters that silent emptinesses occur, from Lily and Everett's avoidance of honest conversation to Martha's illegible and finally burned diary. After *Run, River* Didion accentuates the importance of such failures of communication and links them clearly to a general failure of meaning by embodying vacancy and silence in the shape of the text itself.

In her second novel, seven years after the first, she takes the techniques of curtailment and withholding to their furthest extreme. *Play It As It Lays* is a strikingly bare novel. Simply in the visual sense it is strikingly bare—out of the total 213 pages, 142 have significantly more than the usual inch of bare margin, and 62 of those (by a crudely impressionistic count, but one which yields an accurate enough picture) are one-third or more blank. The mean chapter length is under 2½ pages, the median chapter length is 2, and mode (commonest occurring) is one-half. By comparison with virtually any novel, of any time, these are extremely short chapters.

The minimalism or curtailment of the text that so characterizes *Play It As It Lays* is a result of several interwoven techniques
or types of effects which recur throughout. One of these is compression, simply saying much in little. Didion takes to a sometimes startling, sometimes cryptic extreme the succinctness we
have observed in Austen, Porter, and Cather. She takes to an extreme, even, the succinctness of Hemingway, whom she admires
and echoes in a late chapter. (Maria agrees with BZ that it "would
be very pretty" to "have enough left" to get into a fight over—p.
211). The metonymic opening sentence of the first chapter—
"What makes Iago evil? some people ask"—distills the whole of
Maria's life-meaning into her awareness of evil and compresses
the concept of evil to a single example, one which evokes insoluble mystery. It is also, we should note, associated with the victimization of a woman, Desdemona. At times Didion's compression
technique is used for shock effect, as she lets the reader come to
an independent realization of what is implied, such as: "She won-
dered if Tommy Loew and the starlet had gone back to BZ's later,
and who had watched whom" (p. 27). In addition, Didion regularly employs fragmentation, breaking the continuity of sentences, paragraphs, or chapters; terse, uncontextualized openings
that leap at the reader out of the white blank of a preceding
empty page; unexplained concrete details, frequently ominous in
their starkness ("I try not to think of dead things and plumbing"—p. 8); and snapshots, or better, given the cinematic ambi-
ance, short cuts of events or conversations—chapter 38, for
example, which consists of six brief spoken comments, or chapter
40, a playlet of five spoken lines.

All of these stylistic devices are introduced in the opening
chapter and are readily apparent throughout the novel. They are
quite obvious, in the sense of being easily recognized, though
their full import may not be easily grasped. The technique of
fragmentation, especially, becomes so recurrent as to seem almost
a gimmick. Didion breaks a sentence into grammatical fragments, even one-word units—into sentences, that is, that are
mostly grammatical blanks.[10] Or she inserts paragraph breaks or
breaks chapters into sections separated by a half-inch or so of

blank page. This kind of caesura occurs twice within the first chapter, with the insertion of half-inch blanks between segments of a line of thought. For instance:

> ... I might as well lay it on the line, I have trouble with *as it was*.
>
> [space]
>
> I mean it leads nowhere.   (p. 5)

Or:

> "Don't let them bluff you back there because you're holding all the aces."
>
> [space]
>
> Easy aces.   (p. 7)

Essentially this sort of effect gives the illusion of a halt in a flow of speech, allowing the listener—the reader—to dwell on what has been said, imaginatively realizing its grimness before the screw is tightened even more, or imagining the speaker's realizing it herself. Or similarly these breaks, like the even larger breaking of potentially unified sequences into separate chapters, simply create suspense as to what is coming next. In any case, the effect is to slow our reading, to invite us into the narrative space so that we participate in the "imagination of disaster."[11]

Especially in the opening chapters, beyond serving purposes of reader involvement—that is, the simple stimulation of curiosity—the use of cryptic fragments builds ominousness. Such fragments establish the sense that Maria or the narrator finds some things too depressing or too distasteful to talk about. It is rather like opening the door just a crack to peek at something frightful. In the later part of the book especially, a frequent use of brief, fragmentary chapters establishes the empty, dead-end quality of Maria's life. The surrounding whiteness of the page highlights, by contrast, the few lines of print, implying that what is left out in the void of unsaying is less worthy of verbalization than what is put into words on the page. Since that which is printed is often flat, banal, inconclusive, we realize that the untold must be a dreary void indeed. The blank spaces before and after chapters, as well as various kinds of blanks within chapters, are great arid spaces of depression, sameness, meaninglessness. And for all their brevity, the fragmentary cuts that make up these curtailed chapters or sections of chapters become tedious—purposely tedious— as the ennui or fatigue established in the opening chapter (partly by the flattening effect of punctuating questions with periods rather than interrogative marks) becomes a pervasive mood of futility.

The silences and withholdings we see in these chapters and throughout the novel reflect a complex narrative strategy involving interplay between Didion's, the detached narrator's, morally judging depiction of Maria's world and the expression of Maria's state of mind and her own self-judgment. For instance, the flat, weary tone I have noted at several points conveys both Didion's judgment of the meaningless nature of the morally bankrupt society she is depicting and her created character's, Maria's, fatigue with that world. To a great extent this means her fatigue and depression with being a woman, dealing with the problems either inherent in femaleness or created by societal expectations of women. The occasional hard-boiled terseness of the narrative style is generally Didion's, i.e., the detached narrator's; she shocks the reader with the hard, uncushioned fact. The evasive style is more often Maria's, as she avoids direct, fully verbalized confrontation of elements in her life that are too overwhelming, too anxiety-laden.

What Maria manages not to elaborate on or even mention is, at times, the degeneracy all around her in which she participates even though she finds it unacceptable. The narrator says just enough to let us catch the idea, while Maria refuses to comment. For instance, the narrator intimates that Maria participated in sadomasochism with BZ and Helene, while Maria herself tries to efface the experience from consciousness by shutting out her "flash" of memory and ignoring what is right before her eyes, Helene's bruise. She denies even the intention of talking about it: "'I just don't remember getting here. . . . That's all I was saying'"

(p. 162). The few instances when Maria is talkative are conversational diversions thrown up to steer talk away from the unspeakable. In much the same way, she engages in elaborately patterned freeway driving as a means of evading the shapelessness of her life.

Much of the reality that Maria's evasive nonspeech avoids is, to be sure, ungendered. Sadomasochism is brutalizing to either a man or a woman; lack of purpose or of relational stability demeans any life. However, the personal disorder depicted by Maria and associated with her is particularized as experience essentially or socially attendant upon being female. She inhabits a "realm of misery peculiar to women" (p. 61).

At the center of these miseries is the thwarting of her powerful urge to motherhood. Cut off by her mother's horrible death from any bonding relationship as a daughter, Maria is also cut off from the role of mother. Her child, Kate, is neurologically defective in some devastating way never made clear, and has been removed to an institutional caretaking facility. Early on we see Maria fighting off "a wave of the dread" while clutching Kate's baby pillow as if it were a lifesaver (p. 22). The article "the" attached to "dread" may imply that it is the ultimate dread, fear of the ontological void (and the book sustains that possibility), or that it is a kind of personal dread so recurrent, so familiar, that it is recognizable as *the* dread. Or it may point at the standard feminine dread of pregnancy, *the* dread being roughly analogous to *the* curse. At any rate, Maria's encounter of the void is firmly linked to her being as woman, by means of her focus on her child. Later, her nightmares of the doom of innocence are a Hitlerian horror scene in which she conspires in the gassing of "little children" whom she betrays with comforting words when they "cried or held back" (p. 125). Her preoccupation with threat and disaster, the precariousness of life, is concretized as a mother's nightmare world of "four-year-olds in the abandoned refrigerator, the tea party with Purex, the infant in the driveway, rattlesnake in the playpen" (p. 99).[12] At the end, her fantasies of establishing a fulfilling and orderly life take the form of domestic idyll with her child.

Maria's obsessive grieving for her mother and for her child is compounded by her abortion. Maneuvered into getting the abortion by her husband, Carter, she goes through it in an emotionally dissociated, perceptually heightened way, with the result that later, when guilt and deprivation keep bringing the experience before her, she focuses on details that a more composed mind would have dismissed. After she begins having nightmares about stopped-up plumbing, stemming from having heard the abortionist flush away the contents scraped from her uterus, she moves out of her house when a sink stops up and vomits when the shower in the apartment where she has taken refuge seems slow to drain. She imagines, deep in the subterranean pipes as they are deep in her repressed consciousness, the hacked parts of embryos. On the day that the child would have been born (her certainty about the date is itself an indication of her overwrought state) she bursts into tears.

Despite their clearly personalized particularization, Maria's miseries are seen as being symptomatic of the experience of women generally. She speaks out of the experience of being female, and the awful truths she is reluctant to verbalize are the truths of that experience.

The commonality with women in general is established by the assertion of maternal heritage: "From my mother I inherited my looks and a tendency to migraine" (p. 3). Why from her mother and not her father? Perhaps because women's lives are inherently tension-ridden, producing migraines—generalized, pain. Women's lives are lives of pain; she is her mother's daughter. Further, that "tendency to" pain is verbally linked (grammatically coordinate) to the inherited "looks"—and, perhaps, to emphasis on looks? Maria's life in Los Angeles demonstrates that this is so; indeed, carries it to an extreme. As a minor movie star, she must parley her looks into jobs; her appearance is her life. At one point her husband uses her as sexual bait when trying to sell BZ on a movie venture. Going to incessant parties, for which she dresses strikingly and takes care to set her face into a bright-eyed allure, she sees all around her the dehumanizing valuation of women solely by their appearance, as sex objects. A man at a party, staring fixedly at a young girl, tells BZ that he would "like to get into that" (p. 36)—*that,* an object. Maria reacts by nervously twisting her napkins around her glass. Her friend Helene is so lost in the dehumanizing emphasis on appearance that she falls into panic and weeps when her hairdresser goes out of town.

Fearing engulfment in the role of sex object, Maria fears engulfment in other stereotypes of women as well. Indeed, her life in Los Angeles is dominated by stereotypes. The two films her husband Carter has made of her present her as either a victim or a kind of passive nullity. Those, it seems, are the stereotypes he projects onto her. Neither is acceptable; she reacts with nausea.

Even as she lives an extreme version of the woman as sex object, sleeping with many men and having sex forced on her at least once, she lives the (superficially) conflicting stereotype of the frigid wife—she "lay perfectly still" on nights when she knew her husband was not sleeping, to avoid attracting his advances (p. 184). When Carter accuses her of not wanting sex, she feels apologetic and obscurely guilty and claims, falsely, that she does, avoiding discussion of the many reasons why sex no longer appeals to her. Clinging desperately to the inapplicable stereotype of the loving wife, the woman for whom Love is all, she whispers meaninglessly that she loves Carter at the end a conversation in which he has been haranguing her. She feels guilty for her failure to live up to the image of the cheerleader for her husband's career, and the breakup of her marriage fills her with dread despite the fact that the marriage has scarcely been a satisfying relationship. Grasping at a similar straw, she tells the lover who may or may not have been the father of her aborted child that she is crying because he makes her so happy, when actually she is crying because she is devastated by life in general. She avoids at exaggerated cost the grocery-cart stigmas of the "idle lonely" (p. 121), another engulfing label, and is "plagued" by the possibility that she has fallen irretrievably into the stereotype of the fast woman. She fears that the various men of her acquaintance "recognized her, knew her, had her number" (p. 114). These are, of course, the same men who urge her into promiscuity. Continuing to accumulate one-night stands, she feels herself falling into a pattern that does not represent her real self, but actually obscures it, leaving her a "sleepwalker" (p. 105) in her own life while her personal memories have "ceased to exist" (p. 150), obliterated in the pattern of degeneracy.

Maria's drugged manner and minimal or evasive speech are largely efforts to avoid the fullness of her unhappiness and the emptiness of her life, eloquently conveyed by the blank spaces that surround such minimal chapters as her listing of her few remaining standards of conduct. In that listing, these few standards relate specifically to being a woman. She will not, she promises herself, "*walk through the Sands or Caesar's alone after midnight,*" because to do so would be to lay herself open to being taken as an expensive whore, or "*carry a Yorkshire in Beverly Hills,*" because that would be acting out the frivolous role of movie star/society queen (p. 135). It is left to the reader to flesh out these and other brief phrases expressive of Maria's despair with our understanding of the experiences behind the trite phrases. The evasive style is, after all, one which assumes that some things go without saying. Anomie and the slippage of traditional values are familiar to most Americans of the late twentieth century. Didion, through the sensibility of her character, renders these familiar abstractions as specifically female anxieties.

Such anxieties are intensified by the dominant role played by men. In Maria's world, as in Carter's gang-rape movie, men tend to be oppressors and women victims. Maria's father baited her mother ("'You wouldn't understand that,'" p. 87); Ivan Costello baited Maria ("'there's not going to be any getting married and there's not going to be any baby makes three,'" p. 141) and forces sex on her because "'you'll like it better that way anyway'" (p. 179); Carter baits Maria for her "menopausal depression" and aging ("'*Menopause. Old.* You're going to get *old*'"—p. 195). Sex is a battle zone of beatings with fists and belts. From her father, who insisted she pursue her modeling career in New York even though she wanted to stay home, to BZ, who insists she wants to go to Mexico after she has said she doesn't, to Carter, who insists on her having the abortion that pushes her over the brink, men domineer women. During the abortion ordeal Maria is surrounded by males who have no understanding of what she is enduring but keep telling her what to do. No wonder she is "'tired of listening to you all'" (p. 84)—that is, all men.

The only source of solidarity Maria can feel is the shared grimness of being female. It appears to her that "whatever arrangements were made, they worked less well for women" (p. 46). At the abortionist's, when she tries to avoid the fact of what is happening by focusing on the pattern in the wallpaper and imagining the woman who used to live in that house, she envisions the woman only as a wife, and therefore grievance-laden, a "hoarder of secret sexual grievances" (p. 80). Apparently, to be a wife means only and inevitably that. Later, Maria falls into conversation with a stranger at the small town in the desert where Carter is filming and finds that she, too, shares in the general futility, incessantly sweeping sand off her trailer-house pad to the fence while "new sand blew in as she swept" (p. 198). The woman also shares an understanding that the essence of a woman's life is grief. Claiming not to have shed a tear since she turned to religion, the woman immediately assumes, when Maria starts crying, that the reason is a classic female problem: "'You pregnant or something?'" (p. 198). Typically, Maria makes no comment, only shakes her head.

Maria's conversation, even her verbalized thoughts, are minimal because full expression of her experience would lay it before her in unavoidable and overwhelming specificity. Her conversation flows freely only when she is trying to mask reality with irrelevancy. More often she has "nothing to say" (p. 63). Silence becomes her defense against the void as well as a narrative representation of it. Language, which would put her at risk of having to face her own misery and emptiness, would also be an inadequate representation of that misery and emptiness, and thus a betrayal of it. When she tells Carter about her pregnancy and admits that she doesn't know who the father is, she "wanted to tell him she was sorry, but saying she was sorry did not seem entirely adequate, and in any case what she was sorry about seemed at once too deep and too evanescent for any words she knew, seemed so vastly more complicated than the immediate fact that it was perhaps better left unraveled" (p. 49).

The sense of doom Maria avoids expressing is intensely female, to a degree not usually recognized in commentary on Didion's work. True, the specifically female anxieties that trouble Maria most deeply, and which speak most directly to women readers, are also presented as exempla of the general anxieties of modern society. Everyone, this strategy implies, will experience such problems in individualized ways; this happens to be Maria's way. Moreover, her anxieties are linked to nonsexed anxieties through the technique of reticence itself. One "reads" the phenomenon of evasion and its emotional context even without "reading" the causes themselves from a vantage of shared experience. The application, then, is general. But the focus is specifically gendered.

If Maria's evasive style reveals, in attempting to mask, her unhappiness with her own life, and if that unhappiness is rooted in her being-as-woman, then it is evident how central to the novel is the problem of women's lives in a debased social system. Didion's own (the narrator's own) withholdings and compressions are not evasive but aggressive. When Maria whispers her brief admission to Carter that she had chosen her obstetrician by his office location "near Saks," her reluctance derives from her wish to evade the triviality and randomness of her decision. She explains, "'I was having my hair done at Saks'" (p. 51), but does not explain why her life is such that she would let that factor determine the much more important factor of consulting a physician. When Didion includes Maria's whispered admission in her narrative, without explanation or further comment, she is exposing the entire set of conditions that allow, or perhaps push, women into pursuing their lives in such a misvalued way. Her strategy is to use evasion and suppression to reveal and to criticize. By shocking the reader, by revealing the spotlighted appalling detail or firing the single-bullet phrase, she engineers our realization of the fuller picture and our recoil from it. The absences in her novel, the empty spaces given shape by the bare outlines of her minimal prose, become the positive presence of a feminist exposé that is also a general exposé of mid-twentieth-century malaise. Indeed, the two are not separable.

Didion's next novel, *A Book of Common Prayer,* is perhaps her most remarkable achievement. Not so hard-surfaced as *Play It As It Lays,* nor so accessible in its fictional milieu and the nature of its ethical critique, it is nevertheless quite as aggressive in its exposure of the inadequacies of women's lives. That exposure is couched in a language of regretful irony maintained throughout the book with remarkable consistency. Both the narrator, Grace Strasser-Mendana, and the main character whose life she ponders, Charlotte Douglas, are clearly and distinctively realized, but the encompassing voice remains Grace's. It is a more subtly and solemnly ironic voice than that of Didion's earlier novels.

Neither the compression nor the fragmentation of narrative surface is so obvious here as in *Play It As It Lays.* One is not struck by expanses of blankness. Certain techniques, however, are familiar from the preceding novel; the breaking of sentences into halting, sometimes sarcastic phrases; the evasiveness of the central character (a different quality of evasiveness, however); and the frequent use of unexplained physical details or cryptic phrases for effects of mystification and sinister foreboding. Charlotte, the central character, evades revelation of the truth less by silence than by misrepresentation, but is no less reluctant than Maria Wyeth to confront the facts that are troubling to her. Moreover, she is herself a much more elusive character than Maria, whom we comprehend fairly well by the end of her jigsaw-puzzle novel. A new element of withholding, not present in *Play It As It Lays,* combines with the narrator's reticence to leave this book much more deeply obscured. That element is the narrator's inability to know much of the truth of her story. A scientist, Grace Strasser-Mendana wishes to base her account on observed or at least reliably reported fact. But her access to facts is severely limited. She must finally stake her sense of solidarity with Charlotte, and her willingness to "be her witness" (p. 3), on intuition.[13]

In piecing together her account of how Charlotte came to end her life at Boca Grande, Grace relies on observation of Charlotte's behavior, on Charlotte's own statements, and on what she can learn from brief meetings with Charlotte's two ex-husbands[14] and her daughter Marin. But these sources of information leave a great deal of uncertainty. The evidence is inconclusive in several major respects, notably in giving little clue to the mystery of Charlotte's inner being. One problem is that Charlotte regularly changes her versions of certain key episodes, preferring, it seems, to tell what she wishes had happened rather than what happened. The fact that she does disguise the truth is as important to Grace's understanding, in fact, as what Charlotte actually says. But this means that Grace is thrown back on inference, on the imagination. Grace herself is implicated in her story of Charlotte much as Marlow is implicated in his story of Kurtz in *Heart of Darkness,* because her intuited understanding of her subject grows out of her own experiences and emotions. She confronts the mystery of the separate individual, a mystery which forever resists the achievement of full understanding. But she is able to explore that mystery because of commonalities shared with Charlotte.

Grace says that we all, meaning all of us women, "have the same dreams" (p. 53). The dreams she refers to are Charlotte's dreams of "sexual surrender and infant death," which together Grace labels "commonplaces of the female obsessional life" (p. 53). Charlotte does indeed carry these obsessions. She engages in pointless sexual liaisons—apparently searching for some perfect love relationship which she never achieves—then carries with her an exaggerated guilt, to the point that her body tenses if she finds herself simultaneously in the presence of two men with whom she has slept. Apparently Didion indeed regards sexual guilt as one of the primary constants of the female emotional life; it appears also in Maria's torments in *Play It As It Lays* and in Lily's tortured awareness that she is an object of gossip and her wish that she might have stayed with her husband and avoided the fatal engagement to meet her lover that opens *Run, River.* The two impulses, the one toward sexual vitality as a (frequently spurious) sign of personal fulfillment and the other toward cleanness or inviolateness, are mutually exclusive. Yet neither can be relinquished. The result is acute frustration, even self-hate.

Charlotte and Grace share, as well, the centrality of the maternal experience in their lives and the doom of that experience. As Grace explicitly states, "One thing I share with Charlotte: I lost my child" (p. 13). Charlotte, indeed, has in different ways lost two children. Her older daughter, Marin, she lost "to 'history.'" That is, Marin became caught up in revolutionary movements that carried her beyond her own depth or her mother's ability to reclaim her. The second child, an infant, Charlotte lost, in the words of the medical report, "to 'complications'" (p. 3). Both hydrocephalic, the child is an emblematic representation of the blighting of life that results from hopelessly disordered relationships. The child cannot possibly live. Yet Charlotte, whether from the strength of her urge to mother or the strength of her urge to deny unpleasant realities or from some confused mixture of the two, commits herself to caring for the baby to the end, walking and singing to it and telling it "about the places they would see together" (pp. 152, 149). In much the same way, she had attempted to deny Marin's childhood anxieties and her own "dread" for the doom awaiting children of the present age by providing "weird and unsettling, cheerful but not quite responsive" answers to Marin's questions (p. 111). In neither case is her delusion, if it is that—or her heroism, perhaps—efficacious.

Grace, who also loses her child, morally if not physically, resorts to a different kind of denial, not Charlotte's openly wishful evasion, but the evasive duplicity of a crisp irony that seems to, but does not, give the whole story. Grace acknowledges that she "talk[s] to" her son Gerardo "as an acquaintance" and that he adopts social attitudes she does not "admire" (p. 14). What this seeming frankness manages to conceal is the intensity of disappointment and hurt that go with such admissions. Dying, she feigns sleep when her son comes home from Europe, pretending that "my indifference to his presence derives from my being asleep" (p. 52). For both, the truth is too overwhelming to talk about. Indeed, the disheartening truth for both is much the same, that the adult child is involved in shabby revolutionary acts in which innocent people get hurt. ("By Day Seven Gerardo wanted to get out himself," Grace says, in evident distaste—p. 273.) Like the unscientific Charlotte, who "dreamed her life," Grace preserves "some areas" of her life in which "I, like Charlotte, prefer my own version" (p. 199).

Stylistically, *A Book of Common Prayer* recalls *Play It As It Lays* in the verbal modes of its main character and of its narrator. Grace Strasser-Mendana, like the unpersonalized narrator of the earlier novel, adopts a style of the quick thrust, the stark and often sardonic, understated phrase. In part, this style reflects her chosen stance as the detached research scientist—she is a trained anthropologist and a self-trained biochemist. But as we have already seen, the attempt at detachment proves as inadequate to the emotional content of Grace's experience as it does to its truth content. Like the narrator of the earlier novel, Grace employs a pared-down prose that achieves pointed satirical effects, through bubble-puncturing precision—when summarizing the tarnished social image of her fatuous ex-sister-in-law she comments that the woman is "a national treasure as it were" (p. 75); indicating the inconsequential nature of revolutions in Boca Grande, she makes her point with the one little word "usually" and the present tense: "The final closing of the airport is what we usually call Day One" (p. 271).

Grace's narrative style includes certain devices familiar from *Play It As It Lays*. One is the device of breaking sentences into fragments for effects of spotlighting:

> A not atypical *norteamericana.*
> Of her time and place. (p. 57)

or

> In other words.
> All the markers were on the table. (p. 246)

Another device is repeating empty phrases that not only constitute evasions of the deplorable or the unbearable but also take on a sardonic tone through repetition:

> In short. (p. 19)

or

> In any case. (p. 272)

or

> In any case.
> In the second place. (p. 75)

Grace's narrative, however, takes to a much further extent a device only insinuated in the earlier novel, the echoic, almost incantatory repetition of common or parallel elements in sequences of short phrases:

> Boca Grande is. (p. 235)

then

> Boca Grande is. (p. 240)

then

> Boca Grande is.
> Boca Grande was.
> Boca Grande shall be. (p. 244)

Or:

> Her only child.
> Her oldest child.
> The only child she ever dressed in flowered lawn
> for Easter. (p. 200)

Variations of this sort of effect run throughout the novel in a much more pervasive way than these few quotations can indicate. Cumulatively, they establish a sense of the narrator's brooding over events or impressions and a sense of uncanny parallels between actions, as if some highly significant pattern is almost ritualistically being acted out. Such an effect is quite evident, for instance, in this sequence:

> He had found Marin Bogart in an empty room
> in Buffalo.
> He had buried Warren Bogart in an empty grave
> in New Orleans.
> He had come to save Charlotte from an empty
> revolution in Boca Grande. (p. 254)

Largely because of the sound effects created, these parallelisms convey a prayerlike sense, thus a substantiation of the title.[15]

The sense of a religious import to Grace's account of Charlotte Douglas derives largely from a suggestion of redemptive reenactment developed from the parallels between the two. Charlotte repents the failure of mothering that contributed to the loss of Marin, and atones by her faithful care of the defective infant and by persisting in service to the victims of another foolish revolutionary action. Grace repents, or at any rate deplores, grieves, the loss of her son Gerardo to ethical nonawareness and pointless scheming, and atones by offering up her account of Charlotte's life.[16] Charlotte repents, moreover, her leaving of her first husband without warning him, and atones for that wrong by returning to him as he wishes (indeed demands) and by giving scrupulous warning to her second husband before leaving him to do so. Even more profoundly, she atones for all her past failures to persist in right conduct—for, as Warren accuses her, "the way you walked away from everything else in your life" (p. 179),—by staying with the baby until it dies and by staying to see the revolution through until she dies herself, effectively offering up her life. As she says, "'I walked away from places all my life and I'm not going to walk away from here'" (p. 263). By staying she hopes to redeem, through the essentially religious symbolic action of sacrificial atonement, her previous life.

Similarly, Grace hopes to redeem her own life by "redeeming" Charlotte's, that is, by discovering and setting forth its final meaning, so far as she can discover it. To do so is to walk through the valley of the shadow, to put off her armor of scientific method and assume, so far as she is able, Charlotte's vulnerability. It is to expose herself anew, by choice, to the hurts she has already suffered and repressed, by exposing herself to Charlotte's similar hurts. The novel, then, both enacts and depicts, in a generally underplayed way, an act of martyrdom. Grace's characteristically dry comment describes her own and Charlotte's call to the stringent discipline of redemptive action: "I have noticed that it is never enough to be right. I have noticed that it is necessary to be better" (p. 164). Grace's sense of failure at the end—"I have not been the witness I have wanted to be" (p. 280)—is testimony to the final mystery of personhood, the inability of one person fully to understand another,[17] and also to a kind of sacred humility. She has indeed provided, as her name indicates, an avenue of grace.

If Grace's verbal style, like the narrator's in *Play It As It Lays*, is often drily sardonic, making pointed use of her terseness, it is also at times elliptical in evasive or mystifying ways. As we will see, these latter resemble the characteristic verbal manner of Charlotte herself. The way in which Grace gives the bare outlines of things, for instance her outline of Charlotte's story at the opening of the novel, emphasizes the weight of the untold or even the unfathomed looming behind these cryptic indications. The brief, incomplete phrases such as we have already noted—"in any case," "again as usual"—are sometimes used to let her block out the need to elaborate when doing so would be grievous or futile. Similarly, she simply cuts her account short, leaves a blank, when she does not wish to comment or to hold up to view the full, distressing picture. In narrating one of Charlotte's interviews with FBI men about Marin's disappearance, for example—an account she must first have received from Charlotte herself—she gives a fairly detailed report up to the point of what "Charlotte said before she broke" (p. 63). Breaking the account there allows her to avoid exposing Charlotte's weeping or collapse into weeping or whatever, exactly, it was. We have only the terse word *broke,* followed by a blank space and then a reference to the FBI men's departure. Grace's reticence here implies her discretion or mercy; she does not go into the worst, but lets us guess it for ourselves.

Grace as narrator stimulates us to guess a great deal for ourselves. Her silences open the text to participatory reading even as they close off the provision of information or determinate interpretations. Indeed, the two are inseparable. The terse phrases she uses as formulas of evasion actually invite our conjecture as to the *what* or the *why*. In other ways as well, she introduces brief references to emotions or events, or simply to objects—such as her list of items found on Charlotte's body—that arouse and accommodate the reader's elaboration, even as Grace avoids giving her own. Sentences such as, "I continue to live here only because I like the light" (p. 13) are to be read as metastatements, not even shorthand versions of statements so much as shorthand versions of powerfully emotional nonstatements.

Charlotte, as reported by Grace (we never have a first-person segment of Charlotte's own narration as we do of Maria's in *Play It As It Lays*), also tends to say just enough to evoke speculation. She has a strange way of bringing up bits about her life which no one has asked about and then leaving them unexplained. People are left guessing—as are we; but we can guess more intelligently because of the spatial form of the novel. Like Maria's, her mind hovers over strangely detached objects in a way that can only seem ominous. She remarks, apropos of nothing, upon the "red cardboard patent-leather shoes" worn by "all the children . . . all over the tropics," and explains her intense interest only by remarking, equally abruptly, that she "did have a baby who had red shoes" (pp. 44–45). Only the past tense and the guilt implied by her fretting over having refused to buy Marin a pair of red shoes once can be construed as being explanatory. Much later we discover that the mortician in Merida, where her infant daughter died, had "wrapped the baby in a lavender nylon shawl and put a bow in her hair and tiny red shoes on her feet" (p. 153). Some of her elliptical references, of course, are never explained. Much of our understanding is provided by Grace's or our own guessing based on minimal clues. Charlotte never actually says what a dreadful man her first husband, Warren, was or how she felt about him or about her second husband; mostly we judge for ourselves or guess by drawing inferences from her behavior and from the way she avoids confronting the fact of how Warren disturbs her (p. 123).

Like Maria, Charlotte occasionally becomes very talkative—but only when she is using her words to avoid other words, other realizations. An example, illustrating both her conspicuous eccentricity and her hidden depth, is her behavior at a cocktail party soon after her arrival in Boca Grande. Here she talks "feverishly," in "bizarrely arresting stories" that leave her audience "transfixed" (pp. 29–33). Many of her stories are inspired by absences: the absence of banyan trees reminds her of a banyan tree story, the absence of caviar at the party reminds her of a caviar story. But of course such arbitrary conversational starts can scarcely be stimulated by nonexistent reminders; one is not "reminded" of something by a lack, unless it is the lack of something much more obvious and expected than banyan trees in a Central American consulate. We read that she was reminded, but we know that she didn't need to be reminded; her memories were always with her, hidden away and ready. When she talks, she tries to cover her obsessions and depressions. Often it works even more directly: she lies to avoid what she knows is true. Particularly when dealing with the upbringing of Marin, she constructs stories of what she wishes had happened, leaving unexpressed the actual fear and guilt she feels. In many cases we never know the truth of what happened; nor does it matter. What we know is that Charlotte found it necessary to be reticent about the truth, to misrepresent it.

If the doom of their mothering is one of the primary reasons for Charlotte's reticence, as it is for Grace's, the cruelty and intrusiveness of men is another. There is not a single male in all the novel to whom Didion's troubled women can freely and equally relate. Sex is a mode of domination. In the early chapters we see Charlotte as a virtual pawn shoved back and forth between her former and her present husband. They argue over her preferences and habits as if she were scarcely present. Warren changes her lunch order and then orders for himself what she had wanted. She does not even protest. She has "no need" to act for herself during the crisis of Marin's disappearance because Leonard will act for her, and indeed she "settled many problems that way" (p. 72). During her troubled first marriage, Warren had actually at times struck her and called her demeaning names, and when he drops back into her life after Marin's disappearance he resumes the habit of baiting and harassing her. When she breaks down in tears under the pressure of FBI questioning, he mocks, "'Boo hoo'" (p. 99). It is his own daughter, not Leonard's, who has disappeared.

Charlotte's departure from Leonard's house to join Warren in miserable months of travel is a departure on paths of humiliation and sexual thralldom. Denying that she wants to go with Warren, to have sex with him again, she is told by Leonard, "'Shit. I know you don't *want* to'" (p. 129). Both realize that she will act under a kind of sexual duress, going whether she wants to or not. Warren not only humiliates her with his rudeness and his compulsive sexual adventuring, but becomes, once again, physically abusive, at one point "twist[ing] her arm behind her back" so viciously that the car-rental clerk who witnesses the incident starts to call the police (p. 159). Like the aunt Grace mentions, and perhaps like Grace herself, Charlotte "appeared to locate the marriage bed as the true tropic of fever and disquiet" (p. 82). Marriage is a version of a primitive custom Grace tells Charlotte about, in which "female children were ritually cut on the inner thigh by their first sexual partners, the point being to scar the female with the male's totem" (p. 83).

That primitive custom, it seems, sums up Didion's view of the relations of men and women (at any rate in her first three novels). In *A Book of Common Prayer* the lives of women in a masculinist society—even if those women are, like Grace Strasser-Mendana, very rich and powerful—are so "dark and febrile and outside the range of the normal" (p. 83) that they scarcely bear discussing. Charlotte's despair and confusion can only be redeemed by the grace afforded her by another woman's witnessing, and the silences in her grim witnessing when some things are too grim to be spoken are the fullest possible revelation of that grimness.

In her most recent novel, *Democracy,* Didion writes in the terse, elliptical style we expect of her but with a somewhat different and more highly politicized import. As in *A Book of Common Prayer,* the narrative strategy involves a first-person narrator only slightly distanced from the author herself. Indeed, the distance is even less here. The narrator of the earlier book is particularized with a name, Grace Strasser-Mendana, and a personal background clearly distinct from Didion's own. The narrator of *Democracy* is a thinly fictionalized Joan Didion; we might call her "Joan Didion": a persona in only the most circumstantial of ways. This persona advances and retreats. At those points when she is at the narrative fore, she addresses the reader directly, calling our attention to the difficulties entailed by getting and presenting the story. Several chapters open abruptly with terse one-line "paragraphs" focusing on the act of telling—imperatives: "Call me the author" (p. 16), "See it this way" (p. 75), "Let me establish Inez Victor" (p. 44); personal declarations: "I also have Inez's account" (p. 129), "I am resisting narrative here" (p. 113). The directly accostive narrative voice that such openings establish creates the sense of urgency avowed in the narrator's "warning" to the reader,

> like Jack Lovett and (as it turned out) Inez Victor,
> I no longer have time for the playing out.
>   Call that a travel advisory.
>   A narrative alert.   (p. 164)

The issuance of a "narrative alert," an overt tactic for gaining reader involvement, is a part of the entire strategy by which "Joan Didion" is placed within the novel. The narrator's struggle to understand her characters' story becomes part of the fiction, which is a fiction of reporting rather than creating. "Joan Didion" is here, like Joan Didion in fact, an interpretive journalist, trying to get at the truth and communicate it before the failure of the social situation, represented in the fall of South Vietnam, makes investigation and interpretation impossible. When she says that she does not have time for a fully elaborated narrative, we feel not only the wildly accelerating events of the evacuation of Hanoi and the family tragedy being played out against it but also the impending breakup of the social order and the brevity of human life. The urgency "Didion" asserts is communicated to us, in part, by the rapid succession of terse, often fragmentary phrases.

Though the overall style is characteristically terse, it is not so austere as that of the most extremely bare of Didion's novels, *Play It As It Lays*. The presence and, moreover, the nature of recurrent sensed details—tropical rain and gardenia blossoms and termites falling onto the surface of a cup of tea—soften the stylistic surface, fleshing out what would otherwise be bare narrative bones indeed. Further, the fragmentation of narrative through breaking into brief one-liners is less insistent than in the earlier novel. There is more supple alternation between one-liners and longer, more filled-out paragraphs.

Even so, moderated as it is, Didion's style is still relatively bare, more closely resembling *Play It As It Lays* than *Run, River* in its use of curtailed one-liners, fragments, and vacancies. In all Didion's work, the breaking into brief stand-alone sentences or phrases, or often strings of such sentences or phrases, is a device for emphasis, usually an ironic twist of emphasis. But in *Democracy*, the device gains a faster pace and a more hard-bitten, slangy tone. The rapidity is largely a matter of achievement of a sense of fast-breaking events, even of events being out of control. This is true both of family events and of events on the large scale. Social structures collapse more rapidly than politicians, generals, and weapons dealers can shore them up. The fast verbal pace is achieved also through associative listing of items, such as:

> Certain words and phrases keep recurring.
> Tiger Ops.
> Black flights.
> Extraction.
> Assets.
> AID was without assets.
> USIA was without assets.   (p. 195)

Another example:

> 1) *Shining Star,* Inez had written on the piece of paper.
> 2) *Twinkling Star*
> 3) *Morning Star*
> 4) *Evening Star*
> 5) *Southern Star*
> 6) *North Star*
> 7) *Celestial Star*
> 8) *Meridian Star*
> 9) *Day Star*
> 10) ? ? ?   (p.69)

The reader scans down such a list impressionistically, gaining a kind of snapshot sense of a hectic, unstable situation or, in the latter instance, a sense of the unstable state of mind of a woman who "believed that grace would descend on those she loved and peace upon her household on the day she remembered the names of all ten Star Ferry boats that crossed between Hong Kong and Kowloon" (p. 69).

Rapid exchanges of smart dialogue, often in brief, slangy phrases tossed off sarcastically, also contribute to the fast pace of the dramatized scenes and to the harsh tone. The narrative voice, as well, often employs bitten-off slang to convey a mocking commentary or a sense of world-weariness. Summing up her description of Inez's life with her political campaigner husband, Harry Victor, the narrator tosses out,

> Through the mill.
> Through the wars. (p. 48)

Indeed, all the major characters have been "through the wars." They speak in a rapid-fire lingo of phrases familiar to those who "know the moves" (p. 150), a kind of argot of a governmental in-group. To sample this jaded, fast dialogue, consider:

> You talk to Harry or me, you're talking *in camera.*
> Strictly."
> "Strictly *in camera,*" Frank Tawagata said, "I still can't help you."
> "You can't, you can't. Just say the word."
> "I just said it." (pp. 146–47)

Or another example:

> Frank Tawagata said nothing.
> "Embarrassing Harry. Because face it, the guy to get is Harry."
> "I would say 'was' Harry."
> "Run that down for me."
> "Harry's already been got, hasn't he? In '72?"
> "Free shot, Frank. You deserve it." (pp. 147–48)

Or yet another:

> Inez had looked at Billy Dillon.
> "Well?" Billy Dillon said.
> "Well what?"
> "What should I tell Harry?"

"Tell him he should have advanced it better,"
Inez Victor said. (p. 171)

One does not usually speak of "advancing" a piece of family news
(a death, actually, and the need to attend a funeral) to one's own
adolescent child, as if it were a proposition in the political power
struggle.

The narrator's hard-bitten phrases, not quite hiding a fullness
of emotion sensed behind them, often, though not consistently,
emulate the glibness or sarcasm of this campaigning, image-
building circle in which Inez moves as Harry Victor's wife. Mull-
ing her story, she comments mockingly: "Cards on the table" (p.
17); "Water under the bridge" (p. 17); "The Alliance *qua* Alliance" (p. 111); "His famous single room at the Y" (p. 129). At
other times, it is the laconic, tough yet nostalgic voice of Jack
Lovett that we hear in the narrator's brief phrases. The beauti-
fully taut opening of the novel, for instance, starts in Lovett's
voice, then elides into Didion's own terse identification of the
characters, emphasizing (significantly) Inez's marital state, then
returns to Lovett's distinctive blend of nostalgia and hard-boiled
realism:

> The light at dawn during those Pacific tests was
> something to see.
> Something to behold.
> Something that could almost make you think
> you saw God, he said.
> He said to her.
> Jack Lovett said to Inez Victor.
> Inez Victor who was born Inez Christian.
> He said: the sky was this pink no painter could
> approximate, one of the detonation theorists used to
> try, a pretty fair Sunday painter, he never got it. Just
> never captured it, never came close. The sky was
> this pink and the air was wet from the night rain,
> soft and wet and smelling like flowers, smelling like
> those flowers you used to pin in your hair when you
> drove out to Schofield, gardenias, the air in the
> morning smelled like gardenias, never mind there

> were not too many flowers around those shot is-
> lands.
> > They were just atolls, most of them.
> > Sand spits, actually. (p. 11)

In part, Didion adopts Lovett's savvy understatement as a way of
conveying, through its own cadences, some sense of an elusive
personality, as if, though the mystery cannot be analyzed, it can
be glimpsed:

> According to Jack Lovett himself he was some-
> one who had "various irons in the fire."
> > Someone who kept "the usual balls in the air."
> > Someone who did "a little business here and
> there."
> > Someone who did what he could. (p. 39)

In part, however, she adopts this tone, with its characteristic curtailments, as a protection from the pressure of emotion—just as,
we suspect, Lovett himself adopts it. Indeed, all the people we
respect in this book—Lovett, Inez, and the narrator—are "wary
to the point of opacity" (p. 84). They adopt a tough exterior—
such as Lovett's exclamation, conveying a lifelong caring and a
lifelong frustration, "'Oh shit, Inez, Harry Victor's wife'" (p. 15;
repeated or echoed on pp. 44, 46, 107, and 187)—to cover their
vulnerability, knowing full well even as they do it that toughness
"'never stopped any plane from crashing'" (p. 205). Disaster happens despite the surface toughness that they nevertheless maintain
because, like the Hemingway hero's style, that is the way to do it,
or at any rate their way to do it.

The narrator tells things in a compressed shorthand, sometimes imagistic but sometimes carefully abstract, both for impact
and for control, for protection from the disorder.[18] Inez's mother,
Carol Christian, she tells us, clung to an assortment of romantic
notions "in the face of considerable contrary evidence" (p. 24). It
is not necessary to specify what that evidence was; we get the idea
well enough, and she would rather not go into it. Just as the
device of curtailed references is a means of refraining from specification, implying that that specification would be too unpleas-

ant, so silences in the text, blanks or gaps, serve the same purpose, conveying ideas without spelling them out. In this novel, many blanks are structural, signaling shifts in the action. Many, however, as in the previous novels, tacitly invite the reader's particularized understanding even as they imply the narrator's brooding. After a long, wordy sentence conveying, in its cadences, the jumbled, densely populated quality of Harry Victor's politicizing, the narrator sums up,

> These people had taken their toll.
>
> [space]
>
> By which I mean to suggest that Inez Victor had
> come to view most occasions as photo opportunities.
>
> (p. 50)

After an account of Inez's conference with her daughter Jessie's first therapist, ending in "'What I don't do is shoot heroin,' Inez said," there appears a gap on the page, then, "The second therapist believed . . ." (p. 63). In the gap occurs the whole messy process of breaking off with one and finding the second, a process the narrator spares us all. Indeed, the gap says something that a full account could not say, that that messy process is not worth repeating and that it is so obviously unavoidable at this point that it goes without saying.

Inez Victor herself, in this way a typical Didion heroine, is equally reticent. In part her silences and the oddity of her speech when she does express herself are a result of being squelched. As the daughter of a son of a powerful family in a relatively closed society (Hawaii) and the wife of a powerful man with presidential ambitions, she has had to preserve appearances throughout her life. Her expression of self is subordinated to the building of her husband's political image. She has had to calculate every word, every facial expression, to ensure that that image is not damaged, playing a role in a planned script, repeating empty enthusiastic phrases—"'Marvelous day.' 'You look marvelous.' 'Marvelous to be here'" (p. 42)—and "fixing her gaze in the middle distance" (p. 50). When traveling she always has to go through a routine of phony accessibility, to "'trot out the smile'" and, as her husband's public relations aide puts it, "'move easily through the cabin'" (p. 122). So well trained is she in playing the "tennis" game of public relations that Billy Dillon, the aide, has only to "mim[e] a backhand volley" to get her back on track if she slips into real communication (p. 52). What she says get smoothed over and reinterpreted, polished for press release beyond all recognition. Even the personal interests she is allowed to pursue are selected for their political appeal: a trumped up "special interest" in selecting the paintings to be hung in American embassies is safe; her real interest in "work with refugees" is off-limits because it is controversial and therefore "inappropriate" (p. 56).[19] This is why it is so significant at the end that after Jack Lovett's death she devotes herself, in an almost saintly way, to the administration of refugee relief in Kuala Lampur: it is the most emphatic possible way to express her independence from her husband's control.

Inez's public self has been an "impenetrable performance" (p. 112) protecting the mystery and the vulnerability of her private self. At times she uses silence, as she uses diversionary performances, to protect her self from manipulation and from the intrusion of a curious public, largely the intrusion of journalists. Within that protection, she has developed a "capacity for passive detachment" (p. 70), avoiding verbal acknowledgment of unacceptable things. But she also uses silence more aggressively. After a party at which her husband passes off empty, stale rhetoric she has heard him use "a number of times before" to cover lack of knowledge, she drives fast and says nothing until he finally notices and gets the point. Defensively, he taunts her for her "quite palpable unhappiness" (pp. 57–58). They go to bed in silence. On another occasion, seeing her husband condoning what she regarded as specious activities by their son, she again spoke tersely and then "said nothing." Again Harry gets the point: "'Very eloquent. Your silence,'" he says (p. 206).

Inez Victor, like other women in Didion's novels, and like Didion as narrator, manages to say more than she says and to speak by not speaking. This, of course, is a time-honored way with women—women writers and women generally. Inez Victor speaks out of the frustration of feminine roles that inhibit her self-realization and interfere with her freedom of action. When she tries to assert her own judgment, as a free and intelligent adult, she is muffled and manipulated and her sexual relations with her husband deteriorate: they "had gone to bed in silence, and, the next morning, ... Harry left ... without speaking" (p. 58); they had "slept in the same room but not in the same bed" (p. 179). The marital relation hinges on her being constrained in her self-assertion, on her foregoing a lifelong love relation with another man even though she had repressed her own reactions to her husband's succession of affairs because "girls like that come with the life" (p. 48). Her achievement of communication with "Joan Didion," the narrative persona, despite all the negative constraints of a lifetime of resisting honest personal communication and honest public statements, has to be regarded as a victory—like her victory in asserting her right to pursue the social service work to which she feels drawn. The end of the book, with Inez still in Kuala Lampur, speaking to whomever she wants to when she wants to, stating her reasons in her own terms and with an edge of mockery (asked by Billy Dillon for "one fucking reason" why she is there, she writes back tersely, *"Colors, moisture, heat, enough blue in the air. Four fucking reasons."*—p. 232), is thus, in a limited way, a happy ending, despite its solemnity.

As in the other novels, the frustrating and repressed nature of the central character's life is not hers alone, but a condition she shares with other women. Within *Democracy,* the lives of Inez's mother, sister, and daughter are also troubled. Didion conveys the picture to us in a compressed version, letting us imagine the depressing details for ourselves. Inez's mother, brought from the mainland as a bride and expected to fit into her in-laws' social position in Hawaii, finds herself stifled there. Though she tries to claim her husband's attention, largely through a series of ineffectual and unrealistic romantic ploys picked up in a lifetime of conditioning in femininity, to the point of writing to him in pretended jest, "Who do you f——— to get off this island?" (p. 24), her marriage is essentially the story of a "stubborn loneliness" which she had "perfected" (p. 22). As Didion tersely puts it, she had "miscalculated" in marrying Paul Christian (p. 24). But the same could be said of Inez's marrying Harry Victor and her sister Janet's marrying Dick Ziegler. Marriage itself is a miscalculation. Janet's life is so empty of individual goals and satisfactions that she is driven to fill her time with drinking, shopping, contrived trips for no purpose, and affairs. The inheritor of disorder, Inez's daughter Jessie drifts through adolescence in a narcotic haze, without the slightest notion of a plan or goal for her life. She, too, has learned the lesson of silence in dealing with men; after an overdose, she repeatedly insists, "'Don't tell Daddy'" (p. 61).

The narrator, too, "Joan Didion," shares the frustrations of being a woman in what continues to be a man's world, and a disordered world as well. Because of the unusual narrative strategy, with the author's real self represented in a fictive world that includes events, people, and places we also recognize from the daily newspaper, the figure of "Joan Didion" ("call me the author," the narrator says, but particularizes herself by quoting textbook comments on Didion) becomes a bridge between fiction and fact. Naturally, by the creation of verisimilitude in her fictive world, the author invites (as do authors generally in realistic fiction) a sense of identification which generalizes the import of the story. To the extent that we recognize aspects of the characters' lives as resembling our own, we say that the story represents general experience. Accordingly, women readers will recognize the silences in the marriage bed, the conversational slightings, and other experiences of the fictional Inez and will validate the representational character of her story. But the bridging effect of "Joan Didion" accomplishes such generalizing in a much more direct way.

Clearly, the narrator objects to aspects of her world that are not gender-related. Her difficulty in telling her story does not stem simply from the fact that she is a woman, writing about a woman. The main burden of the story is a stringent objection to the ebbing of traditional values, family values, and a moral horror at the spectacle of America's role in Vietnam. It is an objection to dishonesty. Didion affirms the importance of what we must consider traditional values and traditional sources of satisfaction for women as well—stable relationships with men and with extended family, motherhood. Whether there has ever been a time when these roles alone did in fact provide adequate sources of fulfillment is a question she does not address. At the same time, Didion does not ignore the need for other satisfactions as well, means of achieving personal autonomy and self-definition. At any rate, the uncentered state of American society that undermines public and private honor also makes traditional role-fulfillment impossible. Gender problems are implicated in Didion's broad social criticism, even when they are not specified.

Within the novel, "Joan Didion" is drawn to the story of Inez Victor largely by her own need. Obviously it is, in a journalistic sense, a good story, with interesting social trappings and an odor of scandal. But it is not those aspects that keep the novelist working to find the right narrative approach to what is "a hard story to tell" (p. 15). Those externals are aspects of the story that she has "abandoned," "scuttled," "jettisoned" (p. 19) in favor of a focus on Inez's feelings and on her achievement of a personal value perspective on a world falling apart. That "Joan Didion" shares the need for such a perspective is clear from her account of the genesis of the novel: "I began thinking about Inez Victor and Jack Lovett at a point in my life when I lacked certainty, lacked even that minimum level of ego which all writers recognize as essential to the writing of novels, lacked conviction, lacked patience with the past and interest in memory; lacked faith even in my own technique" (p. 17). She focuses, in the early part of the novel, on the powerful emotional pull of a daughter's feelings toward a mother who has abandoned her and on the liminal position of looking with regret at a disappearing world, giving the "last look through more than one door" (p. 15). If she finds it a "hard story to tell" (p. 15) because of its complexity, occupying as it does the intersection of many issues, she also finds it hard to tell because its emotional impact evokes her own shared feelings.

The narrator's feelings are apparent in her hovering, circling style, with its tone of stiff-upper-lip compression. Her own experience of the breakup of American pretenses and the revelation of the hollowness at the core, epitomized in the fall of Vietnam, leads her to reinterpret the behavior of Inez Victor, also experiencing that breakup in a very direct way, so as to see it as a coping mechanism. "After the events which occurred in the spring and summer of 1975 I thought of it differently. I thought of it as the essential mechanism for living a life in which the major cost was memory. Drop fuel. Jettison cargo. Eject crew" (p. 70). In the same way as Inez jettisons the troubling cargo of memory, "Joan Didion" jettisons the cargo of superficial approaches to the story and Didion jettisons the cargo of excess verbiage. She retains only the words that epitomize emotional states and qualities of experience, not elaborated descriptions of those states and qualities, and the terse sarcasms that pronounce her judgment in the shortest possible fashion. The quickness of her verbal step shows her distaste for the moral muck. These few summary phrases she sets off as significant units ("drop fuel" and the parallel phrases quoted above) and repeats in meditative litanies. Her sense of the preciousness of Inez's long love for Jack Lovett, for instance, is conveyed in the sequence,

> to keep the idea of it quick.
> Quick, alive.
> Something to think about late at night.
> Something private.
> She always looked for him. (p. 92)

The reader's sense of such a sequence encompasses not only its realization of Inez's emotion but its evidence of the narrator's involvement. The selection of the few emphasized phrases conveys a correspondence of feeling which goes far to explain the powerful emotional hold of the story on "Joan Didion," evidenced by her "examining this picture for some years now" to understand Inez's motivation, including Inez's motivation for first concealing and then revealing her memories to the writer "Joan Didion" (p. 215).

We may conjecture that the answer to that puzzle, the puzzle of why Inez finally shares her memories after long concealment, lies in her final achievement of an autonomous personal space. Released from the confusions and trivialization imposed on her by others, notably by both her natal family and her husband, she can at last achieve emotional balance and pursue work that she herself finds important. Only the sense of security gained by achieving that space allows her to communicate freely with "the author." "Didion," too, needs to find such a space, and does find it vicariously in her relationship to Inez—thus becoming enabled to write her novel. "Didion's" relation to Inez, then, becomes a kind of daughter-to-mother relation, a version of the relation that had first drawn her into the story. Inez, through her suffering and her eventual achievement, gives birth to and nurtures the eventual achievement of "the author."

Joan Didion represents a very different achievement in using strategies of reticence than the achievement we see in Austen, Porter, or Cather. Her strategy is more directly aggressive than theirs, employing sarcastic barbs to undermine the dishonesty and specious values that are her target. Conversational sarcasm, too, is often, of course, conveyed in brief phrases and monosyllables. Didion's interrupted style lends itself to our "hearing" a voice of sarcastic stringency, with anger and grief seething in the interstices.[20] At the same time, sarcasm does not attack its object directly, but obliquely. It is another means of saying without saying, of speaking—virulently—by indirection or by not speaking. Didion's acerbic voice is a radical transformation of the traditional female reticence we see brought to fullness in Austen. It is also a continuation of that female strategy.

Afterword

Reticence, she thought, had an important place in artistic creation.

———— JAMES WOODRESS, *Willa Cather: A Literary Life* ————

John Dewey writes, in *Art As Experience,* that "possibilities that are unrealized and that might be realized are when they are put in contrast with actual conditions, the most penetrating 'criticism' of the latter that can be made."[1] It is in Dewey's sense of presenting unrealized possibilities, alongside past and present injustices and discouragements, that the four writers considered here can be said to have produced fiction of social criticism. The persuasive aspects of their work—and these, as I have argued, are both central and powerful—are embedded in nondiscursive "languages" of situation and dramatic interaction, in curtailed and indirect narrative prose, and in the interstices between such elements, where the reader's own persuasions are formed. All of these rhetorical strategies are built on reticence—though, to be sure, reticence does not mean the same thing for all of them. Austen, Cather, Porter, and Didion, all four, employ such rhetorical strategies persistently, I would even say primarily, in persuasive support of their concern with gender issues. Through indirect and elliptical styles, they lead or challenge readers to see the complex situations of women more clearly.

I have not argued, and I do not argue, that women writers uniformly, as a category if you will, are characterized by a reticent "feminine" style. Pluralism, diversity, is as true a perception and as central a value for me when considering women writers as it is when considering our richly plural, diverse world as a whole. I do not accept an essentialist view. At the same time, I have not argued, and I do not argue, that the writers I have discussed here are unique or even unusual among women writers, except insofar as Austen is unique in having been the first to bring a rhetorical technique based on discreet silence to full and definitive realization in the genre of the novel. On the contrary, far from being unique as a group, I believe that these four provide particularly interesting examples of a stylistic quality observable in many women writers.

Other writers might well be chosen for analysis in relation to a stylistic discipline of reticence or withholding. I hope that others will be fully studied in this respect. Virginia Woolf, obviously; the voids, compressions, and incomplete statements in her novels invite careful extended study. Looking back only a little further one encounters the stark grimness of Edith Wharton's *Ethan Frome,* in which the forces that drive a woman toward death and the forces that hold a woman in a bleak life are together glimpsed as an unspeakable darkness lying beyond the spare narrative of discouragement and emotional penury. One thinks of Tillie Olsen's "Tell Me a Riddle," of all the indignation spoken in the few words of the old woman her husband calls "Mrs. Word Miser" and all the heroism enacted in her long, quiet maintenance of youthful ideals. Olsen, too, is an artist whose compressed surfaces open to us vastly more than they say. Or, in our own time, there is that succession of odd and unsettling novels by Anne Tyler, where great mysteries of motivation yawn beneath the small gestures of an eccentric sort of dailiness.

It is Muriel Spark, however, whose work seems to me most conspicuously and most teasingly to invite the kind of study I have pursued here. In mentioning Spark, of course, I turn the trans-Atlantic sequence of this study back toward its beginning. Indeed, Muriel Spark is often compared to Jane Austen in that her fiction displays a "rather dry, sparsely furnished, though elegant and mannered surface" reminiscent of Austen's.[2] Though Spark's growing canon is far more sizable than Austen's, she shows a similar reliance on terse, barbed wittiness and an even heavier reliance on silence. Unlike Austen's, Spark's novels are often so exceedingly slight that they may seem to be mere freaks and capers. But one always has the sense that more is lurking around all the corners—and that that "more" is of an enormous seriousness. In part, the disproportion between slightness of surface and vastness of significance is sacramental, a function of Spark's religious vision. At times, as in *The Hothouse by the East River,* it is a disproportion that verges on perversity. One may feel like protesting, just how much fictional weight can the fall of a shadow sustain? But in a book like *The Driver's Seat* we encounter, I think, a very model of the silent invocation of an overwhelming and—in its implications—a persuasive presence.

Spark's *The Driver's Seat* is a genuinely, even radically, odd book, its oddity lying not only in the bizarre speech and actions of the main character, Lise, but also in the absence of any explanation of them. Lise's strange behavior simply flares out of empty mystery. From the beginning, the reader is invited, incited, to speculate. Why, in the opening chapter, is Lise so offended by a salesclerk's implication that she might have use for a stain-proof dress? She goes on looking for "the necessary dress"[3]—necessary for what? Why does she choose a dress of such clashing colors? Why does she laugh at the salesclerk's suggestion that she might ever need to wash the dress? An answer of sorts is provided in the third chapter, when Lise's violent death is foretold. But we are left wondering how all the odd details relate to her death and why her behavior is so bizarre.

At the end, many of these uncertainties are resolved: she has been flouting convention, proclaiming her imbalance, seeking out destruction. Indeed, she has been seeking it in precisely the way she gets it—as victim of a sex crime and stabbing. She provides her killer the knife and tells him what to do. But that knowledge only opens deeper questions as to why a woman would need to seek out her own death, and in a way that means managing her own enactment of female victimization. On these questions, on the nature of Lise's life before she begins to arrange for death and on the societal context that so disorders her, the book is silent. By

her silence, Spark prompts us to entertain the most radical questions as to women's role in modern society and the factors that
drive women to self-hate.

To say all this is very much to say that Muriel Spark uses silence to much the same effect as Joan Didion, who also raises the
specter of madness growing out of societal constructions of gender. But Austen, Cather, and Porter as well, in less obviously tormented ways, have used silence and cryptic utterance to raise
questions about social construction of gender, and they, too,
though less harshly than Spark or Didion, raise the specter of
resultant emotional breakdown. Austen does so with Marianne,
of *Sense and Sensibility;* Cather with Marian Forrester of *A Lost
Lady;* and Porter with both Amy and Cousin Eva in "Old Mortality." They see very clearly, and persuade their readers to see as
well, that women pay a heavy psychological price for the maintenance of a masculinist social system. The fact that they do not
spell out just how heavy a price it is may be attributable to a
variety of reasons, but I believe we can see some of them fairly
clearly.

Austen is reticent about fully stating her vision out of a dis-
creetness ingrained by long years of alert social experience. She is
reticent, too, because of a fictional theory—that the intelligent
reader's active response can be more forcefully evoked by understatement and ellipsis than by full "telling." Cather uses the understated, indirect, and elliptical style because of her awareness,
from the example of Austen as well as Henry James, of the effects
such a style can achieve and, therefore, from her informed commitment to indirection in narrative. But she is reticent, too, because of the pressure of her own need to conceal and protect.
Porter—who, we know, both understood and admired Cather
precisely because of her novelistic restraint—employs the reticent
style for much the same sort of purposes as did Austen and
Cather, but also, like Austen, as a measure of character. But Porter adds, particularly in "Pale Horse, Pale Rider," a dimension of
bitterness and denunciation that one scarcely feels in the work of
her older contemporary or of her more distant predecessor. It is
this dimension that links her, more directly than Cather or Aus-

ten, to Didion, a woman who writes out of the anguished sense of what it means to inhabit a superficially "liberated" world in which the old misogynistic patterns continue to repeat themselves. Through the silences of her bitterly angry style, Didion expresses a refusal to hold verbal commerce with such a world, even as she communicates her anger to readers caught up in that loud silence.

NOTES

BIBLIOGRAPHY

INDEX

Notes

──────────────── PREFACE ────────────────

1 • Carol P. Christ, *Diving Deep and Surfacing: Women Writers on Spiritual Quest* (Boston: Beacon Press, 1980).

2 • "Talking with Adrienne Rich," *The Ohio Review* 13 (1971):31.

3 • Willa Cather, "The Demands of Art," Lincoln *Courier,* November 23, 1895; reprinted in *The Kingdom of Art: Willa Cather's First Principles and Critical Statements, 1893–1896,* ed. Bernice Slote (Lincoln: University of Nebraska Press, 1966), p. 409.

4 • Mary Jacobus, *Reading Woman: Essays in Feminist Criticism* (New York: Columbia University Press, 1986), p. 108.

──────────────── CHAPTER ONE ────────────────

1 • It is appropriate that the reader's attention be directed first, before all other references, to Booth's magisterial *The Rhetoric of Fiction* (Chicago and London: University of Chicago Press, 1961).

2 • John Auchard, *Silence in Henry James: The Heritage of Symbolism and Decadence* (University Park and London: Pennsylvania State University Press, 1986), p. 3.

3 • Frank Kermode, *The Genesis of Secrecy: On the Interpretation of Narrative* (Cambridge: Harvard University Press, 1979), p. 15.

4 • John Cage, *Silence: Lectures and Writing* (Middletown, Ct.: Wesleyan University Press, 1961); Max Picard, *The World of Silence,* trans. S. Godman (1948; Chicago: H. Regnery, 1952); Susan Sontag, *Styles of Radical Will* (New York: Farrar, Straus and Giroux, 1969); Erich Heller, *The Artist's Journey into the Interior* (New York: Vintage Books, 1968).

5 • Booth, *The Rhetoric of Fiction,* pp. v, 300, 304.

6 • For example, Philip C. McGuire's painstaking *Speechless Dialect: Shakespeare's Open Silences* (Berkeley: University of California Press, 1985) examines specific moments in several of Shakespeare's plays at which the printed text allows the reader or director or actor such great latitude of interpretation that the result is not simply a nuanced version of a text but a distinct collaborative recreation, perhaps at great variance from what custom has dictated or led us to assume as "the" meaning. The idea

of silence as an invitation to interactive reading will be taken up here in relation, especially, to the works of Jane Austen and Joan Didion.

7 • Cage himself makes the analogy between musical "silences" (nonnotated points in the musical text "opening the doors of the music to the sounds that happen to be in the environment") and the "empty" spaces of modern sculpture and architecture. *Silence,* pp. 7–8.

8 • Picard, *The World of Silence,* p. 17. Picard goes on to posit, with great eloquence, the absoluteness of silence even amid our noisy modernity: "Still like some old, forgotten animal from the beginning of time, silence towers above all the puny world of noise; but as a living animal, not an extinct species, it lies in wait, and we can see its broad back sinking ever deeper among the briers and bushes of the world of noise" (p. 22).

9 • George Steiner, *Language and Silence: Essays on Language, Literature, and the Inhuman* (New York: Atheneum, 1967), p. 39. The quotation from Kafka used as an epigraph to this chapter is cited by Steiner.

10 • Steiner, *Language and Silence,* p. 49. I remember hearing someone say, after a performance of "Threnody for the Victims of Hiroshima," by Christof Penderecki, that the reason he did not applaud was not dislike of its experimental style but a sense that the only way to receive such music as the "Threnody" is in silence. A silent reception, presumably, would express the hearer's grief for the victims and perhaps a moral judgment on the atrocity itself.

11 • Ihab Hassan, *The Dismemberment of Orpheus: Toward a Postmodern Literature,* 2d ed. (Madison: University of Wisconsin Press, 1982), pp. 23, 83, 267–68.

12 • Ibid., pp. 13–14.

13 • J. A. Ward, *American Silences: The Realism of James Agee, Walker Evans, and Edward Hopper* (Baton Rouge: Louisiana State University Press, 1985), pp. 65–66.

14 • Ward's view of Hemingway is as a modernist. Hassan explicitly sees Hemingway as a forerunner of postmodernism and hears in his silence only intimations of nonbeing.

15 • Hassan, *The Dismemberment of Orpheus,* pp. xvii, 3.

16 • Mary Jacobus, *Reading Woman: Essays in Feminist Criticism* (New York: Columbia University Press, 1986), p. 31.

17 • Susan M. Gilbert and Susan Gubar, *The War of the Words,* vol. 1 of *No Man's Land: The Place of the Woman Writer in the Twentieth Century* (New Haven and London: Yale University Press, 1988), p. xiv.

18 • Susan Sontag, "The Aesthetics of Silence," in *Styles of Radical Will,* p. 12.

19 • Toril Moi summarizes Gilbert and Gubar's definition of the supposed ideal woman, in *Madwoman in the Attic,* as someone "passive, docile, and above all *selfless.*" That Moi takes this triad of qualities to include, by

implication, silence is clear from her contrasting definition of the "monster woman" as someone who "*has* a story to tell." Toril Moi, *Sexual / Textual Politics: Feminist Literary Theory* (London and New York: Methuen, 1985), p. 58.

20 • John Kucich argues, in *Repression in Victorian Fiction: Charlotte Bronte, George Eliot, and Charles Dickens* (Berkeley: University of California Press, 1987), that Victorian repression and its associated qualities are empowering. A kind of repression "actually heightens interior life libidinally by disrupting it" (p. 23). My own argument differs in that I see repression and allied qualities as constituting a reality which women such as Jane Austen and (in recently republished works) Louisa Mae Alcott were able to use for subversive ends. Both views, however, reinterpret the phenomenon of the silencing of women as something other than an unmitigated ill, because women have been able to react adaptively and to make creative use of an unjust social situation.

21 • Mary Poovey, *The Proper Lady and the Woman Writer: Ideology as Style in the Works of Mary Wollstonecraft, Mary Shelley, and Jane Austen* (Chicago and London: University of Chicago Press, 1984), p. 43.

22 • Ruth Borker, summarizing Roger Abrahams's work on women's speech in Black American communities, notes that it is "expected to be more restrained, less loud, less public, and less abandoned than men's." Borker, "Anthropology: Social and Cultural Perspective," in *Women and Language in Literature and Society,* ed. Sally McConnell-Ginet, Ruth Borker, and Nelly Furman (New York: Praeger Publishers, 1980), p. 38. The phenomenon is more general, however, than the specific culture in which it is demonstrated in this article.

23 • For example, see Don H. Zimmerman and Candace West, "Sex Roles, Interruptions, and Silences in Conversation," in *Language and Sex: Difference and Dominance,* ed. Barrie Thorne and Nancy Henley (Rowley, Mass.: Newbury House, 1975), pp. 105–29.

24 • Gilbert and Gubar, *The War of the Words,* p. xii.

25 • Gilbert and Gubar, *The War of the Words,* p. 6.

26 • Bonnie Costello associates female silence, as well, with the stereotype of nonrationality: being "supposedly intuitive," woman "naturally has trouble being articulate." Costello, "The 'Feminine' Language of Marianne Moore," in *Women and Language in Literature and Society,* p. 229.

27 • Mary Daly, *Beyond God the Father* (Boston: Beacon Press, 1974), p. 47.

28 • Carol P. Christ, *Diving Deep and Surfacing: Women Writers on Spiritual Quest* (Boston: Beacon Press, 1980), pp. 16–17.

29 • Auchard, *Silence in Henry James,* p. 9.

30 • Alicia Suskin Ostriker, *Stealing the Language: The Emergence of Women's Poetry in America* (Boston: Beacon Press, 1986), pp. 53–54.

197

31 • Adrienne Rich, "When We Dead Awaken: Writing as Re-Vision," in *On Lies, Secrets, and Silence: Selected Prose, 1966–1978* (New York: W. W. Norton, 1979), p. 39.

32 • Jane Marcus, "Still Practice, A / Wrested Alphabet: Toward a Feminist Aesthetic," in *Feminist Issues in Literary Scholarship,* ed. Shari Benstock (Bloomington and Indianapolis: Indiana University Press, 1987), p. 81.

33 • Paula Treicher points out that the price the speaker will pay for her "impertinence" toward the end of Charlotte Perkins Gilman's "The Yellow Wallpaper" is surely a sentence of absolute incarceration, a severer version of the imposed "treatment" that has made her ills so much worse. Paula A. Treicher, "Escaping the Sentence: Diagnosis and Discourse in 'The Yellow Wallpaper,'" in *Feminist Issues in Literary Scholarship,* pp. 74–75.

34 • Mary Jacobus, *Reading Woman,* p. 29. I would add my voice to those who express their misgivings that French feminist theory, for all the excitement it has stimulated, returns to the old, old prison of making assumptions about a supposed essential nature of the female. Essentialism is a consistent feature (I would say, a consistent shortcoming) of French feminism, in contrast to Anglo-American pluralistic theory.

35 • King-Kok Cheung, "'Don't Tell': Imposed Silences in *The Color Purple* and *The Woman Warrior," PMLA* 103 (1988): 163.

36 • Ostriker, *Stealing the Language,* p. 6.

37 • Joanna Russ, *How to Suppress Women's Writing* (Austin: University of Texas Press, 1983).

38 • Jacobus, *Reading Woman,* p. 263.

39 • Cheris Kramarae cites an essay by Thomas Higginson, called "Women and the Alphabet: Ought Women to Learn It?" written in 1881 but published in his book *Woman and the Alphabet* in 1900, in which Higginson observed that it was "indelicate" for a woman to "speak in public" (Kramarae, "Proprietors of Language," in *Women and Language in Literature and Society,* p. 60). Frank Lentricchia comments that in the past (an unspecified past) "genteel daughters could be well-read, but they were taught lady-like reticence in matters of publication" (Lentricchia, "Patriarchy Against Itself—The Young Manhood of Wallace Stevens," *Critical Inquiry* 13 [1987]:783). The generally accepted view of the secret or repressed woman writer, denied audience as well as preparation for her art, has recently been challenged, however, by Margaret J. M. Ezell in two articles presenting historical demonstration of the social voice of literary women through the circulation of manuscripts in the seventeenth century. See Ezell, "'To Be Your Daughter in Your Pen': The Social Functions of Literature in the Writings of Lady Elizabeth Brackley and Lady Jane Cavendish," *The Huntington Library Quarterly* 51 (1988): 281–

96; and "The Myth of Judith Shakespeare: Creating the Canon of Women's Literature," *New Literary History* 21 (1990).

40 • An illustrative example is described by Marcia J. Citron in her article "Felix Mendelssohn's Influence on Fanny Mendelssohn Hensel as a Professional Composer," *Current Musicology* 37 / 38 (1984): 9–17. Similarly, Citron notes that the "scarcity of professional singing instruction for women" in the nineteenth century "reflected society's views regarding the impropriety of women's performing in a public forum" (Citron, "Women and the Lied, 1775–1850," in *Women Making Music,* ed. Jane Bowers and Judith Tick [Urbana: University of Illinois Press, 1986], p. 227). Josephine Donovan points out that the genres in which women first began to write in England, in any numbers—personal letters and the memoir or autobiography—were not forms overtly intended for publication (Donovan, "The Silence Is Broken," in *Women and Language in Literature and Society,* pp. 210–12).

41 • Juliet Mitchell, *Psychoanalysis and Feminism* (New York: Random House, 1974), pp. 301–3. Toril Moi also points out that Freud's writings are less univocal than some feminists (she speaks particularly of Kate Millett) have made them out to be and that other feminist critics (among whom she cites Mitchell) have read Freud differently and have appropriated Freudian theory (Moi, *Sexual / Textual Politics,* pp. 27–29). At the very least, however, appropriation of Freud for feminism requires enormous revisionist work from what has been generally accepted and established, and therefore generally influential—in what seems clearly a deleterious way, having the widespread effect of fortifying misogyny with abstruse theory. Mitchell concedes that "there seems overwhelming justification for the charge that the many different psychotherapeutic practices, including those that by formal definition are within psychoanalysis, have done much to re-adapt discontented women to a conservative feminine status quo, to an interiorized psychology and to a contentment with serving and servicing men and children" (p. 299).

42 • Helene Vivienne Wenzel, "Introduction to Luce Irigaray's 'And the One Doesn't Stir without the Other,'" *Signs* 7 (1981): 57.

43 • Jacobus, *Reading Woman,* p. 14.

44 • All of the examples in this text paragraph are quoted by Gilbert and Gubar in *The War of the Words,* pp. 152, 263.

45 • Christ, *Diving Deep,* p. 4.

46 • Tillie Olsen, *Silences* (New York: Dell, 1965), p. 252; Patrick Moore, "Symbol, Mask, and Meter in the Poetry of Louise Bogan," in *Gender and Literary Voice,* ed. Janet Todd (New York: Holmes and Meier, 1980), p. 68; Ostriker, *Stealing the Language,* pp. 3–4.

47 • Jacobus, *Reading Woman,* pp. 38–39. Sandra M. Gilbert and Susan Gubar

ask, "Does the Queen try to sound like the King," or does she "'talk back' to him in her own vocabulary?" (Gilbert and Gubar, *The Madwoman in the Attic: The Woman Writer and the Nineteenth-Century Literary Imagination* [New Haven: Yale University Press, 1979], p. 46).

48 • Janet Perez, "Functions of the Rhetoric of Silence in Contemporary Spanish Literature," *South Central Review* 1 (1984): 129.

49 • Julia Kristeva includes silence among the means by which the mother "unsettles" the paternal symbolic language. See "Place Names" in *Desire in Language: A Semiotic Approach to Literature and Art,* ed. Leon S. Roudiez (New York: Columbia University Press, 1980), 238–42.

50 • Janet Todd gives implicit acknowledgment of the prevalence of verbal restraint among women writers in calling Fanny Burney a "reticent and conventional author." Todd, Introduction to *Gender and Literary Voice,* ed. Janet Todd (New York: Holmes and Meier, 1980), p. 2.

51 • John Kucich's statement that we in the twentieth century have little need to "resort to negative emotional gestures like silence, self-conflict, or renunciation" is, in my view, problematic. The evidence seems to indicate that a great many people, at any rate a great many women, have frequent recourse to silence and self-conflict at least, if not renunciation. Kucich, *Repression in Victorian Fiction,* p. 287.

52 • Susan Jaret McKinstry, "The Speaking Silence of Ann Beattie's Voice," *Studies in Short Fiction* 24 (1987): 117. The "linguistic and temporal elision" of Beattie's stories, McKinstry says, "makes absence present."

53 • Poovey, *The Proper Lady and the Woman Writer,* p. 47.

54 • Bernice Slote, "Willa Cather: The Secret Web," in *Five Essays on Willa Cather,* ed. John J. Murphy (North Andover, Mass.: Merrimack College, 1974), p. 9.

55 • Booth uses Porter as a benchmark example of an author who enlists reader sympathy by employing a limited, isolated narrator. In "Pale Horse, Pale Rider," he says, by confining the point of view "strictly to what Miranda can see and know and feel," Porter creates an "almost unbearably poignant sense of . . . [her] helplessness in a chaotic, friendless world" (*The Rhetoric of Fiction,* pp. 274–75).

───────────── CHAPTER TWO ─────────────

1 • All quotations follow the Chapman edition, 1982 reprint; citations in parentheses give volume and page numbers: *The Novels of Jane Austen,* ed. R. W. Chapman, 5 vols. (Oxford and New York: Oxford University Press, 1923; rpt. 1982).

2 • Mary Mahar Annable, in the abstract of her dissertation "'Not . . . for Such Dull Elves': Rhetorical Strategies for Reader Involvement in *Pride*

and Prejudice and *Mansfield Park," Dissertations Abstracts International* 44 (1984): 2769A-2770A, discusses the "dynamic interaction between text and reader" that is "sparked and given space within the text by what the text does not say—its structural indeterminacy." Annable enumerates several "strategies for reader involvement" but does not mention dialogue.

3 • The "dull elves" phrase is from Austen's letter to Cassandra dated January 29, 1813; see *Jane Austen's Letters to Her Sister Cassandra and Others,* 2d ed., ed. R. W. Chapman (London and New York: Oxford University Press, 1952), p. 298. The phrase occurs in a parodic misquotation of some "jingling lines" (as Mary Lascelles terms them) of Walter Scott in *Marmion* (Mary Lascelles, *Jane Austen and Her Art* [London: Oxford University Press, 1939; rpt. 1966], p. 125).

4 • Tony Tanner, *Jane Austen* (Cambridge: Harvard University Press, 1986), p. 236.

5 • Norman Page identifies the use of excessive speech as a moral index in *The Language of Jane Austen:* "readiness of speech is associated with the vicious, and taciturnity with the virtuous" ([Oxford: Basil Blackwell, 1972], p. 38). Stuart M. Tave, in *Some Words of Jane Austen,* discusses the effects of Willoughby's "say[ing] what he thinks on every occasion": he "hastily forms and gives opinions" and as a result his opinions do not reflect reality; he lives "an imaginary life" ([Chicago and London: University of Chicago Press, 1973], p. 162).

6 • Tanner, *Jane Austen,* p. 201.

7 • David Monaghan, *Jane Austen: Structure and Social Vision* (New York: Barnes and Noble, 1980), p. 49.

8 • I do not mean to imply that, except for *Mansfield Park,* her narrative point of view is unvaried. Varying in the degree to which the narrative voice is identified with one character, her narrative perspective varies also in reliability, from a consistent reliableness in *Sense and Sensibility* toward greater fluidity and fleeting ironic coloration in *Emma.* As Richard F. Patterson argues in "Truth, Certitude, and Stability in Jane Austen's Fiction," there is no "authoritative narrative voice" in Austen's fiction, but "narrative self-consciousness is combined with a deliberate omission" of varying parts of "the 'truth'" (*Philological Quarterly* 60 [1981]: 466–67). For a discussion of how the narrative strategy of *Northanger Abbey* differs from that of the other works, see Howard S. Babb, *Jane Austen's Novels: The Fabric of Dialogue* (New York: Archon Books, 1967), pp. 87–88 ff.

9 • Babb, *Jane Austen's Novels,* p. 144.

10 • Mary Poovey explores the question at length and to thoroughly enlightening effect in *The Proper Lady and the Woman Writer: Ideology As Style in the Works of Mary Wollstonecraft, Mary Shelley, and Jane Austen* (Chicago and London: University of Chicago Press, 1984).

11 • Wayne C. Anderson makes the same point, that silences invite reader participation, with respect to Hardy's fiction in his essay "The Rhetoric of Silence in Hardy's Fiction," *Studies in the Novel* 17 (1985): 53–68. "What makes these silences significant is their rhetorical impact on us as readers. A rhetoric of silence conditions our response to character, landscape, and plot development in Hardy's fiction, eliciting—demanding— our participation in the act of narrative. . . . What the rhetoric of silence requires is an attentiveness from us as readers" (p. 59). Anderson concedes, however, that for the most part Hardy gives "excessive commentary."

12 • Babb, *Jane Austen's Novels,* p. 128.

13 • Frank Kermode, *The Art of Telling: Essays on Fiction* (Cambridge: Harvard University Press, 1983), p. 128. Kermode's reference, earlier in his study, to "half-occulted senses in the text" that are "deep shadows in the story" might well have been (though it was not) written of *Emma,* with the "half-occulted" "shadow" that is Jane Fairfax's story, or of other aspects of Austen's work. In *The Genesis of Secrecy* Kermode refers to the "varying focus, fractured surfaces, over-determinations" and "displacements" that have "constituted a perpetual invitation to all inquirers after latent sense" not only in the postmodern rediscovery of the oracular" but "for centuries" (*The Genesis of Secrecy: On the Interpretation of Narrative* [Cambridge: Harvard University Press, 1979], p. 15).

14 • Susan Morgan, "Why There's No Sex in Jane Austen's Fiction," *Studies in the Novel* 19 (1987): 346–56.

15 • Mary Poovey's phrase in *The Proper Lady,* p. xi.

16 • David Monaghan, in *Jane Austen: Structure and Social Vision,* sees Austen's "principal subject" in all her novels as the "drama of women." This drama, as Monaghan summarizes it, consists in women's sense of themselves as active subjects, their tension with a society that regards them as objects, and their efforts to achieve self-direction. See especially pp. 25–26.

17 • The image of reining ("free rein") comes from A. Walton Litz, citing Frank O'Connor's interpretation in *The Mirror in the Roadway* (p. 25), to the effect that Jane Austen was "a woman afraid of the violence of her own emotions, who rode the nightmare and sometimes rode it on too tight a rein." Litz suggests that the "uncertainty" between the two sisters in *Sense and Sensibility* "provides strong support" for such a view (Litz, *Jane Austen: A Study of Her Artistic Development* [New York: Oxford University Press, 1965], p. 79).

18 • Rachel M. Brownstein, *Becoming a Heroine: Reading about Women in Novels* (New York: Viking Press, 1982), pp. 82–83.

19 • Tave, *Some Words,* p. 109.

20 • Poovey, *The Proper Lady,* p. 47.

21 • What I have called shadow elements Mary Poovey refers to as "substitutions" or "resolutions blocked at one level of a narrative and then displaced by other subjects" (*The Proper Lady*, p. 242).

22 • In Poovey's terms, women in *Persuasion* are seen as being "imprisoned," "confined," "'surrounded and shut in,'" and "legally crippled, sometimes physically crippled, by the actions of men" (p. 233).

23 • Tave, *Some Words*, p. 256.

24 • Poovey, *The Proper Lady*, p. 232.

25 • Brownstein, *Becoming a Heroine*, p. 98.

26 • Poovey, *The Proper Lady*, p. 201.

27 • Lascelles, *Jane Austen and Her Art*, p. 126. Lascelles's language implies a sense that Austen's fictional practice was governed by a kind of delicacy toward her creatures. More directly, Lascelles attributes the occlusion of the love scene to an "instinctive" reticence combined with not simply a lack of personal experience and a "scrupulous fidelity to the evidence at her disposal" but to Austen's awareness that reviewers would assume, if she included scenes of passion, that there *was* experience (pp. 218, 126–27).

28 • Cf. Page, *The Language of Jane Austen*, p. 137: Austen "tends to renounce dialogue when events seem about to precipitate a scene with considerable emotional potential."

29 • See Babb, *Jane Austen's Novels*, pp. 9–15.

30 • Kermode, *The Genesis of Secrecy*, p. 15. Tony Tanner, developing a similar line of thought, speaks of Austen's clarity in style of discourse as being a Heideggerian "clearing" which also "conceals" (Tanner, *Jane Austen*, pp. 66–67).

31 • Alice Chandler, "'A Pair of Fine Eyes': Jane Austen's Treatment of Sex," *Studies in the Novel* 7 (1975): 100. Chandler's concise summary of the general view of Austen's romantic scenes does not indicate, however, her own agreement. Elsewhere in the article Chandler charges that Austen has "wrongly been seen as suspicious of all feeling" (p. 88) and goes on to argue the richness and subtlety of sexual emotion conveyed in the novels.

32 • Chandler, "'A Pair of Fine Eyes,'" p. 100. Another point at which speechlessness conveys intense emotion is the moment when Wentworth lifts the "troublesome little boy" off Anne's neck in *Persuasion*. Her surging emotions "make her perfectly speechless" (Tave, *Some Words*, p. 275).

33 • Lloyd W. Brown, *Bits of Ivory: Narrative Techniques in Jane Austen's Fiction* (Baton Rouge: Louisiana State University Press, 1973), p. 197.

34 • Babb, *Jane Austen's Novels*, p. 198. Tave agrees that in the proposal scene in *Emma* Austen "is not shirking the emotion, but telling us all we want to know at this point with the fullest warmth and pleasure" (*Some Words*, p. 254).

35 • Babb, *Jane Austen's Novels,* pp. 8–15, makes the same point.

36 • James Thompson, "Jane Austen and the Limits of Language," *Journal of English and Germanic Philology* 85 (1986): 510, 526. My own article on which the present chapter draws was published in 1982, but the present treatment has been considerably enriched by reading Thompson's thorough discussion of the subject: Janis P. Stout, "Jane Austen's Proposal Scenes and the Limitation of Language," *Studies in the Novel* 14 (1982): 316–26.

37 • Thompson, "Jane Austen and the Limits of Language," p. 513.

38 • Chandler, " 'A Pair of Fine Eyes,' " p. 100.

39 • Morgan terms the basis of the simpler explanation a "shaky biographical principle" ("Why There's No Sex in Jane Austen's Fiction," p. 350).

40 • "Jane Austen," in *The Essays of Virginia Woolf,* vol. 2, *1912–1918,* ed. Andrew McNeillie (New York and London: Harcourt Brace Jovanovich, 1987), p. 11; Willa Cather, "The Demands of Art," Lincoln *Courier,* November 23, 1895; reprinted *The Kingdom of Art: Willa Cather's First Principles and Critical Statements, 1893–1896,* ed. Bernice Slote (Lincoln: University of Nebraska Press, 1966), p. 409; Katherine Anne Porter, "Virginia Woolf," in *The Collected Essays and Occasional Writings of Katherine Anne Porter* (New York: Delacorte Press, 1970), p. 69.

<hr />

CHAPTER THREE

1 • Katherine Anne Porter, "Afterword" to Willa Cather, *The Troll Garden,* (New York: NAL 1961; rpt. as "Critical Reflections on Willa Cather," in *Critical Essays on Willa Cather,* ed. John J. Murphy (Boston: G. K. Hall, 1984), p. 36. All references to Cather's works are to *The Novels and Stories of Willa Cather,* "Autograph Edition," in 13 vols. (Boston: Houghton Mifflin, 1937–40). Parenthetical references are to volume and page of this edition, with simple abbreviations of the titles added when the references might be unclear.

2 • For example: Louise Bogan stressed Cather's allegiance to "processes of simplification" along with her sure rooting in American materials and sensibility in an overview, "American-Classic," published in the *New Yorker,* August 8, 1931. Edward A. and Lillian D. Bloom, in *Willa Cather's Gift of Sympathy* (Carbondale: Southern Illinois University Press, 1962) attribute her spareness to an aesthetic distaste for the "relentless inclusiveness" of naturalism (rpt. *Critical Essays,* ed. Murphy, p. 45). David Stouck, in "Willa Cather and the Impressionist Novel," links her "classical forms and a reserved, often laconic style" to the selectivity of Flaubert and the aesthetic principles of Prosper Mérimée (*Critical Essays,* ed. Murphy, pp. 49–52). Susan J. Rosowski, in *The Voyage Perilous: Willa*

Cather's Romanticism (Lincoln: University of Nebraska Press, 1986), also treats Cather's selectivity as essentially a matter of aesthetic principle, a deliberate bareness that allows her to focus on essentials.

3 • Stouck, "Willa Cather and the Impressionist Novel," p. 49.

4 • For example: Leon Edel launched the identification of Cather's evasively economic style with her own avoidance of anxieties in 1959 in *Stuff of Sleep and Dreams: Experiments in Literary Psychology* (New York: Harper and Row, 1982), accounting for the absence of explanation of Professor St. Peter's depression, in *The Professor's House,* by reference to Cather's suppression of her own emotions relating to Isabelle McClung's marriage (rpt., *Critical Essays,* ed. Murphy, p. 214). Blanche H. Gelfant's essay "The Forgotten Reaping-Hook: Sex in *My Ántonia*" (first published in *American Literature* 43 [1971]:60–82) attributes the selective narrative method of the novel to a "reluctance to portray sexuality" (*Critical Essays,* ed. Murphy, p. 147). Following a similar argument, Kathleen L. Nichols, in "The Celibate Male in *A Lost Lady:* The Unreliable Center of Consciousness" (first published in *Regionalism and the Female Imagination* 4 [1978]: 13–23), sees the narrator's refusal to "name," or specify, things as a strategy of avoidance (rpt., *Critical Essays,* ed. Murphy, p. 189). On the basis of an intensive study of much seldom-read apprentice work, Sharon O'Brien observes that the early stories reveal "sexual and creative conflicts" which are suppressed in the mature work (O'Brien, *Willa Cather: The Emerging Voice* [Oxford: Oxford University Press, 1987], p. 196).

5 • James Woodress reports that she "had no interest" in such matters as "woman's suffrage" (*Willa Cather: A Literary Life* [Lincoln: University of Nebraska Press, 1987], p. 236).

6 • It is for this reason that she can be read in such conservative ways by people who ignore the deep duplicity of her work. For instance, Susan J. Rosowski applauds, as if it were a victory, Jim Burden's coming to view Ántonia as a "mythic earth mother." In Rosowski's thesis-bound view, his recognition of her as earth mother is one of Cather's "moments of transcendence which ... affirm that universal truths exist and that through the imagination we can experience them" (Rosowski, *The Voyage Perilous,* p. 207).

7 • Homosexual authors are forced to "find a language of reticence and evasion, obliqueness and indirection" (Jeffrey Meyers, *Homosexuality and Literature, 1890–1930* [Montreal: McGill–Queens College University Press, 1977], p. 1). That Cather was keenly aware of the negative impact of existing gender roles is evident from a letter written in 1931 in which she said that it was a "distinct disadvantage" to be a woman writer and that Virginia Woolf (presumably in *A Room of One's Own*) had stated the disadvantages very well (Woodress, *Willa Cather: A Literary Life,* p. 423).

8 • Rosowski, *The Voyage Perilous,* p. 237: In *Sapphira and the Slave Girl,*

"dark revelations are as central as sunny ones were to Cather's early novels."

9 • Gelfant ("The Forgotten Reaping-Hook," p. 147) finds Jim "a more disingenuous and self-deluded narrator than we supposed" with "myriad confusions" behind his "explicit statements." David Laird discusses Jim Burden's "obsessive need" to "bring fixity and stability to the streaming immediacy of things," a need which is opposed to the "spontaneity, vitality, the determined energy" of Ántonia (Laird, "Willa Cather and the Deceptions of Art," in *Interface: Essays on History, Myth, and Art in American Literature,* ed. Daniel Royot [Montpellier, France: University of Montpellier, 1984], p. 53). I am puzzled by William J. Stuckey's comment, in *"My Ántonia: A Rose for Miss Cather" (Studies in the Novel* 4 [1972]: 479), that Cather "kept on using" Jim Burden "even when it must have been apparent that he was not working." It seems to me that Jim Burden works very well indeed—if "working" means developing a polysemous fiction in which meanings beyond the surface meaning deepen and test each other.

10 • Deborah G. Lambert, "The Defeat of a Hero: Autonomy and Sexuality in *My Ántonia," American Literature* 53 (1982): 676–90; Sharon O'Brien, "'The Thing Not Named': Willa Cather as a Lesbian Writer," *Signs* 9 (1984): 576–99; Gelfant, "The Forgotten Reaping-Hook"; Leon Edel, "A Cave of One's Own," pp. 200–217 in *Critical Essays,* ed. Murphy; rpt. from *Literary Biography* (University of Toronto Press, 1957).

11 • I would question, then, Lambert's view in "The Defeat of a Hero" that an approach such as Gelfant's, which focuses on the limitations of the narrator, "assumes traditional sex roles as normative: Jim's experience is central and Antonia's is the subordinate, supporting role" (p. 684).

12 • Similarly, in Benda's ink drawings, which Cather herself commissioned to illustrate the text, the figures of Lena and of Ántonia (plates 7 and 8), in the two drawings most fully immersed in the Nebraska setting, appear in isolation against empty spaces of white page stretching out in every direction. Jean Schwind sees in the openness of these plates a "recognition of a world" beyond human limits (Schwind, "The Benda Illustrations to *My Ántonia:* Cather's 'Silent' Supplement to Jim Burden's Narrative," *PMLA* 100 [1985]: 51–67).

13 • Donald Sutherland remarks with nice precision, in "Willa Cather: The Classic Voice," that Cather's manner is "simple, or simplified" (in *The Art of Willa Cather,* ed. Bernice Slote and Virginia Faulkner [Lincoln: University of Nebraska Press, 1974], p. 173).

14 • James E. Miller, Jr., in "Willa Cather and the Art of Fiction," discusses Cather's idea of novelistic form by analogy with painting. Her "emphasis on spareness, sparseness" and her selectivity led to her achievement of "what painters call 'composition'" (*The Art of Willa Cather,* pp. 121–48).

15 • Eudora Welty, "The House of Willa Cather," in *The Art of Willa Cather,* p. 5.

16 • James Woodress, "Cather and Her Friends," *Critical Essays,* ed Murphy, p. 82.

17 • Woodress denies, as well, that she was lesbian or, if she was, that her lesbianism was expressed in her writing. Her "sexual preferences," he says, never "influenced her writing." There she is "perfectly androgynous" ("Cather and Her Friends," p. 84). But androgyny is an ideal that can be approached equally well from a heterosexual orientation or a lesbian one. Sexual preference is simply irrelevant to the achievement of an androgynous ideal. It is not irrelevant, however, to Cather's oblique, evasive fictional presence.

18 • Bernice Slote, "Willa Cather: The Secret Web," pp. 1–19 in *Five Essays on Willa Cather,* ed. John J. Murphy (North Andover, Mass.: Merrimack College, 1974), pp. 4–5.

19 • Woodress, *Willa Cather: A Literary Life,* p. 55. Sharon O'Brien, however, argues that "the girl became William not because she thought she was male but because she did not want to be female, and that choice suggests self-contempt as well as self-expression" (*Willa Cather: The Emerging Voice,* p. 111). O'Brien views the four-year adoption of a male persona, together with the masculine ideals of art Cather expressed in her youth, as a profound "alienation" from her gender (see especially pp. 147–60).

20 • Susan Gubar, "Blessings in Disguise: Cross-Dressing as Re-Dressing for Female Modernists," *Massachusetts Review* 22 (1981): 495.

21 • It is open to question whether Cather assumed a male persona to free herself for her interests in what she herself called "slicing toads" and similar boyish activities (preceding interests in the "male" activity of literature) or whether she professed such interests as an appropriate expression of her male persona. For "slicing toads," see O'Brien, *Willa Cather: The Emerging Voice,* p. 89, citing Mildred Bennett, *The World of Willa Cather,* rev. ed. (Lincoln: University of Nebraska Press, 1961), pp. 112–13.

22 • Gubar, "Blessings in Disguise," p. 495.

23 • O'Brien, *Willa Cather: The Emerging Voice,* p. 160. O'Brien notes, however, that Cather's use of pseudonyms, including masculine pseudonyms, during her years in Pittsburgh indicates that "concealment" still "held its charms" (p. 202).

24 • Gubar, "Blessings in Disguise," p. 495.

25 • David Daiches, for instance, includes the tale among "episodes" whose "relation to the novel as a whole is somewhat uncertain" (Daiches, *Willa Cather: A Critical Introduction* [Ithaca, N.Y.: Cornell University Press, 1951], p. 47). Blanche Gelfant astutely points out ways in which the interpolated tale is a "paradigm" for Mr. Shimerda's story and the general

view, expressed in Jim Burden's narrative, that "the real danger to man is woman, that his protection lies in avoiding or eliminating her." She sums up unforgettably, "in one way or another, the woman must *go*" ("The Forgotten Reaping-Hook," 157–58, 163).

26 • In her remarkably thought-provoking and scrupulously documented essay examining Cather's own role in the design of the book, "The Benda Illustrations," Jean Schwind finds the resisting undercurrent to be conveyed by the Benda illustrations, which form a "separate account of Jim's heroine" (p. 52).

27 • Gelfant, "The Forgotten Reaping-Hook," p. 147.

28 • The roses Niel brings to Marian Forrester's bedroom window early one morning, and which he then throws into a mud wallow when he discovers that an all too virile man is with her, are fresh and dewy, "just beginning to open" (7:80). That is, in the traditional language of flowers which casts red roses as a figurative vulva, they are beyond the virginal bud stage but still not fully open—just the phase in which Niel would like to arrest Marian's sexuality: somewhat experienced, and therefore mysteriously alluring to the virginal youth, but not obvious or mature (i.e., active). I cannot agree with Kathleen Nichols ("The Celibate Male," p. 193) that these early-morning roses represent his own "budding passion." Only when it was clear that Niel still occupied a safe childhood world could he revel in the fullness of a symbolic female sexuality: on the occasion of a childhood picnic that immediately precedes his literal and symbolic fall, the wild roses in the marsh are "wide open and brilliant" (*ALL* 7:12).

29 • Nichols's comment that he is "much too pessimistic and ineffectual to be a celibate ideal" ("The Celibate Male," p. 187) is a point well taken. I would add, too imperceptive and judgmental. As Woodress says, Cather emphasizes Mrs. Forrester's "strong will and brave spirit" and "does not pass judgment on her" (*Willa Cather: A Literary Life,* pp. 349–50). I should stress again that, while commending Nichols's assessment of the narrative irony in *A Lost Lady,* I do not accept his view that, even though she distance herself from Niel, Cather "merges" her voice with that of Jim Burden. See Dalma H. Brunauer, "The Problem of Point of View in *A Lost Lady,*" *Renascence* 28 (1975): 47–52.

30 • Stouck, "Willa Cather and the Impressionist Novel," p. 52.

31 • O'Brien, *Willa Cather: The Emerging Voice,* p. 217.

32 • James Woodress finds the narrator too "unsophisticated" to "transmit" meanings conveyed by concise allusions such as the aria Myra's guest sings, the "Casta Diva" from Bellini's *Norma.* See *Willa Cather: A Literary Life,* p. 387.

33 • Woodress, for instance, is clear that Oswald had been "the enemy of her soul's peace" and supports his reading by reference to the letter (*Willa*

Cather: A Literary Life, pp. 384–85). See also George Seibel, "Miss Willa Cather from Nebraska," *New Colophon,* September 1949, pp. 207–8.

34 • John H. Randall III, for example, argues that in the stripped-down style of *Death Comes for the Archbishop* "human problems have been ignored rather than transcended" (Randall, "Summary of *Death Comes for the Archbishop:* The Cathedral and the Stagecoach," in *Critical Essays,* ed. Murphy, p. 249; reprinted from Randall's book *The Language and the Looking Glass: Willa Cather's Search for Value* [New York: Houghton Mifflin, 1960]).

35 • The autobiographical view was first asserted by Leon Edel in *Literary Biography,* published in 1957, revised and reprinted in *Stuff of Sleep and Dreams: Experiments in Literary Psychology* (New York: Harper and Row, 1982), pp. 216–40, then reprinted as "A Cave of One's Own" in *Critical Essays,* ed. Murphy, pp. 200–217. Edel's argument is both extended and, in specific ways, challenged by John G. Gleason in "The 'Case' of Willa Cather," *Studies in American Fiction* 20 (1986): 275–99.

36 • O'Brien, *Willa Cather: The Emerging Voice,* p. 240. O'Brien astutely relates the fact that Cather saw the Hambourgs in a permanent residence to the importance she always attached to space and houses in judging that this particular aspect of the trip to visit them was acutely distressing for her.

37 • James F. Maxfield, "Strategies of Self-Deception in Willa Cather's *Professor's House,*" *Studies in the Novel* 16 (1984): 83.

38 • David Laird observes, in "Willa Cather and the Deceptions of Art" (p. 54), that the irony Cather achieves in *My Ántonia* with the first-person point of view is achieved in *The Professor's House* by her choosing to "silence the voice of her narrator"and shift the focus to Outland.

39 • Frederick C. Crews, "Whose American Renaissance?" *New York Review,* October 27, 1988, p. 72.

40 • David Stouck, *Willa Cather's Imagination* (Lincoln: University of Nebraska Press, 1975), p. 135.

41 • A student in my American novels class, Sandra Beckmann, pointed out to me the clue provided by the children's attention to Frances Harling's picture. Their regard for her is evidence that Ántonia believes there is more in life for women than what Jim sees for them.

42 • Warren Motley, "The Unfinished Self: Willa Cather's *O Pioneers!* and the Psychic Cost of a Woman's Success," *Women's Studies* 12 (1986): 151.

43 • O'Brien, *Willa Cather: The Emerging Voice,* pp. 171–72.

44 • John J. Murphy suggests that the silence in the novel that occurs when Alexandra was struggling to build her success is a strategy for avoiding presentation of the conflict between her erotic self and her committed self. That conflict is transposed to her dream of surrender to a gigantic

male being who carries her away across the fields. The suppression allows Cather to project Alexandra's own necessary suppression of the conflict within and to heighten the contrast between the aspiring Alexandra and the fulfilled Alexandra (see Murphy, "A Comprehensive View of Cather's *O Pioneers!*" in *Critical Essays*, pp. 113–27). Motley, in "The Unfinished Self," however, points out that the conflict does enter the novel, but only in subtle and indirect ways. Motley's article provides a perceptive discussion of the emotional cost paid by Alexandra in achieving "what successful men have—autonomous power" (p. 151).

45 • Rosowski, *The Voyage Perilous*, p. 63.

46 • Motley, "The Unfinished Self," p. 149.

47 • Part of the problem with Sapphira, who is a thoroughly disagreeable even while impressive character, is that she has been allowed to usurp too much of the man's rightful role of dominance in the household. That is, Cather presents their relationship as a situation in which the old way of male dominance has been too fully reversed. Sapphira's husband puts down his foot occasionally, and when he does it is on firm moral ground (as when he reminds her that they do not sell their people), but for the most part he defers to her wishes and stays out of the way.

48 • Merrill Maguire Skaggs, "A Good Girl in Her Place: Cather's *Shadows on the Rock*," *Religion and Literature* 17 (1985): 29.

49 • O'Brien, *Willa Cather: The Emerging Voice*, p. 205.

50 • Theodore S. Adams, "Willa Cather's *My Mortal Enemy:* The Concise Presentation of Scene, Character, and Theme," *Colby Library Quarterly* (1973): 148.

CHAPTER FOUR

1 • All of the comments quoted are to be found in Harold Bloom, ed., *Modern Critical Views: Katherine Anne Porter* (New York: Chelsea House, 1986). All of the articles except Bloom's are available elsewhere as well. Robert Penn Warren's essay, "Irony with a Center, Katherine Anne Porter (1941–52)," is included in his *Selected Essays* (New York: Random House, 1941). Eudora Welty's "The Eye of the Story" first appeared in the *Yale Review* in 1965 and was reprinted in *Katherine Anne Porter: A Collection of Critical Essays*, ed. Robert Penn Warren (Englewood Cliffs, N.J.: Prentice-Hall, 1979). Robert Heilman's "*Ship of Fools:* Notes on Style" appeared in *Katherine Anne Porter: A Critical Symposium*, ed. Lodwick Hartley and George Core (Athens: University of Georgia Press) in 1969, after original publication in *Four Quarters*, 1962. Debra A. Moddelmog's "Narrative Irony and Hidden Motivations in Katherine Anne Porter's

'He'" was first published in *Modern Fiction Studies* 28 (1982); 405–13. References to Porter's work are to *The Collected Stories of Katherine Anne Porter* (New York: Harcourt, Brace and World, 1965).

2 • Barbara Thompson, "Katherine Anne Porter: An Interview," in *Katherine Anne Porter: A Critical Symposium,* ed. Hartley and Core, p. 18; first published, *Paris Review* 29 (1963).

3 • Heilman, "*Ship of Fools:* Notes on Style," in *Modern Critical Views,* pp. 34, 27.

4 • Darlene Harbour Unrue, *Truth and Vision in Katherine Anne Porter's Fiction* (Athens: University of Georgia Press, 1985), p. 219.

5 • The list of Miranda stories varies according to who is making the list. "Flowering Judas" and "Hacienda" are customarily included even though the main character, who seems to be the same in both, is called, in "Flowering Judas," Laura. Her characteristics, particularly her reticence or tendency toward withdrawal, so closely resemble those of Miranda that the grouping is inevitable. Both Jane DeMouy (in *Katherine Anne Porter's Women: The Eye of Her Fiction* [Austin: University of Texas Press, 1983]) and William Nance (*Katherine Anne Porter and the Art of Rejection* [Chapel Hill: University of North Carolina Press, 1963]), extend the list much further, Nance including even "Leaning Tower" with its male protagonist.

6 • Porter in a letter to Donald Sutherland, June 2, 1953, quoted in Unrue, *Truth and Vision,* p. 8.

7 • Welty, "The Eye of the Story," in *Katherine Anne Porter: A Collection of Critical Essays,* p. 74.

8 • Porter quoted by Bloom in his Introduction to the *Modern Critical Views* volume, p. 4. The author's nephew, Paul Porter, also mentions her dislike of off-color language: "When confronted with the big F, she would compress her lips and make a fnnf sound. 'What's that,' we would say, 'what did you say?' 'You know.'" From unpublished comments by Paul Porter at a conference at Texas A&M University on "Katherine Anne Porter and Texas: An Uneasy Relationship," April 23, 1988.

9 • Jane Krause DeMouy opens a genuinely new and long-overdue path in criticism of Porter in her book *Katherine Anne Porter's Women: The Eye of Her Fiction,* the basic thesis of which is that the single most encompassing principle of Porter's work is "an unfolding of a particular understanding of feminine experience" (p. 203).

10 • M. M. Liberman, *Katherine Anne Porter's Fiction* (Detroit: Wayne State University Press, 1971), p. 52.

11 • Warren, "Irony with a Center," p. 144.

12 • Thompson, "An Interview," p. 107.

13 • Thomas F. Walsh, "Deep Similarities in 'Noon Wine,'" *Mosaic* 9 (1975): 87.

14 • M. Wynn Thomas, "Strangers in a Strange Land: A Reading of 'Noon Wine,'" *American Literature* 47 (1975): p. 245.

15 • Frederick J. Hoffman, *The Art of Southern Fiction: A Study of Some Modern Novelists* (Carbondale: Southern Illinois University Press, 1967), p. 45.

16 • Walsh, "Deep Similarities," p. 90.

17 • Hoffman, *The Art of Southern Fiction,* p. 46.

18 • Thomas, "Strangers in a Strange Land," p. 246.

19 • Joan Givner cites a letter in which Porter traces Miranda's name to an early lover's playful reference to himself as Ariel and Porter as Miranda. Givner seems to offer the letter as refutation of critics' assumption that the name was taken from *The Tempest,* but it indicates only that the derivation was indirect. Joan Givner, *Katherine Anne Porter: A Life* (New York: Simon and Schuster, 1982), p. 170.

20 • Beverly Gross, "The Poetic Narrative: A Reading of 'Flowering Judas,'" *Style* 2 (1968): 131.

21 • DeMouy, *Katherine Anne Porter's Women,* p. 117.

22 • Robert Penn Warren comments in his Introduction to *Katherine Anne Porter: A Collection of Critical Essays* (p. 9), that "the most powerful tension in her work is between the emotional involvement and the detachment." The phrase adumbrates the tension DeMouy defines more narrowly, in *Katherine Anne Porter's Women,* as a "conflict between their natural desire for the warmth, security, and community of love, and their innate human desire to be autonomous and independent" (p. 203).

23 • Gross, "The Poetic Narrative," p. 132.

24 • For a provocative interpretation of the horse-race sequence and its connection to parts 1 and 3 of "Old Mortality," see Jane Flanders, "Katherine Anne Porter and the Ordeal of Southern Womanhood," *Southern Literary Journal* 9 (1976): 47–60.

25 • Liberman, *Katherine Anne Porter's Fiction,* p. 48.

26 • Nance comments that Miranda is "more romantic than she realizes with her vision of unobstructed autonomy and self-sufficiency" (p. 130). Also, DeMouy points out that Miranda's marriage was "an impetuous elopement" (p. 157)—that is, rather Amy-like.

27 • J. A. Ward comments in *American Silences: The Realism of James Agee, Walker Evans, and Edward Hopper* ([Baton Rouge: Louisiana State University Press, 1985], pp. 65–66, 56), that Hemingway "consistently identifies speech with falsity, and encumbers his protagonists with a surrounding chorus of banal voices that urge sentiment, manliness, and responsibility." In contrast, "when the conversation reaches a significant issue" Hemingway's center of consciousness "ceases to talk"; he has "a compulsion to be honest" that makes him "monosyllabic." Ward could as well have written these words about Porter's center of consciousness. Indeed, her contemporaneity with the male artists discussed by Ward sug-

gests that Porter's own moral and stylistic standards emphasizing reserve and inwardness are a part of a larger modernist pattern. However, the fact that she writes out of a woman's experience in the world adds new dimensions to the pattern.

28 • DeMouy, *Katherine Anne Porter's Women*, p. 161.

29 • I have pointed out in my article "Miranda's Guarded Speech: Porter and the Problem of Truth-Telling" (*Philological Quarterly* 66 [1987]: 259–78, note 2), the distortion created by critics' disregard for the gender of Porter's central, and clearly autobiographical, character. A particularly influential summation of the central plot of her fiction, offered by James William Johnson in "Another Look at Katherine Anne Porter," *Virginia Quarterly Review* 36 (1960): 598–613, makes insistent use of the masculine pronoun in speaking of a sequence of seventeen protagonists, twelve of whom are, in fact, female.

30 • W. J. Cash, *The Mind of the South* (New York: Knopf, 1941).

31 • I am closely following DeMouy's work here, though I do not share DeMouy's emphasis on biological threat.

CHAPTER FIVE

1 • David J. Geherin observes that the reader is "struck most profoundly" by the "silences between the chapters" ("Nothingness and Beyond: Joan Didion's *Play It As It Lays*," *Critique: Studies in Modern Fiction* 16 [1974]: 76; rpt. *Joan Didion: Essays and Conversations*, ed. Ellen G. Friedman [Princeton: N.J.: Ontario Review Press, 1984], p. 114). Some critics, however, seem to find the most notable attribute of Didion's novels to be the broken or fragmented quality of her narrative, that is, the juxtaposition of abrupt images and sequences in the verbalized prose itself. Geherin finds that it recalls T. S. Eliot's "heap of broken images." Katherine Usher Henderson, in *Joan Didion*, views the fragmented style as evidence that the narrator, a sometime model, views life as "a series of images flashed on a screen" ([New York: Ungar, 1981], pp. 28–29). Samuel Coale similarly comments on the "cinematic juxtaposition" of her prose ("Didion's Disorder: An American Romancer's Art," *Critique* 25 [1984]: 160). The two stylistic attributes are, of course, related.

2 • Page references to Didion's four novels will appear in parentheses without other indication. References to *Play It As It Lays, Run River,* and *A Book of Common Prayer* are to the readily available Pocket Books editions. For *Democracy* I use the first edition, New York: Simon and Schuster, 1984.

3 • Rodney Simard, "The Dissociation of Self in Joan Didion's *Play It as It Lays,*" in *Narcissism and the Text: Studies in Literature and the Psychology*

of Self, ed. Lynne Layton and Barbara Ann Schapiro (New York: New York University Press, 1986), p. 279.

4 • Sandra K. Hinchman, "Making Sense and Making Stories: Problems of Cognition and Narration in Joan Didion's *Play It as It Lays,*" *Centennial Review* 29 (1985): 460.

5 • Geherin, "Nothingness and Beyond," p. 68. C. B. Charbat, however, finds the novel—and apparently Geherin's article as well—essentially pretentious and finally lacking in content. Charbat, "Joan Didion's *Play It As It Lays* and the Vacuity of the Here and Now," *Critique* 21 (1980): 53–60.

6 • Mark Royden Winchell, *Joan Didion* (Boston: Twayne, 1980), p. 128.

7 • Hinchman, "Making Sense and Making Stories," 472.

8 • Henderson, *Joan Didion,* p. 59.

9 • This "contradiction between Didion's epistemology and Didion's art" is pointed out by Hinchman in "Making Sense and Making Stories," p. 473. In attributing the epistemology to "radical empiricism, passively registering sense-impressions and non-commitally witnessing events," however, Hinchman misrepresents radical empiricism. As William James enunciates the theory that he designates by that term, it is a belief that not only the isolated sense impressions and phenomena but also the connections between them—that is, the inferences we make about relational structures—are *experienced.* The theory does not deny but validate interpretive inferences, so long as those inferences originate pragmatically, that is, from direct experience within a context of purpose.

10 • Hinchman's observation ("Making Sense and Making Stories," p. 460) that by "failing to deliver a smoothly flowing narrative, Didion seems to be denying that discrete experiences can be aggregated into a logically satisfying whole" is cogent, though I would say, not "failing to deliver," but refusing to deliver.

11 • The phrase is Henry James's in a personal letter, describing himself: "I have the imagination of disaster and see life indeed as ferocious and sinister" (*Letters to A. C. Benson and Auguste Monod,* ed. E. F. Benson [London: Elkin Mathews and Marrot, 1930], p. 35). It was picked up by J. A. Ward for his title *The Imagination of Disaster: Evil in the Fiction of Henry James* (Lincoln: University of Nebraska Press, 1961).

12 • We might want to observe that this could simply be called a parent's nightmare world, but in Didion's fiction, parent is mother.

13 • Henderson considers the narrator to be limited by an assumption that the scientific method should be applied to human problems (*Joan Didion,* pp. 80–88). I do not find this view sustained by the text. Grace, the narrator, explicitly acknowledges the limitation of scientific knowledge or methods in remarking, "I am less and less convinced that the word 'unstable' has any useful meaning except insofar as it describes a chemical compound" (p. 104).

14 • It is not clear from the narrative whether Charlotte was divorced from her second husband, Leonard. I say ex-husband because, whatever the technicalities, she had left him.

15 • The connection between Didion's fragmented style and the religious overtone of the novels, particularly *A Book of Common Prayer*, is hinted in Geherin's comment that her "narrative technique" recalls T. S. Eliot's "heaps of broken images" (Geherin, "Nothingness and Beyond," p. 114). Eliot's broken images are, of course, the representations of a lost spiritual wholeness that he mourns and prays to have restored. More directly, Winchell says the prose of *A Book of Common Prayer* has "a liturgical cadence," its "repetition of key phrases" and its "frequent paragraph divisions" giving it a "sound and an appearance not unlike that of the Anglican prayer book" (Winchell, *Joan Didion*, p. 142). Henderson, however, while agreeing that the style uses rhythm and parallel sentence structure to "achieve a liturgical effect," regards it as seeming to "mock the rhythms of prayer" (Henderson, *Joan Didion*, p. 87).

16 • I reject, then, in regard to Grace Strasser-Mendana, the judgment summarized in the abstract of Mary Linda Bush's doctoral dissertation on Didion, "The Use of Narrative Devices in the Fiction and Non-Fiction of Joan Didion," that Didion's fiction is "beset" by "insufficient character motivation" (*Dissertations Abstracts International* 451 [1984]: 181A-182A). By the same token, as my comments on Charlotte's acts of atonement indicate, I reject Winchell's judgment that Charlotte is altogether an "unreflective protagonist." Mark Winchell, *Joan Didion*, p. 141.

17 • Grace has earlier acknowledged the inability of the scientist to penetrate the mystery of other selves, or even of her own deepest self: "I did not know why any one of those female children [the subjects of her anthropological study] did or did not do anything at all. Let me go further. I did not know why I did or did not do anything at all" (p. 4).

18 • Joyce Carol Oates's title for her review of *Play It As It Lays*, "A Taut Novel of Disorder," puts its finger quite precisely not only on the quality of that novel but of this one as well (*New York Times Book Review*, April 3, 1977, pp. 1, 34-35; rpt. in *Joan Didion: Essays and Conversations*, ed. Friedman, pp. 138-41.

19 • The constant pressure of such enforced fakery explains the mocking delight she manifests when her husband loses the presidential nomination: flying back to New York after the California primary, she parties with newspaper people on the airplane, singing "It's All Over Now, Baby Blue."

20 • Didion's career as novelist also has spaces in which we glimpse (in her journalism) anger seething. Curiously, those gaps are strangely patterned: her novels have appeared at seven-year intervals—1963, 1970, 1977, 1984.

———————— AFTERWORD ————————

1 • John Dewey, *Art As Experience* (1934; New York: Putnam, 1958), p. 346.

2 • Bernard Harrison, "Muriel Spark and Jane Austen," in *The Modern English Novel: The Reader, the Writer, and the Work,* ed. Gabriel Josipovici (New York: Barnes and Noble, 1976), p. 225.

3 • Muriel Spark, *The Driver's Seat* (New York: Alfred A. Knopf, 1970), p. 5.

Bibliography

PRIMARY TEXTS

For Jane Austen, I have used the standard edition by R. W. Chapman in five volumes, published by Oxford University Press in 1923, reprinted in 1982. In addition, I have referred to *Jane Austen's Letters to Her Sister Cassandra and Others,* Second Edition, also edited by Chapman and published by Oxford University Press, 1952.

There is no definitive edition of Willa Cather's complete works. One reasonable solution is to use the texts readily available in quality paperback editions. However, I have chosen to use the Autograph Edition published by Houghton Mifflin from 1937 through 1940.

Among Joan Didion's works I have used the following editions: *A Book of Common Prayer,* 1977; New York: Pocket Books, 1978. *Democracy,* New York: Simon and Schuster, 1984. *Play It As It Lays,* 1970; New York: Pocket Books, 1978. *Run River,* 1963; New York: Pocket Books, 1978.

For Katherine Anne Porter I have used *The Collected Stories of Katherine Anne Porter.* New York: Harcourt, Brace and World, 1965.

SCHOLARSHIP AND CRITICISM

Adams, Theodore S. "Willa Cather's *My Mortal Enemy:* The Concise Presentation of Scene, Character, and Theme." *Colby Library Quarterly* (1973): 138–48.

Anderson, Wayne C. "The Rhetoric of Silence in Hardy's Fiction." *Studies in the Novel* 17 (1985): 53–68.

Annable, Mary Mahar. "'Not ... for Such Dull Elves': Rhetorical Strategies for Reader Involvement in *Pride and Prejudice* and *Mansfield Park.*" *Dissertations Abstracts International* 44 (1984): 2769A-2770A.

Auchard, John. *Silence in Henry James: The Heritage of Symbolism and Decadence.* University Park and London: Pennsylvania State University Press, 1986.

Babb, Howard S. *Jane Austen's Novels: The Fabric of Dialogue.* New York: Archon Books, 1967.

Bennett, Mildred. *The World of Willa Cather.* Revised Edition. Lincoln: University of Nebraska Press, 1961.

Bloom, Edward A., and Lillian D. Bloom. *Willa Cather's Gift of Sympathy.* Carbondale: Southern Illinois University Press, 1962.

Bloom, Harold. Introduction to *Modern Critical Views: Katherine Anne Porter.* Edited by Harold Bloom. New York: Chelsea House, 1986.

Bogan, Louise. "American-Classic." *New Yorker,* August 8, 1931.

Booth, Wayne. *The Rhetoric of Fiction.* Chicago and London: University of Chicago Press, 1961.

Borker, Ruth. "Anthropology: Social and Cultural Perspective." In *Women and Language in Literature and Society.* Edited by Sally McConnell-Ginet, Ruth Borker, and Nelly Furman. New York: Praeger Publishers, 1980. Pp. 26–44.

Brown, Lloyd W. *Bits of Ivory: Narrative Techniques in Jane Austen's Fiction.* Baton Rouge: Louisiana State University Press, 1973.

Brownstein, Rachel M. *Becoming a Heroine: Reading about Women in Novels.* New York: Viking Press, 1982.

Brunauer, Dalma H. "The Problem of Point of View in *A Lost Lady.*" *Renascence* 28 (1975): 47–52.

Bush, Mary Linda. "The Use of Narrative Devices in the Fiction and Non-Fiction of Joan Didion." *Dissertations Abstracts International* 451 (1984): 181A–182A.

Cage, John. *Silence: Lectures and Writing.* Middletown, Ct.: Wesleyan University Press, 1961.

Cash, W. J. *The Mind of the South.* New York: Knopf, 1941.

Cather, Willa. "The Demands of Art." Lincoln *Courier,* November 23, 1895. Reprinted in *The Kingdom of Art: Willa Cather's First Principles and Critical Statements.* Edited by Bernice Slote. Lincoln: University of Nebraska Press, 1966.

Chandler, Alice. "'A Pair of Fine Eyes': Jane Austen's Treatment of Sex." *Studies in the Novel* 7 (1975): 88–103.

Charbat, C. B. "Joan Didion's *Play It As It Lays* and the Vacuity of the Here and Now." *Critique* 21 (1980): 53–60.

Cheung, King-Kok. "'Don't Tell': Imposed Silences in *The Color Purple* and *The Woman Warrior.*" *PMLA* 103 (1988): 162–74.

Christ, Carol P. *Diving Deep and Surfacing: Women Writers on Spiritual Quest.* Boston: Beacon Press, 1980.

Citron, Marcia J. "Felix Mendelssohn's Influence on Fanny Mendelssohn Hensel as a Professional Composer." *Current Musicology* 37 / 38 (1984): 9–17.

———. "Women and the Lied, 1775–1850." In *Women Making Music.* Edited by Jane Bowers and Judith Tick. Urbana: University of Illinois Press, 1986. Pp. 224–48.

Coale, Samuel. "Didion's Disorder: An American Romancer's Art." *Critique* 25 (1984): 160–70.

Costello, Bonnie. "The 'Feminine' Language of Marianne Moore." In *Women and Language in Literature and Society.* Edited by Sally McConnell-Ginet, Ruth Borker, and Nelly Furman. New York: Praeger Publishers, 1980. Pp. 222–38.

Crews, Frederick C. "Whose American Renaissance?" *New York Review,* October 27, 1988. Pp. 68–76.

Daiches, David. *Willa Cather: A Critical Introduction.* Ithaca, N.Y.: Cornell University Press, 1951.

Daly, Mary. *Beyond God the Father.* Boston: Beacon Press, 1974.

DeMouy, Jane. *Katherine Anne Porter's Women: The Eye of Her Fiction.* Austin: University of Texas Press, 1983.

Donovan, Josephine. "The Silence Is Broken." In *Women and Language in Literature and Society.* Edited by Sally McConnell-Ginet, Ruth Borker, and Nelly Furman. New York: Praeger Publishers, 1980. Pp. 205–18.

Edel, Leon. "A Cave of One's Own." In *Critical Essays on Willa Cather,* edited by John J. Murphy. Boston: G. K. Hall, 1984. Pp. 200–217. Reprinted from Edel, *Stuff of Sleep and Dreams: Experiments in Literary Psychology.* New York: Harper and Row, 1982. Pp. 216–40.

Ezell, Margaret J. M. "The Myth of Judith Shakespeare: Creating the Canon of Women's Literature." *New Literary History* 21 (1990).

———. "'To Be Your Daughter in Your Pen': The Social Functions of Literature in the Writings of Lady Elizabeth Brackley and Lady Jane Cavendish." *The Huntington Library Quarterly* 51 (1988): 281–96.

Flanders, Jane. "Katherine Anne Porter and the Ordeal of Southern Womanhood." *Southern Literary Journal* 9 (1976): 47–60.

Geherin, David J. "Nothingness and Beyond: Joan Didion's *Play It As It Lays.*" *Critique: Studies in Modern Fiction* 16 (1974): 64–78. Reprinted in *Joan Didion: Essays and Conversations,* edited by Ellen G. Friedman. Princeton, N.J.: Ontario Review Press, 1984.

Gelfant, Blanche H. "The Forgotten Reaping-Hook: Sex in *My Ántonia.*" *American Literature* 43 (1971): 60–82. Reprinted in *Critical Essays on Willa Cather.* Edited by John J. Murphy. Boston: G. K. Hall, 1984. Pp. 147–64.

Gilbert, Sandra M., and Susan Gubar. *The Madwoman in the Attic: The Woman Writer and the Nineteenth-Century Literary Imagination.* New Haven: Yale University Press, 1979.

———. *The War of the Words.* Volume 1 of *No Man's Land: The Place of the Woman Writer in the Twentieth Century.* New Haven and London: Yale University Press, 1988.

Givner, Joan. *Katherine Anne Porter: A Life.* New York: Simon and Schuster, 1982.

Gleason, John G. "The 'Case' of Willa Cather." *Studies in American Fiction* 20 (1986): 275–99.

Gross, Beverly. "The Poetic Narrative: A Reading of 'Flowering Judas.'" *Style* 2 (1968): 129–39.

Gubar, Susan. "Blessings in Disguise: Cross-Dressing as Re-Dressing for Female Modernists." *Massachusetts Review* 22 (1981): 477–508.

Harrison, Bernard. "Muriel Spark and Jane Austen." In *The Modern English Novel: The Reader, the Writer, and the Work*. Edited by Gabriel Josipovici. New York: Barnes and Noble, 1976.

Hassan, Ihab. *The Dismemberment of Orpheus: Toward a Postmodern Literature.* 2d ed. Madison: University of Wisconsin Press, 1982.

Heilman, Robert B. "*Ship of Fools:* Notes on Style." *Four Quarters,* 1962. Reprinted in *Katherine Anne Porter: A Critical Symposium*. Edited by Lodwick Hartley and George Core. Athens: University of Georgia Press, 1969.

Heller, Erich. *The Artist's Journey into the Interior.* New York: Vintage Books, 1968.

Henderson, Katherine Usher. *Joan Didion.* New York: Ungar, 1981.

Hinchman, Sandra K. "Making Sense and Making Stories: Problems of Cognition and Narration in Joan Didion's *Play It as It Lays.*" *Centennial Review* 29 (1985): 457–73.

Hoffman, Frederick J. *The Art of Southern Fiction: A Study of Some Modern Novelists.* Carbondale: Southern Illinois University Press, 1967.

Jacobus, Mary. *Reading Woman: Essays in Feminist Criticism.* New York: Columbia University Press, 1986.

Johnson, James William. "Another Look at Katherine Anne Porter." *Virginia Quarterly Review* 36 (1960): 598–613.

Kermode, Frank. *The Art of Telling: Essays on Fiction.* Cambridge: Harvard University Press, 1983.

———. *The Genesis of Secrecy: On the Interpretation of Narrative.* Cambridge: Harvard University Press, 1979.

Kramarae, Cheris. "Proprietors of Language." In *Women and Language in Literature and Society.* Edited by Sally McConnell-Ginet, Ruth Borker, and Nelly Furman. New York: Praeger Publishers, 1980. Pp. 58–68.

Kristeva, Julia. "Place Names." In *Desire in Language: A Semiotic Approach to Literature and Art.* Edited by Leon S. Roudiez. New York: Columbia University Press, 1980.

Kucich, John. *Repression in Victorian Fiction: Charlotte Bronte, George Eliot, and Charles Dickens.* Berkeley: University of California Press, 1987.

Laird, David. "Willa Cather and the Deceptions of Art." In *Interface: Essays on History, Myth and Art in American Literature.* Edited by Daniel Royot. Montpellier, France: University of Montpellier, 1984. Pp. 51–59.

Lambert, Deborah G. "The Defeat of a Hero: Autonomy and Sexuality in *My Ántonia.*" *American Literature* 53 (1982): 676–90.

Lascelles, Mary. *Jane Austen and Her Art.* London: Oxford University Press, 1939; rpt. 1966.

Lentricchia, Frank. "Patriarchy Against Itself—The Young Manhood of Wallace Stevens." *Critical Inquiry* 13 (1987): 742–86.

Liberman, M. M. *Katherine Anne Porter's Fiction.* Detroit: Wayne State University Press, 1971.

Litz, A. Walton. *Jane Austen: A Study of Her Artistic Development.* New York: Oxford University Press, 1965.

McGuire, Philip C. *Speechless Dialect: Shakespeare's Open Silences.* Berkeley: University of California Press, 1985.

McKinstry, Susan Jaret. "The Speaking Silence of Ann Beattie's Voice." *Studies in Short Fiction* 24 (1987): 111–17.

Marcus, Jane. "Still Practice, A / Wrested Alphabet: Toward a Feminist Aesthetic." In *Feminist Issues in Literary Scholarship.* Edited by Shari Benstock. Bloomington and Indianapolis: Indiana University Press, 1987. Pp. 79–97.

Maxfield, James F. "Strategies of Self-Deception in Willa Cather's *Professor's House.*" *Studies in the Novel* 16 (1984): 72–86.

Miller, James E., Jr. "Willa Cather and the Art of Fiction." In *The Art of Willa Cather.* Edited by Bernice Slote and Virginia Faulkner. Lincoln: University of Nebraska Press, 1974. Pp. 121–48.

Mitchell, Juliet. *Psychoanalysis and Feminism.* New York: Random House, 1974.

Moddelmog, Debra A. "Narrative Irony and Hidden Motivations in Katherine Anne Porter's 'He.'" *Modern Fiction Studies* 28 (1982): 405–13. Reprinted in *Modern Critical Views: Katherine Anne Porter.* Edited by Harold Bloom. New York: Chelsea House, 1986. Pp. 117–26.

Moi, Toril. *Sexual / Textual Politics: Feminist Literary Theory.* London and New York: Methuen, 1985.

Monaghan, David. *Jane Austen: Structure and Social Vision.* New York: Barnes and Noble, 1980.

Moore, Patrick. "Symbol, Mask, and Meter in the Poetry of Louise Bogan." In *Gender and Literary Voice.* Edited by Janet Todd. New York: Holmes and Meier, 1980. Pp. 67–80.

Morgan, Susan. "Why There's No Sex in Jane Austen's Fiction." *Studies in the Novel* 19 (1987): 346–56.

Motley, Warren. "The Unfinished Self: Willa Cather's *O Pioneers!* and the Psychic Cost of a Woman's Success." *Women's Studies* 12 (1986): 149–65.

Murphy, John J. "A Comprehensive View of Cather's *O Pioneers!*" In *Critical Essays on Willa Cather.* Edited by John J. Murphy. Boston: G. K. Hall, 1984. Pp. 113–27.

Nance, William. *Katherine Anne Porter and the Art of Rejection.* Chapel Hill: University of North Carolina Press, 1963.

Nichols, Kathleen L. "The Celibate Male in *A Lost Lady:* The Unreliable Center of Consciousness." *Regionalism and the Female Imagination* 4 (1978): 13–23. Reprinted in *Critical Essays on Willa Cather.* Edited by John J. Murphy. Boston: G. K. Hall, 1984. Pp. 186–97.

Oates, Joyce Carol. "A Taut Novel of Disorder." *New York Times Book Review.* April 3, 1977. Reprinted in *Joan Didion: Essays and Conversations.* Edited by Ellen G. Friedman. Princeton: Ontario Review Press, 1984.

O'Brien, Sharon. "'The Thing Not Named': Willa Cather as a Lesbian Writer." *Signs* 9 (1984): 576–99.

———. *Willa Cather: The Emerging Voice.* Oxford: Oxford University Press, 1987.

Olsen, Tillie. *Silences.* New York: Dell, 1965.

Ostriker, Alicia Suskin. *Stealing the Language: The Emergence of Women's Poetry in America.* Boston: Beacon Press, 1986.

Page, Norman. *The Language of Jane Austen.* Oxford, Basil Blackwell, 1972.

Patterson, Richard F. "Truth, Certitude, and Stability in Jane Austen's Fiction." *Philological Quarterly* 60 (1981): 455–69.

Perez, Janet. "Functions of the Rhetoric of Silence in Contemporary Spanish Literature." *South Central Review* 1 (1984): 108–30.

Picard, Max. *The World of Silence.* Translated by S. Godman. 1948; Chicago: H. Regnery, 1952.

Porter, Katherine Anne. "Afterword" to Willa Cather, *The Troll Garden.* New York: NAL, 1961. Reprinted as "Critical Reflections on Willa Cather." In *Critical Essays on Willa Cather.* Edited by John J. Murphy. Boston: G. K. Hall, 1984. Pp. 31–39.

———. "Virginia Woolf." In *The Collected Essays and Occasional Writings of Katherine Anne Porter.* New York: Delacorte Press, 1970. Pp. 68–71.

Poovey, Mary. *The Proper Lady and the Woman Writer: Ideology As Style in the Works of Mary Wollstonecraft, Mary Shelley, and Jane Austen.* Chicago and London: University of Chicago Press, 1984.

Randall, John H., III. "Summary of *Death Comes for the Archbishop:* The Cathedral and the Stagecoach." In *Critical Essays on Willa Cather.* Edited by John J. Murphy. Boston: G. K. Hall, 1984. Pp. 247–51. Reprinted from Randall, *The Language and the Looking Glass: Willa Cather's Search for Value.* New York: Houghton Mifflin, 1960.

Rich, Adrienne. "When We Dead Awaken: Writing as Re-Vision." In *On Lies, Secrets and Silence: Selected Prose, 1966–1978.* New York: W. W. Norton, 1979. Pp. 33–49.

Rosowski, Susan J. *The Voyage Perilous: Willa Cather's Romanticism.* Lincoln: University of Nebraska Press, 1986.

Russ, Joanna. *How to Suppress Women's Writing.* Austin: University of Texas Press, 1983.

Schwind, Jean. "The Benda Illustrations to *My Ántonia:* Cather's 'Silent' Supplement to Jim Burden's Narrative." *PMLA* 100 (1985): 51–67.

Seibel, George. "Miss Willa Cather from Nebraska." *New Colophon,* September 1949. Pp. 195–208.

Simard, Rodney. "The Dissociation of Self in Joan Didion's *Play It as It Lays.*" In *Narcissism and the Text: Studies in Literature and the Psychology of Self.* Edited by Lynne Layton and Barbara Ann Schapiro. New York: New York University Press, 1986. Pp. 273–89.

Skaggs, Merrill Maguire. "A Good Girl in Her Place: Cather's *Shadows on the Rock.*" *Religion and Literature* 17 (1985): 27–36.

Slote, Bernice. "Willa Cather: The Secret Web." In *Five Essays on Willa Cather.* Edited by John J. Murphy. North Andover, Mass.: Merrimack College, 1974). Pp. 1–19.

Sontag, Susan. *Styles of Radical Will.* New York: Farrar, Straus and Giroux, 1969.

Steiner, George. *Language and Silence: Essays on Language, Literature, and the Inhuman.* New York: Atheneum, 1967.

Stouck, David. "Willa Cather and the Impressionist Novel." In *Critical Essays on Willa Cather.* Edited by John J. Murphy. Boston: G. K. Hall, 1984. Pp. 48–66.

———. *Willa Cather's Imagination.* Lincoln: University of Nebraska Press, 1975.

Stout, Janis P. "Jane Austen's Proposal Scenes and the Limitation of Language." *Studies in the Novel* 14 (1982): 316–26.

———. "Miranda's Guarded Speech: Porter and the Problem of Truth-Telling." *Philological Quarterly* 66 (1987): 259–78.

———. "Mr. Hatch's Volubility and Miss Porter's Reserve." *Essays in Literature* 12 (1985): 285–94.

Stuckey, William J. "*My Ántonia:* A Rose for Miss Cather." *Studies in the Novel* 4 (1972): 473–83.

Sutherland, Donald. "Willa Cather: The Classic Voice." In *The Art of Willa Cather.* Edited by Bernice Slote and Virginia Faulkner. Lincoln: University of Nebraska Press, 1974. Pp. 156–79.

"Talking with Adrienne Rich." *Ohio Review* 13 (1971): 29–46.

Tanner, Tony. *Jane Austen.* Cambridge: Harvard University Press, 1986.

Tave, Stuart M. *Some Words of Jane Austen.* Chicago and London: University of Chicago Press, 1973.

Thomas, M. Wynn. "Strangers in a Strange Land: A Reading of 'Noon Wine.'" *American Literature* 47 (1975): 230–46.

Thompson, Barbara. "Katherine Anne Porter: An Interview." *Paris Review* 29 (1963). Reprinted in *Katherine Anne Porter: A Critical Symposium.* Edited by Lodwick Hartley and George Core. Athens: University of Georgia Press, 1969. Pp. 3–23.

Thompson, James. "Jane Austen and the Limits of Language." *Journal of English and Germanic Philology* 85 (1986): 510–31.

Todd, Janet. Introduction to *Gender and Literary Voice*. Edited by Janet Todd. New York: Holmes and Meier, 1980.

Treicher, Paula A. "Escaping the Sentence: Diagnosis and Discourse in 'The Yellow Wallpaper.'" In *Feminist Issues in Literary Scholarship*. Edited by Shari Benstock. Bloomington and Indianapolis: Indiana University Press, 1987. Pp. 62–78.

Unrue, Darlene Harbour. *Truth and Vision in Katherine Anne Porter's Fiction*. Athens: University of Georgia Press, 1985.

Walsh, Thomas F. "Deep Similarities in 'Noon Wine.'" *Mosaic* 9 (1975): 83–91.

Ward, J. A. *American Silences: The Realism of James Agee, Walker Evans, and Edward Hopper*. Baton Rouge: Louisiana State University Press, 1985.

Warren, Robert Penn. Introduction to *Katherine Anne Porter: A Collection of Critical Essays*. Edited by Robert Penn Warren. Englewood Cliffs, N.J.: Prentice-Hall, 1979.

———. "Irony with a Center, Katherine Anne Porter (1941–52)." In Warren, *Selected Essays*. New York: Random House, 1941. Reprinted in *Modern Critical Views: Katherine Anne Porter*. Edited by Harold Bloom. New York: Chelsea House, 1986. Pp. 7–22.

Welty, Eudora. "The Eye of the Story." *Yale Review* 55 (1965): 265–74. Reprinted in *Katherine Anne Porter: A Collection of Critical Essays*. Edited by Robert Penn Warren. Englewood Cliffs, N.J.: Prentice-Hall, 1979. Pp. 72–80.

———. "The House of Willa Cather." In *The Art of Willa Cather*. Edited by Bernice Slote and Virginia Faulkner. Lincoln: University of Nebraska Press, 1974. Pp. 3–20. Also in *Modern Critical Views: Willa Cather*. Edited by Harold Bloom. New York: Chelsea House, 1986. Pp. 145–59.

Wenzel, Helene Vivienne. "Introduction to Luce Irigaray's 'And the One Doesn't Stir without the Other.'" *Signs* 7 (1981): 56–59.

Winchell, Mark Royden. *Joan Didion*. Boston: Twayne, 1980.

Woodress, James. "Cather and Her Friends." In *Critical Essays on Willa Cather*. Edited by John J. Murphy. Boston: G. K. Hall, 1984. Pp. 81–95.

———. *Willa Cather: A Literary Life*. Lincoln: University of Nebraska Press, 1987.

Woolf, Virginia. "Jane Austen." In *The Essays of Virginia Woolf*, Volume 2: *1912–1918*. Edited by Andrew McNeillie. New York and London: Harcourt Brace Jovanovich, 1987.

Zimmerman, Don H., and Candace West. "Sex Roles, Interruptions, and Silences in Conversation." In *Language and Sex: Difference and Dominance*. Edited by Barrie Thorne and Nancy Henley. Rowley, Mass.: Newbury House, 1975. Pp. 105–29.

INDEX